POPULAR
ENTERTAINMENT

PERFORMANCE AND SPECTACLE
CULTURE AND COMPETITION

First Edition

Edited by Barbara McKean
and Carrie J. Cole
University of Arizona

San Diego, CA

Bassim Hamadeh, CEO and Publisher
Christopher Foster, General Vice President
Michael Simpson, Vice President of Acquisitions
Jessica Knott, Managing Editor
Kevin Fahey, Cognella Marketing Manager
Jess Busch, Senior Graphic Designer
Marissa Applegate, Acquisitions Editor
Stephanie Sandler, Licensing Associate

First published in the United States of America in 2013 by Cognella, Inc.

Trademark Notice: Product or corporate names may be trademarks or registered trademarks, and are used only for identification and explanation without intent to infringe.

16 15 14 13 12   1 2 3 4 5

Printed in the United States of America

ISBN: 978-1-62131-139-3 (pbk) / 978-1-62131-140-9 (br)

www.cognella.com 800.200.3908

Acknowledgments

Many thanks to our colleagues who initiated this idea!

Peter Beudert
Jerry Dickey
Christin Essin
Mary Beth Haralovich
Dorothy Roome
Brad Schauer
Beverly Seckinger
Barbara Selznick

and

Bruce Brockman, Director, School of Theatre, Film and Television
Jory Hancock, Dean, College of Fine Arts
University of Arizona

Contents

Part 3: When Culture Becomes Entertainment 195

Introduction to the First Edition

> **Popular** (adjective) … regarded with favor, approval, or affection by people in general. (Dictionary.com)
>
> *It's all about popular*
> *It's not about aptitude*
> *It's the way you're viewed*
> *So it's very shrewd to be*
> *Very very Popular*
> *Like me!*
> "Popular," *Wicked* (2003)

> **Entertainment** (noun) … the act of entertaining; agreeable occupation for the mind; diversion; amusement (Dictionary.com)
>
> *Let me entertain you*
> *And we'll have a real good time,*
> *yes, sir!*
> *We'll have… A real good time!*
> "Let Me Entertain You," *Gypsy* (1959)

Welcome to Popular Entertainment: Performance and Spectacle, Culture and Competition. This textbook for lower-division general education courses introduces students to the ways in which performance, spectacle, culture, and competition interrelate with forms of popular entertainment. We also examine the ways in which those forms influence society's interactions and choices in terms of producing and/or receiving popular entertainment.

Our intentions are to encourage students to foster an appreciation of the historical and cultural legacies within selected forms of popular entertainment and to develop a critical lens for viewing contemporary entertainment. The readings in this book provide theoretical tools and analysis that prepare students to respond more fully and effectively to an increasingly complex and ambiguous field.

The textbook is divided into four parts. Part One begins with an overview of popular entertainment as an industry. Entertainment has become an international marketplace with an ever-increasing emphasis on spectacle. Examining how the industry packages entertainment experiences and how in turn those experiences influence social behavior and appetites is an important first step in analyzing society's choices and interactions. Entertainment is a performed experience. Whether live or mediated, entertainment is created and performed by real people who train and prepare for the performance and who make deliberate choices along the way. Likewise, entertainment is performed for real people who receive the experience in a variety of ways. Theories of performance, of adaptation as process and product, and of modes of engagement provide important threads for analysis that are revisited throughout the textbook.

Convergence adds another important analytical thread. Part Two starts off with a seminal reading on the phenomenon of convergence, the interconnectedness of the multiple ways entertainment is created, distributed, and consumed. The process of convergence focuses less on the product but rather on the changing landscape of media flow. In Part Two, we take a look at the historical foundations of three forms of storytelling: circus, theatre, and film and the ways spectacle, performance, adaptation, and convergence influence the contemporary manifestation of these forms.

The convergence of multiple technologies has led to a global culture where societies around the world can participate or partake in a variety of cultural traditions and performances. Part Three opens with the idea of cultural tourism. As more and more people have access to cultures throughout the world, people can participate as either real or virtual tourists to experience performances of the "other" or of the past. Extending beyond the tourist experience are examples of cultural entertainment where the lines between producer, performer, and audience are increasingly blurred. Performances of ritual and tradition intersect with issues of authenticity and identity to complement and complicate the study and analysis of popular entertainment.

Part Four builds on these ideas of ritual, authenticity, and identity and broadens the study of entertainment to include performances of competition. Spectator sports are one of the most popular forms of entertainment either enjoyed in person or through media. One of the first radio broadcasts in the United States was a baseball game. Today sports are experienced live or mediated or both simultaneously, exemplifying the kind of multi-laminated experience the convergence of performance and technology creates. Extending our study of cultural entertainment, the first section focuses on teams and nations. Modern Olympic Games bring together a study of competition, culture, performance, and ritual on the global stage.

Spectator sports are spontaneous and immediate. They are watched and mediated in real time. Even when audiences record games to be watched at later time, there is still the attraction of not knowing the outcome until the game is watched. While producers cannot control the outcome of the game itself, they can control the spectacle of the overall performance in order to maximize the entertainment value and continue to build audiences. Both professional and college sports are subject to these enhancements of spectacle. The second section turns our attention to the big business of college sports and the specific challenges posed to the industry, the institutions, and the individual student athletes.

Competition is also a solid feature of televised reality programming. Beginning with popular game shows in the 1950s, audiences have continually been attracted to watching "ordinary" folks compete for their chance at fame or fortune. In recent decades, reality programming has amped up the volume on these types of competitions. Today shows such as American Idol test the illusion of authenticity by combining what Schechner refers to in Part One as "make-believe" with "make-belief" (77). Further, the line between those who watch and those who participate is purposely blurred. Audiences vote for their favorites each week and regularly audition or interview to be contestants. Just as in sports, producers of reality programming need an audience to be not just casual viewers but committed enthusiasts or fans.

A Note on the Structure of this Text

At the end of each part, we offer a listing of ideas and questions to consider, along with additional resources to view and read. The threads of spectacle, performance, adaptation, and convergence and the readings presented here offer tools for students to embark on their own analysis of whatever form of popular entertainment they choose. As an example, we offer the following to frame the introduction:

Ideas

Competition
Culture
Performance
Popular Entertainment
Spectacle

Questions

1. What is meant by popular? How does an event become popular?
2. When you think of popular entertainment, what comes to mind first?
3. How do you define culture? What culture(s) do you call your own?
4. How do you define spectacle? What kinds of performances do you use as examples?
5. Do you consider competition as entertainment? As performance?

View

Web:

The Official Wicked the Musical page. http://www.wickedthemusical.com/

Film/Video

The Wizard of Oz (1939)

Gypsy (1962)

That's Entertainment (1974)

Baseball: The Tenth Inning (2010)

Read

Ashby, LeRoy. *With Amusement for All: A History of American Popular Culture since 1830*. Lexington: University Press of Kentucky, 2006. Print.

Gans, Herbert J. *Popular Culture and High Culture: An Analysis and Evaluation of Taste*. New York: Basic Books, 1975. Print.

Matlaw, Myron (Ed). *American Popular Entertainment: Papers and Proceedings of the Conference on the History of American Popular Entertainment*. Westport, Conn: Greenwood Press, 1977.

Modleski, Tania, ed. *Studies in Entertainment: Critical Approaches to Mass Culture*. Bloomington and Indianapolis, IN: Indiana University Press, 1986. Print.

Postman, Neil. *Amusing Ourselves to Death: Public Discourse in the Age of Show Business*. New York: Penguin Books, 1986. Print.

Sayre, Shay and Cynthia King. *Entertainment and Society: Influences, Impacts, and Innovations.* 2nd ed. New York: Routledge, 2010. Print.

Schwartz, Stephen. *Wicked: A New Musical: Original Broadway Cast Recording.* Decca Broadway, 2003. CD.

Wilmeth, Don B. *Language of American Popular Entertainment.* Westport, Conn: Greenwood Press, 1981. Print.

At the end of each of the four parts, we have included exercises aimed at engaging the theories and ideas with examples that are particular to the students' experiences with popular entertainment.

Exercise

Throughout the book, apply these ideas and perspectives to a form of popular entertainment you most enjoy. Write a case study focusing on one performance of popular entertainment. Some examples:

A musical

A circus company

A blockbuster movie

A reality television show

A sporting event

A cultural or historical re-enactment

Part 1

Understanding Popular Entertainment as Industry, Performance and Adaptation

Part One explores definitions, concepts, and theories that provide the foundation for critically viewing and analyzing performances of popular entertainment. The first section of readings takes a broad view of the field and focus on the business of entertainment. Within this view, we look at the economic impact of popular entertainment and the role of the consumer. The ways in which the demand for spectacle throughout a global marketplace drives decisions are discussed to enhance our understanding of the tight relationship between the industry and the products.

The second section narrows the focus to a particular lens for viewing all forms of popular entertainment as performance. This lens forms the basis for analysis of the forms and media introduced throughout the rest of the text. Schechner's essay "What Is Performance?" introduces the key elements within the foundational frame of performance as "restored behavior."

Given that all performance is "restored behavior" or a series of adaptations responding to events, people, and ideas, Hutcheon's chapter on theories of adaptation extends our understanding of performance as both a process and a product by investigating the creative appropriation and acknowledgment of other works and recognizing the deliberate strategies of narrative structure in that process. Audience reception is also part of the process of adaptation and Hutcheon provides categories for understanding modes of engagement. Understanding the process gives both makers and consumers the ability to analyze individual products of entertainment.

Industry, Entertainment, and Society
Popular Entertainment as Performance
Performance and Adaptation

Industry, Entertainment, and Society

Looking at popular entertainment as an industry helps us understand performances of popular entertainment and the role of the spectator and consumer. The Cusic and Faulk essay introduces the US Department of Commerce Bureau of Economic Analysis. The Bureau divides popular entertainment into two basic sectors, which allows scholars to analyze the overall and economic impact of specific forms of entertainment. From the industry perspective, revenue drives the creation of popular entertainment. As the reading points out, consumers "vote with their pocketbooks," which in turn measures perceptions of popularity. "Popular" is an acknowledgment that a key purpose of entertainment is to generate dollars. In today's world much of popular entertainment is produced by large corporations with a variety of divisions that provide specific types of products. Corporate influences affect both the creation and the consumption of much of popular entertainment.

The second essay continues to explore the role of the corporate influences by introducing the concept of spectacle and the influence of spectacle in all forms of popular entertainment. Another key discussion centers on the multimedia culture of popular entertainment and is foundational to the convergence theories discussed further in Part Two. Live or mediated spectacle is dependent on the relationship between the performance and the spectator, who actively chooses *and* passively accepts any forms of entertainment available. Finally, Kellner's take on the changing relationship between information technology and entertainment provides an interesting view on the information we receive through the media.

Ideas

Consumer/Spectator/Audience
US Department of Commerce Bureau of Economic Analysis
Spectacle
Multimedia culture
"Infotainment"

Popular Culture and the Economy

By Don Cusic and Gregory K. Faulk

T he definition of popular culture is kaleidoscopic. It concerns the arts, culture, and entertainment in a market-based economy but encompasses a wide variety of other activities as well. The purpose of this article is to focus on one aspect of popular culture, its impact on the economy. This issue has been researched before. Using government data, Cusic identified the popular culture economy as having a US$251 billion impact on the U.S. economy in 1995. The purpose of this study is to follow up and expand on this topic.

As noted by Gary Hoppenstand in his inaugural editorial in *The Journal of Popular Culture,* the definition of popular culture is amorphous:

> Uncomfortable with the seemingly indefinable nature of the subject, some scholars consider popular culture to be strictly equated with mass culture, something that is manufactured and distributed to a large audience. Others believe it to be entirely economic in nature, as a product that is designed and sold for consumption on a tremendous scale. There are those who think of popular culture as ideology, as something that reinforces or invents a political or social agenda. Then there are those who insist that popular culture is entwined with social class, defined only as working-class culture or middle-class culture. Certainly all of these concepts hold true for much of what we think of as popular culture, but they are, even collectively, not the entire answer to the question "What is popular culture?"
>
> (Hoppenstand 3)

This study focuses on one of these topics, the economic aspect of popular culture.

The U.S. Department of Commerce, through its Bureau of Economic Analysis (BEA), tracks the economic importance of various industries within the economy. The BEA, in conjunction with the U.S. Census Bureau classifies industries utilizing the North American Industry Classification System (NAICS). These agencies have defined cultural products and services as they relate to the economy. "Cultural products are those that directly express attitudes, opinions, ideas, values, and artistic creativity; provide entertainment; or offer information and analysis concerning the past and present. Included in this definition are popular, mass-produced products as well as cultural products that normally have a more limited audience, such as poetry books, literary magazines, or classical records" (United States Census Bureau). The BEA has identified both the Information as well as the Arts, Entertainment, and Recreation sectors of the economy as providing popular culture products, goods, and services. In 2004, industries involved in creating and producing popular culture products, goods, and services contributed US$565 billion to the economy, 2.9% of the output in the United States.

Information Sector

The notion that we live in an "information economy" is indisputable, but exactly what is the "information economy" and why does it include some popular culture products? The BEA categorizes companies in the Information sector if they transform information into a commodity that is produced and distributed. Included in this categorization are popular culture products: "The Information sector groups three types of establishments: (1) those engaged in producing and distributing information and cultural (emphasis added) products; (2) those that provide the means to transmit or distribute these products as well as data or communications; and (3) those that process data."[1]

The unique characteristics of information and cultural products, and of the processes involved in their production and distribution, distinguish the Information sector. Unlike traditional goods, an information or cultural product such as a newspaper online or television program does not necessarily have tangible qualities nor is it necessarily associated with a particular form. A movie can be shown at a movie theater, on a TV broadcast, through video on demand, or rented at a local video store. A sound recording can be aired on radio, embedded in multimedia products, or sold at a record store. The value of these products to the consumer lies in their informational, educational, cultural, or entertainment content, not in the format in which they are distributed.

A distinguishing feature of most cultural products within the Information sector is that they are protected from unlawful reproduction by copyright laws. The intangible property aspect of information and cultural products makes the processes involved in their production and distribution very different from goods and services. Only those possessing the rights to these works are authorized to reproduce, alter, improve, and distribute them. Acquiring and using these rights often involves significant costs. In addition, technology is revolutionizing the distribution of these products. It is possible to distribute them in a physical form, via broadcast, or online.

Distributors of information and cultural products can easily add value to the products they distribute. For instance, broadcasters add advertising not contained in the original product. This capacity means that unlike traditional distributors, they derive revenue not from sales of the distributed product to the final consumer, but from those who pay for the privilege of adding information to the original product. Similarly, a publisher can acquire the rights to thousands of previously published newspaper and periodical articles and add new value by providing search and software and organizing the information in a way that facilitates research and retrieval. These products often command a much higher price than the original information.

The Census Bureau identifies industries normally associated with popular culture within the Information sector of the economy. It states:

> The main components of this sector are the publishing industries, including software publishing, and both traditional publishing and publishing exclusively on the Internet; the motion picture and sound recording industries; the broadcasting industries, including traditional broadcasting and those broadcasting exclusively over the Internet; the telecommunications industries; the industries known as Internet service providers and web search portals, data processing industries, and the information services industries.
>
> (United States Census Bureau 2002)

Of these industries, those usually considered predominantly popular culture based are newspaper publishers, periodical publishers, book publishers, motion picture and video industries, sound recording industries, radio and TV broadcasting, and cable networks and program distribution. Although popular culture-related products are included in some of the excluded categories (e.g., gaming programs are a component of software publishing, cable distribution networks are a component of the telecommunications industry), the lack of subcategorization within the industry by the BEA precludes their inclusion in this analysis. Popular culture industries comprise about thirty-five percent of the economic output of the "information economy." In 2004, information-related popular culture industries contributed US$385 billion to the U.S. economy.

Arts, Entertainment, and Recreation

In addition to being a significant component of the Information sector of the economy, establishments providing popular culture services comprise the whole of the Arts, Entertainment, and Recreation sector of the economy. According to the Census Bureau, this sector

> includes a wide range of establishments that operate facilities or provide services to meet varied cultural (emphasis added), entertainment, and recreational interests of their patrons. This sector comprises (1) establishments that are involved in producing, promoting, or participating in live performances, events, or exhibits intended for public viewing; (2) establishments that preserve and exhibit objects and sites of historical, cultural, or educational interest; and (3) establishments that operate facilities or provide services that enable patrons to participate in recreational activities or pursue amusement, hobby, and leisure-time interests.
> (United States Census Bureau 2002)

The Arts, Entertainment, and Recreation sector of the economy contributed US$180 billion to the U.S. economy in 2004.

There are some industries that offer Arts-, Entertainment-, and Recreation-related popular culture services in conjunction with other services that are not included in this study. Examples include establishments that provide both accommodations and recreational facilities, such as resorts and casino hotels; restaurants and night clubs that provide live entertainment in addition to the sale of food and beverages; and establishments using transportation equipment to provide recreational and entertainment services, such as those operating sightseeing buses, dinner cruises, or helicopter rides.

Popular Culture, Leisure Time, and the Economy

One perspective of popular culture is that it can be viewed as the leisure time activities of consumers. Some are "free" public goods (e.g., check out a book at the public library) while others have costs (e.g., see the movie that is based on the book). The producers, creators, and distributors of "fee-based" popular culture goods and services have to receive financial rewards commensurate with risk or they will invest in other areas. In other words, those popular cultural activities that survive have withstood the test of the marketplace. In still other words, consumers vote for the most "popular" cultural items with their pocket books (or credit cards). An analysis of the relative economic importance of popular culture-related industries in the economy is simply a measurement of the importance consumers place on

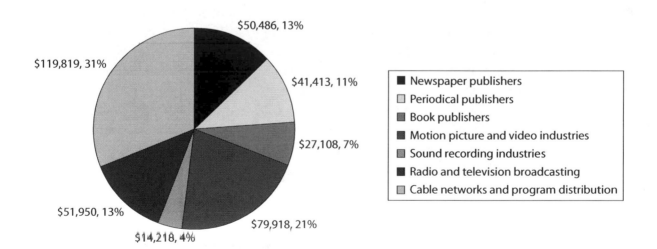

$50,486, 13%
$119,819, 31%
$41,413, 11%
$27,108, 7%
$51,950, 13%
$14,218, 4%
$79,918, 21%

■ Newspaper publishers
□ Periodical publishers
▨ Book publishers
■ Motion picture and video industries
▨ Sound recording industries
■ Radio and television broadcasting
▨ Cable networks and program distribution

Chart A: Information Based Popular Culture Gross Output 2004

the popular culture choices available to them. Trends in popular culture spending reflect shifting tastes.

The marketplace is characterized by the free exchange of goods and services; however, it is not unfettered. Changes in technology, government regulation and mergers, and acquisitions affect consumer popular culture choices. Moreover, some corporations are engaged in many sectors of the popular culture economy.

Contribution of Popular Culture in the Information Sector of the Economy

Information sector-based popular culture industries include publishers (newspapers, periodicals, and books), motion picture and video industries, sound recording industries, radio and TV broadcasters, and cable networks. A common feature of these industries is that some type of media is utilized in production and/or distribution. Altogether these industries accounted for US$385 billion of economic activity in 2004, about sixty-eight percent of the output of popular culture industries (Table 1).

Some large, multinational U.S. domiciled public corporations capitalize on the fact that the preponderance of U.S. consumer popular culture expenditures are on media-based entertainment and have a significant presence in multiple industries. The six major players are General Electric (Universal studios, NBC TV network, CNBC, USA Bravo and SciFi cable programs, Universal theme parks), Disney (Disney, Buena Vista, Touchstone and Hollywood studios, ABC TV network, ESPN, Disney Channel and ABC Family cable programs, seventy radio stations, Disney and Lyric Street records, Disney and Hyperion books, Disney theme parks), News Corporation (20th Century Fox studios, FOX TV network, FOX cable programming, TV guide, New York Post, Harper-Collins book publishing), Time-Warner (Warner and New Line studios, HBO and TBS cable programming, Time magazine, Little Brown book publisher), Sony (Sony, Columbia, Tri-Star studios, programming for ABC, CBS, and NBC TV, Sony/BMG music), and Viacom (Paramount, DreamWorks studios, MTV and Nickelodeon cable programming, Famous music). Viacom owned CBS until December 2005, when it was spun off as a separate corporation. CBS focuses on home-based entertainment (CBS TV network, Showtime cable programming), publishing (Simon and Schuster), and radio ownership (179 stations).

TABLE 1 Popular Culture Gross Output by Category 1998–2004 ($ 000's)

Information	1998	1999	2000	2001	2002	2003	2004
Newspaper publishers	$45,667	$48,634	$51,772	$47,439	$47,828	$48,921	$50,486
Periodical publishers	$36,382	$38,919	$40,848	$40,626	$39,874	$39,608	$41,413
Book publishers	$21,794	$23,801	$25,216	$26,472	$27,041	$25,659	$27,108
Motion picture and video industries	$54,706	$60,415	$63,693	$65,384	$70,432	$74,396	$79,918
Sound recording industries	$11,269	$12,613	$13,265	$13,010	$13,398	$13,805	$14,218
Radio and television broadcasting	$45,105	$47,692	$51,672	$46,357	$49,646	$49,556	$51,950
Cable networks and program distribution	$62,611	$72,646	$85,098	$88,658	$97,364	$108,626	$119,819
Total	$277,534	$304,720	$331,564	$327,946	$345,583	$360,571	$384,912
Arts, Entertainment, Recreation	1998	1999	2000	2001	2002	2003	2004
Performing arts companies	$9,600	$10,059	$10,457	$10,467	$10,885	$11,202	$11,573
Spectator sports	$18,019	$19,494	$21,590	$22,434	$24,380	$25,109	$26,519
Promoters of performing arts and sports and agents for public figures	$10,980	$11,859	$12,575	$13,648	$14,952	$15,764	$16,636
Independent artists, writers, and performers	$14,382	$14,344	$14,620	$16,122	$17,451	$18,766	$18,131
Museums, historical sites, zoos, and parks	$5,482	$6,096	$6,688	$7,883	$7,744	$8,115	$7,972
Fitness and recreational sports centers	$13,084	$14,178	$15,113	$16,403	$18,163	$19,585	$20,101
Bowling centers	$3,460	$3,622	$3,657	$3,814	$4,060	$4,338	$4,631
Other amusement, gambling, and recreation industries	$54,791	$58,243	$62,399	$63,370	$65,595	$68,656	$74,239
Total	$129,798	$137,895	$147,099	$154,141	$163,230	$171,535	$179,802
Total popular culture	$407,332	$442,615	$478,663	$482,087	$508,813	$532,106	$564,714
% US Output	2.8%	2.9%	2.9%	2.9%	3.0%	3.0%	2.9%
Information/popular culture (%)	68.1%	68.8%	69.3%	68.0%	67.9%	67.8%	68.2%
Arts, Entertainment, Recreation/popular culture (%)	31.9%	31.2%	30.7%	32.0%	32.1%	32.2%	31.8%

The above-listed companies are involved in multiple industries within the Information sector. Within these industries there are significant players that are not highly diversified. Newmarket Entertainment Group distributes films created by itself and other independent filmmakers and its release, *The Passion of the Christ*, had the highest box office revenues (US$370 million) of any R-rated film released between 1968 and 2005 (U.S. Entertainment Industry). The highest ranked cable program (Discovery) is owned by a company that is primarily in the cable industry. Regardless of ownership, however, the significant capital investment made by corporations in order to provide entertainment highlights the substantive economic undergirding of media-based popular culture.

A major factor in consolidation within the media industry has been governmental lifting of concentration and cross ownership restrictions primarily through the Telecommunications Deregulation Act of 1996 and actions by the Federal Communications Commission (FCC). The Act removed statutory and court-ordered barriers to competition between segments of the telecommunications industry, enabling baby bells, long distance carriers, cable companies, broadcasters, and others to compete head to head. The FCC relaxed ownership concentration rules in the TV and radio industries and relaxed cross-ownership rules for newspaper/broadcasting and radio/TV.

Another major competitive factor in the media industry is technology. The introduction of readily available broadband technology allows cable companies to deliver on-demand home movies. Digital technology allows radio and TV broadcasters to increase the quality and reach of their transmissions. The Internet has changed output venues (and revenues) of radio, recorded music, and traditional print media such as newspapers and magazines.

Cable TV

The heavy investment by corporations in films, TV, and cable programming is based on consumer preferences. Consumers spend more money on entertainment that they can see and hear than they do on print-based media or sound recordings. Within the Information sector over half of popular culture industry output is centered on cable TV programming, which contributed about US$120 billion to the economy in 2004, about thirty-one percent of popular culture output in the Information sector, and the motion picture and video industries, which contributed about US$80 billion, twenty-one percent of popular culture output in the Information sector (Chart A).

The fact that cable programming is the largest popular culture-based component of the Information sector comes as no surprise because the industry has continually expanded offerings since the introduction of Home Box Office (HBO) in 1975. Because of packaged programming by cable providers, there is little variation in the number of subscribers to the top twenty programming networks. As of December 2005, they all have approximately ninety million subscribers (National Cable & Telecommunications Association). Cable programming has created icons of popular culture: ESPN, CNN, QVC, Nickelodeon, and MTV, among others.

The creation of cable programming is separately categorized by the BEA and is discussed above. The delivery of cable programs (cable service providers) is an element of the Telecommunications sector and not separately categorized by the BEA. In addition to cable service the Telecommunications sector includes cellular and landline phone services, Internet service providers, and satellite communications. Because the value of cable service providers cannot be isolated, it is not included in this analysis of the value of popular culture. However, because the cable service providers play an important part in the distribution of popular culture, a brief discussion of this sector of the industry is in order.

Currently cable has penetrated 59.1 percent of TV households (National Cable & Telecommunications Association). Cable companies benefited from the Telecommunications Deregulation Act of 1996. The Act removed rate regulations on all cable services except the "basic tier" (over-the-air channels, public, and educational channels). Since the passage of the Act, the cable industry has consolidated, with the top five players (Comcast, Time Warner, Charter Communications, Cox Communications, and Adelphia Communications) comprising seventy-four percent of the market.

Films

The second largest player in the media sector is motion picture and video industries. As noted above, the same corporations that provide cable programming are also engaged in motion pictures and have the investment capacity necessary to fund the enormous production and distribution costs associated with movie making. The availability of TV, cable, and other home video devices has created new outlets for movie producers (made for TV and cable movies, original movies shown on TV or cable, rental, and purchased movie DVDs, etc.). The common ownership of movie studios and cable and TV production facilitates have enabled media conglomerates to tap both the movie theater and home viewing audiences. The industry has also fostered technological innovation. It has invested in computer-aided design, which has birthed computer animation in both cartoons and regular films.

The BEA also includes motion picture exhibitors in its motion picture and video industries category. As in the case of motion picture production, exhibition is dominated by several chains: Regal Entertainment Group (United Artists, Edwards Theaters, Hoyts and Regal Cinemas), Loews Cineplex (Sony, Plitt, Walter Reade and RKO), AMC Entertainment (American Multi-Cinema), Carmike Cinemas, Redstone (National Amusements), Cinemark USA, and Marcus Corporation. These chains account for about sixty-five percent of the screens in the United States but account for eighty percent of revenues (Vogel 48).

Broadcasting

Transmission of entertainment over the airwaves is smaller than cable broadcast but still economically significant. Radio and TV broadcasting contributed approximately US$52 billion to the U.S. economy in 2004, thirteen percent of popular culture output in the Information sector. Industry income is derived primarily from advertising revenues allowing radio and TV broadcasters to provide "free" entertainment.

As previously discussed, three of the four major TV broadcasters (ABC, NBC, and FOX) are owned by media conglomerates. The fourth, CBS, is effectively but not officially a subsidiary of the media giant Viacom. CBS also owns the Showtime cable network. In addition to providing TV programming, all of the networks either own and operate or have affiliates in major metropolitan areas. ABC owns ten local TV stations, NBC owns twenty-five (Corporate Disney, NBC Universal). Both of these networks have over two hundred affiliates, and their programming reaches ninety-nine percent of TV viewing households. Of the two other major networks, CBS owns thirty-nine stations and FOX has thirty-five (CBS Corporation, Corporate Disney, NBC Universal, News Corporation). The major impetus for increased station ownership was the Telecommunications Deregulation Act of 1996. Because of the Act, a broadcast company can own two TV stations in markets of five or more, as long as audience coverage does not exceed thirty-nine percent. A broadcaster can own up to eight radio stations in a market as long as the market has at least forty-five stations. Although network programming reaches most TV viewing households, ownership of TV broadcasting stations is diffused. The major media companies own 109 of the 1,371 TV broadcasting stations in the United States; the remainder are locally or regionally owned (Federal Communications Commission).

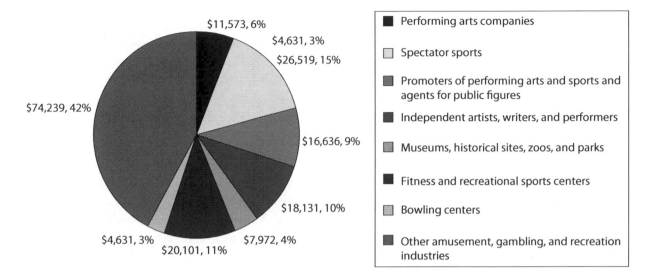

$11,573, 6%

$4,631, 3%

$26,519, 15%

$74,239, 42%

$16,636, 9%

$18,131, 10%

$4,631, 3%

$20,101, 11%

$7,972, 4%

- ■ Performing arts companies
- ☐ Spectator sports
- ■ Promoters of performing arts and sports and agents for public figures
- ■ Independent artists, writers, and performers
- ■ Museums, historical sites, zoos, and parks
- ■ Fitness and recreational sports centers
- ☐ Bowling centers
- ■ Other amusement, gambling, and recreation industries

Chart B: Arts, Entertainment and Recreation Based Popular Culture Gross Output 2004

Radio programming and broadcasting, the other significant component of broadcasting, is also dominated by large media corporations. As noted above, the major media corporations own radio stations. Disney (ABC) owns seventy radio stations and CBS owns 179 stations through its Infinity Broadcasting division. However, the major player in this area is Clear Channel Communications. Of the 11,002 AM and FM commercial radio stations in the United States, Clear Channel owns 1,200 or approximately eleven percent of all U.S. radio stations. The company also owns over thirty TV stations. Other corporations with a significant presence in the radio industry include Cumulus Broadcasting, which owns 306 radio stations; Citadel Broadcasting, which owns 213 stations; and American Family Association, which owns 107 stations. Altogether the top five companies own fourteen percent of the total number of stations; smaller companies, partnerships, and investors own the remaining eighty-six percent. The top companies focus on the major markets. Clear Channel has an eleven percent ownership share by number of stations but a twenty-seven percent market share. Infinity has a two percent share by number of stations but fifteen percent market share ("The State of The News Media 2004").

Sound Recording Industry

Although music epitomizes a culture, its economic impact is relatively small: US$14 billion, or four percent of Information sector popular culture output. The music industry has a symbiotic relation with the broadcasting industry because record labels rely on airplay by radio stations to introduce or popularize a song and generate sales. Only one of the four major record distributors in the United States is owned by a media giant, Sony/BMG. Warner Music Group is owned by a private investor group. Warner and Sony/BMG handle approximately half the albums sold in the United States (Vogel 208–09). One of the other two major U.S. record distributors, Universal Music Group, is a division of Vivendi, a French cable TV, and mobile phone operator. The other, EMI, is based in England and focuses solely on recorded music. The major record labels control about seventy-five percent of U.S.-recorded music sales, smaller independent record labels distribute the remainder. Smaller labels may gain a larger market share as recorded music distribution morphs to the Internet.

Newspapers, Periodicals, and Books

Consumers still have an affinity for traditional print-based media, which represents thirty-one percent of popular culture output in the Information sector. Newspaper publishing contributed over US$50 billion to the U.S. economy in 2004, thirteen percent of popular culture output in the Information sector. Periodical publishers account for eleven percent (US$41 billion), and book publishers account for seven percent (US$27 billion).

Not surprisingly, the major newspaper publishers have diversified into other areas of the Information sector (Media Owners). The New York Times company prints its namesake newspaper along with the *Boston Globe* and twenty other regional newspapers. It also owns eight TV stations, two radio stations, and has a stake in the Boston Red Sox baseball team. The Tribune Company publishes its flagship *Chicago Tribune* and ten other leading daily newspapers. It has twenty TV stations, the cable superstation WGN, WGN-AM radio station, and the Chicago Cubs baseball team. The Washington Post company has interests in newspaper and magazine publishing, TV broadcasting, and cable TV systems. The McClatchy company, lesser known than its counterparts, is the second largest U.S. daily circulation newspaper company and has an interest in the Pittsburgh Pirates baseball team. Other major newspaper publishers (Gannett, E. W. Scripps, Hearst, Journal Communications, and Media General) also own TV stations. As is the case with broadcasting, medium and small town newspapers are mostly regionally or locally owned (Media Owners).

Two organizations primarily associated with newspaper publishing also have a significant presence in magazines, Hearst (*Cosmopolitan, Esquire, Good Housekeeping, Popular Mechanics, Seventeen*, and others) and the Washington Post *(Newsweek)*. The media giant Time Warner publishes its signature magazine along with other high circulation magazines *(People, Sports Illustrated, Fortune,* and *Entertainment Weekly).* Advance Publications focuses primarily on magazine publication and produces *The New Yorker, Vanity Fair, Condé Nast Traveller,* and the *Parade* Sunday newspaper supplement, among other titles. Hachette Filipacchi Media US, a subsidiary of a French conglomerate also involved in aerospace and defense, reaches over fifty million U.S. readers with such magazines as *American Photo, Boating, Car and Driver, Cycle World, File, Metropolitan Home, Premiere,* and *Woman's Day.* Primedia is the number one special interest magazine publisher in the United States with well-known brands such as *Motor Trend, Automobile, In-Fisherman, Power and Motoryacht, Hot Rod, Snowboards, Stereophile,* and *Surfer.*

Book publishing in the United States is characterized by the textbook audience and the market-based fiction and nonfiction audience. Publishers focusing on fiction and nonfiction include Little Brown and Company, controlled by Time-Warner, Simon and Schuster, owned by CBS and Penguin (US), owned by Pearson, a United Kingdom-based company that also owns Pearson textbook publishing and the Financial Times Group. Of the other major book publishers, McGraw-Hill focuses primarily on textbooks but has interests in magazines (*Business Week)* and TV stations. John Wiley and Sons focuses on textbooks and journals for the scientific, technical, and medical communities.

Summary

The Information sector contains media-based companies that produced US$385 billion of economic output in 2004, about two-thirds of the output of popular culture industries. Over half of the economic output in this sector is in films, TV, and cable programming; content consumers can see and hear. Consumers still have an affinity for traditional print-based media, which comprises thirty-one percent of popular culture output in the sector. Transmission of entertainment over the airwaves is thirteen percent of popular culture output in the sector. Although a cultural giant, music is a relative economic midget consisting of four percent of Information sector popular culture output.

Economic production of this magnitude requires substantive investment and a willingness to take risks. The preponderance of popular culture oriented economic output in the Information sector is produced by large multinational public corporations with a presence in various subsectors. This is *ipso facto* a natural economic phenomena. A large capital base is necessary for the huge investment in the production and distribution of media entertainment (films, cable and broadcast TV, radio programs, recorded music, newspapers, magazines, and books). Consumer tastes are fickle, and huge investments in movies, new cable, or TV programs must be made before the film or program is released. If consumers are not impressed and the movie or program "bombs," the producer is saddled with a huge loss. Of course, some films and programs are wildly successful. Diversification is necessary to deal with the risk inherent in such ventures (a movie can flop while a new cable program flourishes). The bottom line is affected if companies do not produce content accepted by the public. In short, consumers would not have the choices available in media-based entertainment without the financial capacity, and risks assumed by these corporations.

In addition to economic capacity, other major factors in consolidation within the media industry have been governmental deregulation and technological change. Government deregulation removed barriers to competition between segments of the telecommunications industry, relaxed ownership concentration rules in the TV and radio industries, and relaxed cross-ownership rules for newspaper/broadcasting and radio/TV. The innovation of broadband technology allows cable companies to deliver on demand home movies. The Internet has introduced new outlets for radio, recorded music, and traditional print media. Although the subsidiaries of the corporations discussed above have changed and will most certainly change over time, for the reasons enumerated in this section the phenomena of consolidation and cross-industry ownership will change but will not vanish.

Contribution of Popular Culture in the Arts, Entertainment, and Recreation Sector of the Economy

In contradistinction to the media-based orientation of companies involved in the Information sector of the economy, the Arts, Entertainment, and Recreation sector of the economy focuses on live entertainment. This sector is divided into three primary categories: (1) Performing Arts, Spectator Sports, and Related Industries; (2) Amusement, Gambling, and Recreation Industries; and (3) Museums, Historical

Sites, and Similar Institutions. Altogether this sector of the economy contributed US$180 billion to the U.S. economy in 2004, about thirty-two percent of popular culture-related economic output (Table 1). Economic output in the Performing Arts, Spectator Sports, and Related Industries subsector was almost US$73 billion, about forty-one percent of all economic output in the Arts, Entertainment, and Recreation sector (Chart B). Those individuals, groups, and teams that attract the public to live venues generate significant revenue. Approximately twenty-five percent (US$18.1 billion) of the US$73 billion output generated in the Performing Arts, Spectator Sports, and Related Industries subsector was by performers. Those individuals and organizations that make the investment and take the risks involved in staging live events also generate significant economic output, US$16.6 billion or twenty-three percent of this subsector's output. The Amusement, Gambling, and Recreation subsector had the largest impact, almost US$99 billion, or fifty-five percent of the Arts, Entertainment, and Recreation output. Museums and Historical sites had the least economic contribution, approximately US$8 billion, or four percent of the economic impact of the Arts, Entertainment, and Recreation sector. Unlike the Information sector, which is characterized by large public corporations with ownership interests in various subsectors, the brunt of the economic output in the Arts, Entertainment, and Recreation sector is produced by private corporations, partnerships, and individual investors.

Performing Arts Companies

The Performing Arts, Spectator Sports, and Related Industries subsector comprises establishments that produce or organize and promote live presentations involving the performances of actors and actresses, singers, dancers, musical groups and artists, athletes, and other entertainers, including independent (i.e. freelance) entertainers and the establishments that manage their careers. The classification recognizes four basic processes: (1) producing (i.e. presenting) events; (2) organizing, managing, and/or promoting events; (3) managing and representing entertainers; and (4) providing the artistic, creative, and technical skills necessary to the production of these live events.

Performing arts companies contributed over US$11 billion to the economy in 2004. The three major categories of performing arts companies include theater, symphony orchestras, and opera. Broadway, the theater district of New York, defines the theater industry and has the greatest economic and historical significance (Vogel 422). Like the film industry, the theater industry comprises production and distribution. Funding for theater production is offered to investors through a limited liability company. Because of the risks involved and the potential to turn the play into a film, large entertainment companies may also provide funding (Vogel 440). Major theater owners (distribution) on Broadway include the Shubert Organization, the Nederlander Organization, and Jujamcyn Theaters. These organizations offer plays on Broadway as well as road tours. They may also participate in the production of a play. In addition to Broadway-based theater companies, regional and local theater companies also produce plays.

There are approximately 1,600 orchestras in the United States. Most rely on patrons for support. Orchestras in major cities such as Boston, Chicago, Los Angeles, and New York attract the bulk of expenditures at concerts staged by professional groups (Vogel 428).

Opera is drama set to music and as such must have singer/actors as well as orchestration.

As a result of the complexity and cost of staging an opera, there are currently four major opera companies in the United States: The Metropolitan, the San Francisco Opera, the Chicago Lyric Opera, and the New York City Opera.

Spectator Sports

This subsector comprises (1) sports teams or clubs primarily participating in live sporting events before a paying audience; (2) establishments primarily engaged in operating racetracks; (3) independent athletes engaged in participating in live sporting or racing events before a paying audience; (4) owners of racing participants, such as cars, dogs, and horses, primarily engaged in entering them in racing events or other spectator sports events; and (5) establishments, such as sports trainers, primarily engaged in providing specialized services to support participants in sports events or competitions. The sports teams and clubs included in this industry may or may not operate their own arena, stadium, or other facility for presenting their games or other spectator sports events. Spectator sports contributed over US$26 billion to the 2004 economy.

The major components of this subsector are professional sports teams and collegiate athletics. The primary professional organizations include the National Football League, Major League Baseball, the National Basketball Association, the National Hockey League, and the National Association for Stock Car Auto Racing. The major collegiate athletic events include teams with membership in the Division I of the National Collegiate Athletic Association. Although ticket sales are a significant revenue component for spectator sports, radio, TV, and cable broadcasting rights are the predominant income source. One impetus for widespread sports coverage through broadcasting is wagering. Betting on any sport is legal in Nevada and restricted to horses, dogs, and jai-alai in several other states. Legal sanctions have not stopped people from betting tens of billions of dollars each year on the results of sporting events (Vogel 397–98).

Given the close tie-in between sports and the media, it is no surprise that media companies also have an ownership interest in sports franchises: News Corp (Los Angeles Dodgers), Time-Warner (Atlanta Braves), Tribune (Chicago Cubs), Rogers Communications (Toronto Blue Jays), McClatchy (Pittsburgh Pirates). Most professional sports franchises are privately held. The only publicly traded professional sports companies are operators of motor sports racetracks (International Speedway Corporation, Speedway Motorsports Inc., and Dover Motorsports Inc. (DVD).

Amusement, Gambling, and Recreation Industries

Industries in the Amusement, Gambling, and Recreation Industries subsector (1) operate facilities where patrons can primarily engage in sports, recreation, amusement, or gambling activities and/or (2) provide other amusement and recreation services, such as supplying and servicing amusement devices in places of business operated by others; operating sports teams, clubs, or leagues engaged in playing games for recreational purposes; and guiding tours without using transportation equipment. This subsector includes gambling industries (except casino hotels), theme parks, skiing facilities, fitness and recreational centers, bowling centers, golf courses, racetracks, and marinas. This subsector contributed over US$99 billion to 2004's economy.

The most auspicious component of the gambling industry, the casino hotels in Las Vegas and elsewhere, are categorized as accommodation and food services, not gambling, by the government and not included in this study. Components of the gambling industry subsector include state lotteries, off-track betting, bookies, and coin-operated gambling devices.

The major economic output within the Amusement, Gambling, and Recreation subsector is primarily produced by private organizations. State governments operate lotteries and regulate gambling casinos. As noted in the discussion on the Information sector, the major theme parks, Disney and Universal, are owned by media conglomerates.

The major public companies in gaming activities include Churchill Downs (horse racing, off-track betting) and Life Time Fitness (indoor recreation) (Yahoo! Finance).

Museums, Historical Sites, and Similar Institutions

Museums comprise establishments primarily engaged in the preservation and exhibition of objects of historical, cultural, and/or educational value. Historical sites comprise establishments primarily engaged in the preservation and exhibition of sites, buildings, forts, or communities that describe events or persons of particular historical interest. Archeological sites, battlefields, historical ships, and pioneer villages are included in this industry. Similar industries include zoological gardens, which comprise establishments primarily engaged in the preservation and exhibition of live plant and animal life displays, and nature parks, establishments primarily engaged in the preservation and exhibition of natural areas or settings. Ownership and management of museums and historical parks is primarily by state/local government or historical organizations. This sector contributed about US$8 billion to the economy in 2004.

Summary

The Arts, Entertainment, and Recreation sector of the economy provides live entertainment and has contributed US$180 billion to the U.S. economy in 2004, roughly one-third of popular culture-related economic output. Most spending in this sector occurred in amusement, gambling, and recreation, which made up fifty-five percent of the sector output. The attraction of performing artists and athletes also generated significant economic impact. Economic output in the performing arts, spectator sports, and related industries was about forty-one percent of all economic, output in the sector. Museums and historical sites had the least economic contribution, four percent of the sector's economic impact.

In keeping with its smaller economic stature compared with the popular culture component of the Information sector, ownership in the Arts, Entertainment, and Recreation sector is mainly concentrated in private individuals, partnerships, and corporations that focus primarily on individual industries within a subsector. The interaction between organizations in the Arts, Entertainment, and Recreation sector and the Information sector is primarily in spectator sports.

Summary and Conclusions about Popular Culture and the Economy

The economic impact of popular culture can be measured using definitions and data from the Bureau of Economic Analysis. Cultural products are identified as those that directly express attitudes, opinions, ideas, values, and artistic creativity. They provide entertainment or offer information and analysis. Both the Information as well as the Arts, Entertainment, and Recreation sectors of our economy provide popular culture products, goods, and services.

About two-thirds of popular culture-related economic output is concentrated in the Information sector of the economy. Popular culture-related output in this sector includes publishing, motion picture and video industries, sound recording industries, radio and TV broadcasters, and cable networks. This sector is dominated by six large corporations that operate in multiple industries: General Electric, Disney, News Corporation, Time-Warner, Sony, and Viacom. These companies have the financial capacity to assume the risks inherent in offering consumers choices in media-based entertainment. Governmental deregulation and technological innovation have also fostered consolidation.

The Arts, Entertainment, and Recreation sector of the economy focuses on live entertainment and includes performing arts, spectator sports, amusement, gambling, recreation, museums, and historical sites. Most of the economic output in the Arts, Entertainment, and Recreation sector is produced by private corporations, partnerships, and individual investors.

In 2004, industries involved in creating and producing popular culture products, goods, and services contributed US$565 billion to the economy. This figure understates the economic value of popular culture. Because of data limitations caused by activities that cross industry classifications, the significant economic output of popular culture in areas such as hotel casinos, cable service providers, and computer games are not captured. Nonetheless the economic importance of popular culture is significant enough to have been identified and measured by the U.S. government. Popular culture can be defined and studied based on its economic impact.

Notes

1. Gross Output by Industry in Current Dollars, Quantity Indexes by Industry, Price Indexes by Industry. The figures cited are for the value of the Gross Output of products created within

the United States, regardless of whether the labor and property inputs are domestically or foreign owned. United States Department of Commerce, Bureau of Economic Analysis (http://www.bea.gov).

Works Cited

CBS Corporation. (14 Jun. 2006). *Our Company.* (http://www.cbscorporation.com/our_company/overview/index.php).

Corporate Disney. (14 Jun. 2006). *Company Overview.* (http://corporate.disney.go.com/corporate/overview.html).

Cusic, Don. (2001). "The Popular Culture Economy." *The Journal of Popular Culture,* 35.3: 1–10.

Federal Communications Commission. (6 Jun. 2006). *Broadcast Stations totals as of 31 Mar. 2006.* (http://www.fcc.gov/mb/audio/totals/bt060331.htm).

Hoppenstand, Gary. (2003). "Inaugural Editorial." *The Journal of Popular Culture,* 37.1: 1–6.

Media Owners. (21 Jun. 2006). *America's Leading Media Companies.* (http://www.mediaowners.com).

National Cable & Telecommunications Association. (19 Jun. 2006). (http://www.ncta.com).

NBC Universal. (14 Jun. 2006). *Company Overview.* (http://www.nbcuni.com/About_NBC_Universal/Company_Overview).

News Corporation. (14 Jun. 2006). *Overview.* (http://www.newscorp.com/operations/overview, html).

Journalism.com. (3 Apr. 2006). "The State of the News Media 2004." (http://www.stateorthenewsmedia.org).

United States Census Bureau, 2002. (23 Jun. 2006). NAICS Codes and Titles, 51 Information. (http://www.census.gov/epcd/naics02/naicod02.htm).

U.S. Entertainment Industry (2005). MPA Market Statistics, *Top Grossing Films by Rating 1968–2005.* (p. 15).

Vogel, Harold L. *(2004). Entertainment Industry Economics.* 6th ed. Cambridge, UK: Cambridge UP.

Yahoo! Finance. (12 Jul. 2006). (http://www.biz.yahoo.com).

Media Culture and the Triumph of the Spectacle

By Douglas Kellner

During the past decades, the culture industries have multiplied media spectacles in novel spaces and sites, and spectacle itself is becoming one of the organizing principles of the economy, polity, society, and everyday life. The Internet-based economy deploys spectacle as a means of promotion, reproduction, and the circulation and selling of commodities. Media culture itself proliferates ever more technologically sophisticated spectacles to seize audiences and increase the media's power and profit. The forms of entertainment permeate news and information, and a tabloidized infotainment culture is increasingly popular. New multimedia, which synthesize forms of radio, film, TV news and entertainment, and the mushrooming domain of cyberspace become extravaganzas of techno-culture, generating expanding sites of information and entertainment, while intensifying the spectacle form of media culture.

Political and social life are also shaped more and more by media spectacle. Social and political conflicts are increasingly played out on the screens of media culture, which display spectacles such as sensational murder cases, terrorist bombings, celebrity and political sex scandals, and the explosive violence of everyday life. Media culture not only takes up always-expanding amounts of time and energy, but also provides ever more material for fantasy, dreaming, modeling thought and behavior, and identities.

Of course, there have been spectacles since premodern times. Classical Greece had its Olympics, thespian and poetry festivals, its public rhetorical battles, and its bloody and violent wars. Ancient Rome had its orgies, its public offerings of bread and circuses, its titanic political battles, and the spectacle of empire with parades and monuments for triumphant Caesars and their armies, extravaganzas put on display in the 2000 film *Gladiator*. And, as Dutch cultural historian Johan Huizinga (1986; 1997) reminds us, medieval life too had its important moments of display and spectacle.

In the early modern period, Machiavelli advised his modern prince of the productive use of spectacle for government and social control, and the emperors and kings of the modern states cultivated spectacles as part of their rituals of governance and power. Popular entertainment long had its roots in spectacle, while war, religion, sports, and other domains of public life were fertile fields for the propagation of spectacle for centuries. Yet with the development of new multimedia and information technologies, technospectacles have been decisively shaping the contours and trajectories of contemporary societies and cultures, at least in the advanced capitalist countries, while media spectacle has also become a defining feature of globalization.

In this opening chapter, I will provide an overview of the dissemination of media spectacle throughout the major domains of the economy, polity, society, culture, and everyday life in the contemporary era and indicate the theoretical approach that I deploy. This requires a brief presentation of the influential analysis of spectacle by Guy Debord and the Situationist International, and how I build upon this approach.

Guy Debord and the Society of the Spectacle

The concept of the "society of the spectacle," developed by French theorist Guy Debord and his comrades in the Situationist International, has had a major impact on a variety of contemporary theories of society and culture.[1] For Debord, spectacle "unifies and explains a great diversity of apparent phenomena" (Debord 1967: Section 10). Debord's conception, first developed in the 1960s, continues to circulate through the Internet and other academic and subcultural sites today. It

---

1 Debord's *The Society of the Spectacle* (1967) was published in translation in a pirate edition by Black and Red (Detroit) in 1970 and reprinted many times; another edition appeared in 1983 and a new translation in 1994. Thus, in the following discussion, I cite references to the numbered paragraphs of Debord's text to make it easier for those with different editions to follow my reading. The key texts of the Situationists and many interesting commentaries are found on various websites, producing a curious afterlife for Situationist ideas and practices. For further discussion of the Situationists, see Best and Kellner (1997: Chapter 3); see also the discussions of spectacle culture in Best and Kellner (2001), upon which I draw in these studies.

describes a media and consumer society organized around the production and consumption of images, commodities, and staged events.

Building on this concept, I argue that media spectacles are those phenomena of media culture that embody contemporary society's basic values, serve to initiate individuals into its way of life, and dramatize its controversies and straggles, as well as its modes of conflict resolution. They include media extravaganzas, sporting events, political happenings, and those attention-grabbing occurrences that we call news—a phenomenon that itself has been subjected to the logic of spectacle and tabloidization in the era of the media sensationalism, political scandal and contestation, seemingly unending cultural war, and the new phenomenon of Terror War. Thus, while Debord presents a rather generalized and abstract notion of spectacle, I engage specific examples of media spectacle and how they are produced, constructed, circulated, and function in the present era.

As we enter a new millennium, the media are becoming more technologically dazzling and are playing an ever-escalating role in everyday life. Under the influence of a multimedia culture, seductive spectacles fascinate the denizens of the media and consumer society and involve them in the semiotics of a new world of entertainment, information, and consumption, which deeply influences thought and action. In Debord's words: "When the real world changes into simple images, simple images become real beings and effective motivations of a hypnotic behavior. The spectacle as a tendency *to make one see the world* by means of various specialized mediations (it can no longer be grasped directly), naturally finds vision to be the privileged human sense which the sense of touch was for other epochs" (ibid.: Section 18). According to Debord, sight, "the most abstract, the most mystified sense corresponds to the generalized abstraction of present day society" (ibid.).

Experience and everyday life are thus shaped and mediated by the spectacles of media culture and the consumer society. For Debord, the spectacle is a tool of pacification and depoliticization; it is a "permanent opium war" (ibid.: Section 44), which stupefies social subjects and distracts them from the most urgent task of real life—recovering the full range of their human powers through creative practice. The concept of the spectacle is integrally connected to the concept of separation and passivity, for in submissively consuming spectacles one is estranged from actively producing one's life. Capitalist society separates workers from the products of their labor, art from life, and consumption from human needs and self-directing activity, as individuals inertly observe the spectacles of social life from within the privacy of their homes (ibid.: Sections 25 and 26). The Situationist project, by contrast, involved an overcoming of all forms of separation, in which individuals would directly produce their own life and modes of self-activity and collective practice.

The correlate of the spectacle, for Debord, is thus the spectator, the reactive viewer and consumer of a social system predicated on submission, conformity, and the cultivation of marketable difference. The concept of the spectacle therefore involves a distinction between passivity and activity, consumption and production, condemning lifeless consumption of spectacle as an alienation from human potentiality for creativity and imagination. The spectacular society spreads its wares mainly through the cultural mechanisms of leisure and consumption, services and entertainment, ruled by the dictates of advertising and a commercialized media culture. This structural shift to a society of the spectacle involves a commodification of previously non-colonized sectors of social life and the extension of bureaucratic control to the realms of leisure, desire, and everyday life. Parallel to the Frankfurt School conception of a "totally administered" or "one-dimensional" society (Marcuse 1964; Horkheimer and Adorno 1972), Debord states that: "The spectacle is the moment when the consumption has attained the *total occupation* of social life" (1967: Section 42). Here, exploitation is raised to a psychological level; basic physical privation is augmented by "enriched privation" of pseudo-needs; alienation is generalized, made comfortable, and alienated consumption becomes "a duty supplementary to alienated production" (ibid.: Section 42).

Since Debord's theorization of the society of the spectacle in the 1960s and 1970s, spectacle culture has expanded in every area of life. In the culture of the spectacle, commercial enterprises have to be entertaining to prosper and, as Michael J. Wolf (1999) argues, in an "entertainment economy," business and fun fuse, so that the E-factor is becoming a major aspect of business.[2] Through the "entertainmentization" of the economy, entertainment forms such as television, film, theme parks, video games, casinos, and so forth become major sectors of the national economy. In the United States, the entertainment industry is now a $480 billion industry, and consumers spend more on having fun than on clothes or health care (Wolf 1999: 4).[3]

2 Wolf's book is a detailed and useful celebration of the "entertainment economy," although he is a shill for the firms and tycoons that he works for and celebrates them in his book. Moreover, while entertainment is certainly an important component of the infotainment economy, it is an exaggeration to say that it drives it and is actually propelling it, as Wolf repeatedly claims. Wolf also downplays the negative aspects of the entertainment economy, such as growing consumer debt and the ups and downs of the infotainment stock market and vicissitudes of the global economy.

3 Another source notes that "the average American household spent $1,813 in 1997 on entertainment—books, TV, movies, theater, toys—almost as much as the $1,841 spent on health care per family, according to a survey by the US Labor Department." Moreover, "the price we pay to amuse

In a competitive business world, the "fun factor" can give one business the edge over another. Hence, corporations seek to be more entertaining in their commercials, their business environment, their commercial spaces, and their websites. Budweiser ads, for instance, feature talking frogs that tell us nothing about the beer, but which catch the viewers' attention, while Taco Bell deploys a talking dog and Pepsi uses *Star Wars* characters. Buying, shopping, and dining out are coded as an "experience," as businesses adopt a theme-park style. Places such as the Hard Rock Cafe and the House of Blues are not renowned for their food, after all; people go there for the ambience, to purchase House of Blues paraphernalia, and to view music and media memorabilia. It is no longer good enough just to have a website, it has to be an interactive spectacle, featuring not only products to buy, but music and videos to download, games to play, prizes to win, travel information, and "links to other cool sites."

To succeed in the ultracompetitive global marketplace, corporations need to circulate their image and brand name, so business and advertising combine in the promotion of corporations as media spectacles. Endless promotion circulates the McDonald's "golden arches," Nike's "swoosh," or the logos of Apple, Intel, or Microsoft. In the brand wars between commodities, corporations need to make their logos or "trademarks" a familiar signpost in contemporary culture. Corporations place their logos on their products, in ads, in the spaces of everyday life, and in the midst of media spectacles, such as important sporting events, TV shows, movie product placement, and wherever they can catch consumers' eyeballs, to impress their brand name on potential buyers. Consequently, advertising, marketing, public relations, and promotion are an essential part of commodity spectacle in the global marketplace.

Celebrity too is manufactured and managed in the world of media spectacle. Celebrities are the icons of media culture, the gods and goddesses of everyday life. To become a celebrity requires recognition as a star player in the field of media spectacle, be it sports, entertainment, fashion, or politics. Celebrities have their handlers and image managers, who make sure that their clients continue to be seen and positively perceived by the public. Just as with corporate brand names, celebrities become brands to sell their Madonna, Michael Jordan, Tom Cruise, or Jennifer

---

ourselves has, in some cases, risen at a rate triple that of inflation over the past five years" (*USA Today*, April 2, 1999: E1). The NPD Group provided a survey that indicated that the amount of time spent on entertainment outside the home—such as going to the movies or a sporting event—was up 8 percent from the early to the late 1990s and the amount of time spent on home entertainment, such as watching television or surfing the Internet, went up 2 percent. Reports indicate that in a typical US household, people with broadband Internet connections spent 22 percent more time on all-electronic media and entertainment than the average household without broadband. See "Study: broadband in homes changes media habits" (pcworld.com, October 11, 2000).

Lopez product and image. In a media culture, however, celebrities are always prey to scandal and thus must have at their disposal an entire public relations apparatus to manage their spectacle fortunes and to make sure that they not only maintain high visibility but keep projecting a positive image. Of course, within limits, "bad" and transgressions can also sell, and so media spectacle contains celebrity dramas that attract public attention and can even define an entire period, as when the O. J. Simpson murder trials and Bill Clinton sex scandals dominated the media in the mid and late 1990s.

Entertainment has always been a prime field of the spectacle, but in today's info-tainment society, entertainment and spectacle have entered into the domains of the economy, politics, society, and everyday life in important new ways. Building on the tradition of spectacle, contemporary forms of entertainment from television to the stage are incorporating spectacle culture into their enterprises, transforming film, television, music, drama, and other domains of culture, as well as producing spectacular new forms of culture, such as cyberspace, multimedia, and virtual reality.

For Neil Gabler, in an era of media spectacle, life itself is becoming like a movie and we create our own lives as a genre like film, or television, in which we become "at once performance artists in, and audiences for, a grand, ongoing show" (Gabler 1998: 4). In Gabler's view, we star in our own "lifies," making our lives into entertainment acted out for audiences of our peers, following the scripts of media culture, adopting its role models and fashion types, its style and look. Seeing our lives in cinematic terms, entertainment becomes, for Gabler, "arguably the most pervasive, powerful and ineluctable force of our time—a force so overwhelming that it has metastasized into life" to such an extent that it is impossible to distinguish between the two (ibid.: 9). As Gabler sees it, Ralph Lauren is our fashion expert; Martha Stewart designs our sets; Jane Fonda models our shaping of our bodies; and Oprah Winfrey advises us on our personal problems.[4]

Media spectacle is indeed a culture of celebrity which provides dominant role models and icons of fashion, look, and personality. In the world of spectacle,

---

4   Gabler's book is a synthesis of Daniel Boorstin, Dwight Macdonald, Neil Poster, Marshall McLuhan, and various trendy theorists of media culture, but without the brilliance of a Baudrillard, the incisive criticism of an Adorno, or the understanding of the deeper utopian attraction of media culture of a Bloch or a Jameson. Likewise, Gabler does not, à la cultural studies, engage the politics of representation, or its ideologies and political economy. He thus ignores mergers in the culture industries, new technologies, the restructuring of capitalism, globalization, and shifts in the economy that are driving the impetus toward entertainment. Gabler also does not address how new technologies are creating new spheres of entertainment and forms of experience and in general describes rather than theorizes the trends he is engaging.

celebrity encompasses every major social domain from entertainment to politics to sports to business. An ever-expanding public relations industry hypes certain figures, elevating them to celebrity status, and protects their positive image in the never-ending image wars. For there is always the danger that a celebrity will fall prey to the hazards of negative image and thus lose celebrity status, or become a negative figure, as will some of the players and institutions of media spectacle that I examine in these studies.

Sports have long been a domain of the spectacle, with events such as the Olympics, World Series, Super Bowl, soccer World Cup, and NBA Championships attracting massive audiences while generating sky-high advertising rates. These cultural rituals celebrate society's deepest values (i.e., competition, winning, success, and money), and corporations are willing to pay top dollars to get their products associated with such events. Indeed, it appears that the logic of the commodity spectacle is inexorably permeating professional sports, which can no longer be played without the accompaniment of cheerleaders, giant mascots that clown with players and spectators, and raffles, promotions, and contests that feature the products of various sponsors.

Sports stadiums themselves contain electronic reproduction of the action, as well as giant advertisements for various products that rotate for maximum saturation—previewing environmental advertising, in which entire urban sites are becoming scenes to boost consumption spectacles. Arenas such as the United Center in Chicago, the America West Arena in Phoenix, or Enron Field in Houston are named after corporate sponsors. Of course, following major corporate scandals or collapses, such as the Enron spectacle, the ballparks must be renamed!

The Texas Rangers' Ballpark in Arlington, Texas, supplements its sports arena with a shopping mall, office buildings, and a restaurant in which, for a hefty price, one can watch the athletic events while eating and drinking.[5] The architecture of the Texas Rangers' stadium is an example of the implosion of sports and entertainment

---

5 The project was designed and sold to the public in part through the efforts of the then floundering son of a former president, George W. Bush. Young Bush was bailed out of heavy losses in the Texas oil industry in the 1980s by his father's friends and used his capital gains, gleaned from what some say was illicit insider trading, to purchase part-ownership of a baseball team (the Texas Rangers). The soon-to-be Governor of Texas, and future President of the United States, sold the new stadium to local taxpayers, getting them to agree to a higher sales tax to build the stadium, which would then become the property of Bush and his partners. This deal allowed Bush to generate a healthy profit when he sold his interest in the Texas Rangers franchise to buy his Texas ranch, paid for by Texas taxpayers (for sources on the life of George W. Bush and his surprising success in politics, see Kellner (2001) and the discussion on Bush Jr. in Chapter 6).

and postmodern spectacle. An artificial lake surrounds the stadium, the corridor inside is modeled after Chartres Cathedral, and the structure is made of local stone that provides the look of the Texas Capitol in Austin. Inside there are Texas long-horn cattle carvings, panels depicting Texas and baseball history, and other iconic signifiers of sports and Texas. The merging of sports, entertainment, and local spectacle is now typical in sports palaces. Tropicana Field in Tampa Bay, Florida, for instance, "has a three-level mall that includes places where 'fans can get a trim at the barber shop, do their banking and then grab a cold one at the Budweiser brew pub, whose copper kettles rise three stories. There is even a climbing wall for kids and showroom space for car dealerships'" (Ritzer 1998: 229).

Film has long been a fertile field of the spectacle, with "Hollywood" connoting a world of glamour, publicity, fashion, and excess. Hollywood has exhibited grand movie palaces, spectacular openings with searchlights and camera-popping paparazzi, glamorous Oscars, and stylish, hi-tech films. Although epic spectacle became a dominant genre of Hollywood film, from early versions of *The Ten Commandments* through *Cleopatra* and *2001* in the 1960s, contemporary film has incorporated the mechanics of spectacle into its form, style, and special effects. Films are hyped into spectacle through advertising and trailers that are ever louder, more glitzy, and razzle-dazzling. Some of the most popular films of the late 1990s were spectacle films, including *Titanic*, *Star Wars—Phantom Menace*, *Three Kings*, and *Austin Powers*, a spoof of spectacle, which became one of the most successful films of summer 1999. During the fall of 1999, there was a cycle of spectacles, including *Topsy Turvy*, *Titus*, *Cradle Will Rock*, *Sleepy Hollow*, *The Insider*, and *Magnolia*, with the last featuring the biblical spectacle of the raining of frogs in the San Fernando Valley, in an allegory of the decadence of the entertainment industry and its deserved punishment for its excesses.

The 2000 Academy Awards were dominated by the spectacle *Gladiator*, a mediocre film that captured the best picture award and the best acting award for Russell Crowe, thus demonstrating the extent to which the logic of the spectacle now dominates Hollywood film. Some of the most critically acclaimed and popular films of 2001 were also hi-tech spectacle, such as *Moulin Rouge*, a film that itself is a delirious ode to spectacle, from cabaret and the brothel to can-can dancing, opera, musical comedy, dance, theater, popular music, and film. A postmodern pastiche of popular music styles and hits, the film uses songs and music ranging from Madonna and the Beatles to Dolly Parton and Kiss.

Other 2001 film spectacles included *Pearl Harbor*, which re-enacts the Japanese attack on the United States that propelled the country to enter World War II, and which provided a ready metaphor for the September 11 terrorist attacks. Major 2001 film spectacles ranged from David Lynch's postmodern surrealism in *Mulholland Drive* to Steven Spielberg's blending of his typically sentimental spectacle of the family with the vision of Stanley Kubrick in *AI*. And the popular 2001 military film *Black Hawk Down* provided a spectacle of US military heroism, which some critics believed sugar-coated the real problems with the US military intervention in Somalia. This created fears that future US adventures involving the Bush administration and the Pentagon would meet similar problems. There were reports, however, that in Somalian cinemas there were loud cheers as the Somalians in the film shot down the US helicopter, and pursued and killed US soldiers, attesting to growing anti-US sentiment in the Muslim world against the Bush administration's policies.

Television has been, from its introduction in the 1940s, a promoter of consumption spectacle, selling cars, fashion, home appliances, and other commodities along with consumer lifestyles and values. It is also the home of sports spectacles such as the Super Bowl or World Series, political spectacles such as elections, scandals, and entertainment spectacles such as the Oscars or Grammies, and its own specialties such as breaking news or special events. Following the logic of spectacle entertainment, contemporary television exhibits more hi-tech glitter, faster and glitzier editing, computer simulations, and, with cable and satellite television, a diverse array of every conceivable type of show and genre.

Television is today a medium of spectacular programs such as *The X-Files* or *Buffy, the Vampire Slayer* and spectacles of everyday life such as MTV's *The Real World* and *Road Rules*, or the globally popular *Survivor* and *Big Brother* series. Real-life events, however, took over TV spectacle in 2000–2001 in, first, an intense battle for the White House in a dead-heat election that arguably constitutes the greatest political crime and scandal in US history (see Kellner 2001). After months of the Bush administration pushing the most hard-right political agenda in memory and then deadlocking as the Democrats took control of the Senate in a dramatic party reaffiliation of Vermont's Jim Jeffords, the world was treated to the most horrifying spectacle of the new millennium, the September 11 terrorist attacks and unfolding Terror War. These events promise an unending series of deadly spectacles for the foreseeable future (see Kellner, forthcoming).

Theater is a fertile field of the spectacle, and thus contemporary stage has exploited its dramaturgical and musical past to create current attractions for large audiences. Plays such as *Bring in 'Da Noise, Bring in 'Da Funk, Smokey Joe's Cafe, Fosse, Swing!,* and *Contact* draw on the history of musical spectacle, bringing some of the most spectacular moments of the traditions of jazz, funk, blues, swing, country, rock, and other forms of pop entertainment to contemporary thespian audiences. Many of the most popular plays of recent years on a global scale have been musical spectacles, including *Les Misérables*, *Phantom of the Opera*, *Rent*, *Ragtime*, *The Lion King*, *Mama Mia*, and *The Producers*, a stunningly successful musical spectacle that mocks the Nazis and show business. These theatrical spectacles are often a pastiche of previous literature, opera, film, or theater, and reveal the lust of contemporary audiences for nostalgia and participation in all types of cultural extravaganzas.

Fashion is historically a central domain of the spectacle, and today producers and models, as well as the actual products of the industry, constitute an enticing sector of media culture. Fashion designers are celebrities, such as the late Gianni Versace, whose murder by a gay ex-lover in 1997 was a major spectacle of the era. Versace brought together the worlds of fashion, design, rock, entertainment, and royalty in his fashion shows and emporia. When Yves Saint-Laurent retired in 2002, there was a veritable media frenzy to celebrate his contributions to fashion, which included bringing in the aesthetic and images of modern art and catering for the demands of contemporary liberated women as he developed new forms of style and couture.

In fashion today, inherently a consumer spectacle, laser-light shows, top rock and pop music performers, superstar models, and endless hype publicize each new season's offerings, generating highly elaborate and spectacular clothing displays. The consumption spectacle is fundamentally interconnected with fashion, which demonstrates what is in and out, hot and cold, in the buzz world of style and vogue. The stars of the entertainment industry become fashion icons and models for imitation and emulation. In a postmodern image culture, style and look become increasingly important modes of identity and presentation of the self in everyday life, and the spectacles of media culture show and tell people how to appear and behave.

Bringing the spectacle into the world of high art, the Guggenheim Museum's Thomas Krens organized a retrospective on Giorgio Armani, the Italian fashion designer. Earlier, Krens had produced a Guggenheim show exhibiting motorcycles and showing plans to open a Guggenheim gallery in the Venetian Resort Hotel Casino in Las Vegas with a seven-story Guggenheim art museum next to it. Not to be outdone, in October 2000, the Los Angeles County Art Museum opened its largest show in history, a megaspectacle "Made in California: Art, image, and identity, 1900–2000," featuring multimedia exhibitions of everything from canonical Californian painting and photography to Jefferson Airplane album covers, surf boards, and a 1998 *Playboy* magazine with "the babes of Baywatch" on its cover.

In 2001, the Los Angeles County Art Museum announced that it would become a major spectacle itself, provisionally accepting a design by Rem Koolhaas that would create a spectacular new architectural cover for the museum complex. As described by the *Los Angeles Times* architectural critic, the "design is a temple for a mobile, post-industrial age ... Capped by an organic, tent-like roof, its monumental form will serve as both a vibrant public forum and a spectacular place to view art" (December 7, 2001: F1).

Contemporary architecture too is ruled by the logic of the spectacle, and critics have noticed how art museums are coming to trump the art collection by making the building and setting more spectacular than the collections.[6] The Frank Gehry Guggenheim Museum in Bilbao, Spain, the Richard Meier Getty Center in Los Angeles, the retrofitted power plant that became the Tate Modern in London, Tadao Ando's Pulitzer Foundation building in Saint Louis, and Santiago Calatrava's addition to the Milwaukee Museum of Art all provide superspectacle environments in which to display their art works and museum fare. Major architectural projects for corporations and cities often provide postmodern spectacles whereby the glass and steel structures of high modernism are replaced by buildings and spaces adorned with signs of the consumer society and complex structures that attest to the growing power of commerce and technocapitalism.

Popular music is also colonized by the spectacle, with music-video television (MTV) becoming a major purveyor of music, bringing spectacle into the core of musical production and distribution. Madonna and Michael Jackson would never have become global superstars of popular music without the spectacular production values of their music videos and concert extravaganzas. Both also performed their lives as media spectacle, generating maximum publicity and attention (not always positive!). Michael Jackson attracted attention in 2001 in a TV spectacle in which he reportedly paid hundreds of thousands of dollars to digitally redo the concert footage he appeared in. Jackson had his images retooled so that he would be free of sweat and appear darker than the "real" image, in order to blend in better with his family members, who were performing with him, and to appear as a cooler black to appeal to his fans. In June 2002, the Michael Jackson spectacle took a bizarre turn when the onetime superstar called the president of Sony records a "racist," in a rally with African–American activist Al Sharpton, for not releasing a September 11 single that Jackson had helped to produce and for not adequately promoting his recent album. Within days, there were reports, however, that Jackson

6   See Nicholai Ouroussoff, "Art for architecture's sake," *Los Angeles Times*, March 31, 2002.

was co-producing the September 11 fund-raising song with a child pornography producer, that McDonald's had dropped its sponsorship when it learned of this, and that Sony too had issues with the project.[7] In a culture of the spectacle, public relations and image can thus make or break its celebrities. Indeed, one cannot fully grasp the Madonna phenomenon without analyzing her marketing and publicity strategies, her exploitation of spectacle, and her ability to make herself a celebrity spectacle of the highest order (Kellner 1995).

In a similar fashion, younger female pop music stars and groups, such as Mariah Carey, Britney Spears, Jennifer Lopez, or Destiny's Child, also deploy the tools of the glamour industry and media spectacle to make themselves spectacular icons of fashion, beauty, style, and sexuality, as well as purveyors of music. Male pop singers, such as Ricky Martin, could double as fashion models, and male groups, such as 'N Sync, use hi-tech stage shows, music videos, and PR to sell their wares. Moreover, hip-hop culture has cultivated a whole range of spectacle, from musical extravaganzas to lifestyle cultivation to real-life crime wars among its stars.

Musical concert extravaganzas are more and more spectacular (and expensive!) and the Internet is providing the spectacle of free music and a new realm of sound through Napster and other technologies, although the state has been battling attempts by young people to utilize P2P (peer to peer) technologies to decommodify culture. Indeed, films, DVDs, sports events, and musical spectacles have been circulating through the Internet in a gift economy that has generated the spectacle of the state attacking those who violate copyright laws that some would claim to be outdated in the culture of hi-tech spectacle.

Food too is becoming a spectacle in the consumer society, with presentation as important in the better restaurants as taste and substance. Best-selling books such as Isabel Allende's *Aphrodite* and Jeffrey Steingarten's *The Man Who Ate Everything* celebrate the conjunction of eroticism and culinary delight. Magazines such as *Bon Appetite* and *Saveur* glorify the joys of good eating, and the food sections of many magazines and newspapers are among the most popular parts. Films such as *Babette's Feast*, *Like Water for Chocolate*, *Big Night*, and *Chocolat* fetishize food and eating, presenting food with the pornographic excesses usually reserved for sex.

Eroticism has frequently permeated the spectacles of Western culture, and is prominently on display in Hollywood film, as well as in advertisements, clubs, and pornography. Long a major component of advertising, eroticized sexuality has

---

7   See Chuck Philips, "New spin on collapse of Jackson's charity project," *Los Angeles Times*, July 13, 2002.

been used to sell every conceivable product. The spectacle of sex is also one of the staples of media culture, permeating all cultural forms and creating its own genres in pornography, one of the highest-grossing domains of media spectacle. In the culture of the spectacle, sex becomes shockingly exotic and diverse through the media of porn videos, DVDs, and Internet sites that make available everything from teen-animal sex to orgies of the most extravagant sort. Technologies of cultural reproduction, such as home video recorders (VCRs), DVDs, and computers, bring sex more readily into the private recesses of the home. And today the sex spectacle attains more and more exotic forms with multimedia and multisensory eroticism, as envisaged in Huxley's *Brave New World*, on the horizon.[8]

The spectacle of video and computer games has been a major source of youth entertainment and industry profit. In 2001, the US video game industry hit a record $9 billion in sales and it expects to do even better in the next couple of years (*Los Angeles Times*, January 1, 2002: C1). For decades now, video and computer games have obsessed sectors of youth and provided skills needed for the hi-tech dot.com economy, as well as for fighting postmodern war. These games are highly competitive, violent, and provide allegories for life under corporate capitalism and Terror War militarism. In the game *Pacman*, as in the corporate jungle, it's eat or be eaten, just as in air and ground war games, it's kill or be killed. *Grand Theft Auto 3* and *State of Emergency* were two of the most popular games in 2002, with the former involving high-speed races through urban jungles and the latter involving political riots and state repression! While some women and game producers have tried to cultivate kinder, gentler, and more intelligent gaming, the best-selling corporate games are spectacles for predatory capitalism and macho militarism and not a more peaceful, playful, and co-operative world. Indeed, in 2002, the US military developed a highly popular and critically acclaimed computer game, freely available to anyone online for downloading and playing upon registration with the US Army (www.goarmy.com/aagame/index.htm). Promoted as "The Official Army Game," it

---

8　There is little doubt but that the emergent technologies of virtual reality, holograms, and computer implants of sensory experience (if such exotica emerge) will be heavily invested in the reproduction of sex. In a webpost by Richard Johnson, "Virtual sex is here" (www.ThePosition.com, January 4, 2001), British Professor Kevin Warwick's latest experiment is described, which involves the implanting of a computer chip, which, if successful, will make possible the communication of a wide range of sensory experience and new types of sexual stimulation. The 1995 film *Strange Days* portrayed a futuristic culture, with addictive virtual reality devices, in which spectators become hooked on videos of extreme sex and violence. *The 13th Floor* (1999) portrayed a virtual reality gadget whereby players are transported to recreations of other times, places, and identities, experiencing full bodily fears and pleasures.

allows the user to participate in simulated military basic training activities. The *Go Army* spectacle provides at once propaganda for the military, a recruitment tool, and participation in simulated military action. As military activity itself becomes increasingly dependent on computer simulation, the line between gaming and killing, simulation and military action, blurs, and military spectacle becomes a familiar part of everyday life.

The terrifying spectacle of fall 2001 revealed that familiar items of everyday life, such as planes or mail, could be transformed into instruments of spectacular terror. The al-Qaeda network hijacking of airplanes turned ordinary instruments of transportation into weapons as they crashed into the World Trade Center twin towers and the Pentagon on September 11. Mail delivery evoked fears of disease, terror, and death, as the anthrax scare of fall and winter 2001 made ordinary letters threatening items. And rumors spread that terrorist networks were seeking instruments of mass destruction, such as chemical, biological, and nuclear weapons, to create spectacles of terror on a hitherto unforeseen scale.

The examples just provided suggest that media spectacle is invading every field of experience, from the economy to culture and everyday life to politics and war. Moreover, spectacle culture is moving into new domains of cyberspace that will help to generate future multimedia spectacle and networked infotainment societies. My studies of media spectacle will strive to contribute to illuminating these developments and to developing a critical theory of the contemporary moment. Building on Debord's analyses of the society of spectacle, I will develop the concept in terms of salient phenomena of present-day society and culture.

But while Debord's notion of spectacle tended to be somewhat abstract and theoretical, I will attempt to make the concept concrete and contemporary. Thus, whereas Debord presents few actual examples of spectacle culture, I develop detailed analyses that strive to illuminate the present age and to update and develop Debord's notion. Moreover, although Debord's concepts of "the society of the spectacle" and of "the integrated spectacle" (1990) tended to present a picture of a quasi-totalitarian nexus of domination,[9] it is preferable to perceive a plurality and heterogeneity of contending spectacles in the contemporary moment and to see spectacle itself as a contested terrain. Accordingly, I will unfold contradictions within dominant spectacles, showing how they give rise to conflicting meanings and effects, and constitute a field of domination and resistance.

---

9   For a critique of Debord, see Best and Kellner 1997: 118ff.

These "dialectics of the present" will disclose both novelties and discontinuities in the current epoch, as well as continuities with the development of global capitalism. The in-depth studies that follow in this book [*Media Spectacle*, by Douglas Kellner] attempt to articulate defining features of the existing and emergent society, culture, and everyday life in the new millennium. Yet my studies suggest that novel and distinctive features are embedded in the trajectory of contemporary capitalism, its creation of a global economy, and ongoing "creative destruction," which has been a defining feature of capitalist modernity from the beginning. Hence, the cultural studies in [the] book will be rooted in critical social theory and will themselves contribute to developing a critical theory of society by illuminating key features and dynamics of the present age. The studies will illustrate, in particular, the dynamics of media spectacle and an infotainment society in the current stage of technocapitalism.[10]

The Infotainment Society and Technocapitalism

Today the society and culture of spectacle is creating a new type of information-entertainment society, or what might be called the "infotainment society." The changes in the current conjuncture are arguably as thoroughgoing and dramatic as the shift from the stage of market and the competitive and *laissez-faire* capitalism theorized by Marx to the stage of state-monopoly capitalism critically analyzed by the Frankfurt School in the 1930s. Currently, we are entering a new form of *technocapitalism* marked by a synthesis of capital and technology and the information and entertainment industries, all of which is producing an "infotainment society" and spectacle culture.[11]

In terms of political economy, the emerging postindustrial form of technocapitalism is characterized by a decline of the state and enlarged power for the market, accompanied by the growing strength of transnational corporations and governmental bodies and the decreased strength of the nation-state and its institutions.

---

10   The analyses in this book [*Media Spectacle*, by Douglas Kellner] are primarily cultural studies, and I explore in more detail elsewhere the consequences for social theory of the phenomena explored. Theoretical grounding, in turn, for the investigations is found in past works, such as Kellner and Ryan (1988), Kellner (1989a, b), Best and Kellner (1991; 1997; 2001), Kellner (1995).

11   On the various stages of development of the Frankfurt School and for an earlier introduction of the concept of technocapitalism, see Kellner (1989b). For more recent reflections on the roles of new technologies in the current stage of capitalist development, see Best and Kellner (2001) and Kellner (2000a).

To paraphrase Max Horkheimer, whoever wants to talk about capitalism must talk about globalization, and it is impossible to theorize globalization without addressing the restructuring of capitalism. Culture and technology are increasingly important constituent parts of global capitalism and everyday life in the contemporary world and permeate major domains of life, such as the economy and polity, as well as constituting their own spheres and subcultures.

The term "infotainment" suggests the synergies of the information and entertainment sectors in the organization of contemporary societies, the ways in which information technologies and multimedia are transforming entertainment, and the forms in which entertainment is shaping every domain of life from the Internet to politics. It is now well documented that the knowledge and information sectors are key domains of our contemporary moment, although how to theorize the dialectics of the present is highly contested. While the theories of Harvard sociologist Daniel Bell (1976) and other postindustrial theorists are not as ideological and far off the mark as some of us once argued, the concept of "postindustrial" society is highly problematic. The concept is negative and empty, failing to articulate positively what distinguishes the alleged new stage. Hence, the discourse of the "post" can occlude the connections between industrial, manufacturing, and emergent hi-tech industries and the strong continuities between the previous and present forms of social organization, as well as covering over the continued importance of manufacturing and industry for much of the world.

Yet discourses of the "post" also serve positively to highlight the importance of significant novelties, of discontinuities with modern societies, and thus force us to rethink the original and defining features of our current social situation (see Best and Kellner 1997; 2001). Notions of the "knowledge" or "information" society rightly call attention to the role of scientific and technical knowledge in the formation of the present social order, the importance of computers and information technology, the materialization of biotechnology, genetic engineering, and the rise of new societal elites. It seems wrong, however, to characterize knowledge or information as *the* organizing or axial principles of a society still constructed around the accumulation of capital and maximization of profit. Hence, in order to avoid the technological determinism and idealism of many forms of postindustrial theory, one should theorize the information or knowledge "revolution" as part and parcel of a new form of technocapitalism. Such a perspective focuses on the interconnections between new technologies, a networked global society, and an expansion of the culture of spectacle in an emergent mode of the "infotainment society," rather than merely obsessing about "new technologies" or "globalization," without seeing the articulations of these phenomena.[12]

The limitations of earlier theories of the "knowledge society," or "postindustrial society," as well as current forms of the "information society," revolve around the extent to which they exaggerate the role of knowledge and information. Such concepts advance an idealist vision that excessively privileges the role of knowledge and information in the economy, in politics and society, and in everyday life. These optics downplay the role of capitalist relations of production, corporate ownership and control, and hegemonic configurations of corporate and state power with all their massive and momentous effects. As I argue below, while discourses of the "post" help describe key defining features of contemporary societies, at least in the overdeveloped world, they neither grasp the specificity of the current forms of global technocapitalism, nor do they sufficiently mark the continuities with previous stages of societal development.

Consequently, to grasp the dynamics of our current social situation, we need to perceive the continuities between previous forms of industrial society and the new modes of society and culture described by discourses of the "post," *and* also grasp the novelties and discontinuities (Best and Kellner 1997; 2001).[13] In the studies in this book, I argue that current conceptions of the information society and the emphasis on information technology as its demiurge are by now too limited. The new technologies are modes of information *and* entertainment that permeate work, education, play, social interaction, politics, and culture. In all of these domains, the form of spectacle is changing areas of life ranging from work and communication to entertainment and diversion.

Thus, "new technologies" are much more than solely information technology, and involve important components of entertainment, communication, and multimedia, as well as knowledge and information, in ways that are encompassing and

---

12 It is striking how many theories of globalization neglect the role of information technology, often falling prey to economic determinism, while many theories of information technology fail to theorize their embeddedness in the global economy, thus falling prey to technological determinism. See Kellner (2000b) and Best and Kellner (2001).

13 Frank Webster (1995: 5, *passim*) wants to draw a line between "those who endorse the idea of an information society" and "writers who place emphasis on continuities." Although he puts me in the camp of those who emphasize continuities (p. 188), I would argue that we need to grasp both continuities and discontinuities in the current societal transformation we are undergoing and that we deploy a both/and logic in this case and not an either/or logic. In other words, we need to theorize both the novelties and differences in the current social restructuring and the continuities with the previous mode of societal organization. Such a dialectical optic is, I believe, consistent with the mode of vision of Marx and neo-Marxists such as those in the Frankfurt School.

restructuring both labor and leisure. Previous forms of culture are rapidly being absorbed within the Internet, and the computer is coming to be a major household appliance and source of entertainment, information, play, communication, and connection with the outside world. To help grasp the enormity of the transformation going on, and as indicators of the syntheses of knowledge and cultural industries in the infotainment society, I would suggest reflecting on the massive mergers of the major information and entertainment conglomerates that have taken place in the United States during the past decades. This process has produced the most extensive concentration and conglomeration of these industries in history, as well as an astonishing development and expansion of technologies and media products.

During the 1980s, television networks amalgamated with other major sectors of the cultural industries and corporate capital, including mergers between CBS and Westinghouse; MCA and Seagram's; Time Warner and Turner Communications; Disney, Capital Cities, and ABC; and GE, NBC, and Microsoft. Dwarfing all previous information/entertainment corporation combinations, Time Warner and America On-Line (AOL) proposed a $163.4 billion amalgamation in January 2000, which was approved a year later. The fact that "new media" Internet service provider and portal AOL was initially the majority shareholder in the deal seemed at the time to be the triumph of the new online Internet culture over the old media culture. The merger itself called attention to escalating synergy among information and entertainment industries and old and new media in the form of the networked economy and cyberculture. But the dramatic decline of its stock price after the merger and a reorganization of the corporation in June 2002 called attention to the difficulties of merging old and new media and complexities and uncertainties within the culture industries that are producing spectacle culture.

These amalgamations bring together corporations involved in TV, film, magazines, newspapers, books, information databases, computers, and other media, suggesting a conflictual and unpredictable coming together of media and computer culture, and of entertainment and information, in a new networked and multimedia infotainment society. There have also been massive mergers in the telecommunications industry, as well as between cable and satellite industries, with major entertainment and corporate conglomerates. By 2002, ten gigantic multinational corporations, including AOL-Time Warner, Disney-ABC, GE-NBC, Viacom-CBS, News Corporation, Vivendi, Sony, Bertelsmann, AT&T, and Liberty Media controlled most of the production of information and entertainment throughout the globe.[14] The result is less competition and diversity and more corporate control of newspapers and journalism, television, radio, film, and other media of information and entertainment.

The corporate media, communications, and information industries are frantically scrambling to provide delivery for a wealth of services. These will include increased Internet access, wireless cellular telephones, and satellite personal communication devices, which will facilitate video, film, entertainment, and information on demand, as well as Internet shopping and more unsavory services such as pornography and gambling. Consequently, the fusions of the immense infotainment conglomerates disclose a synergy between information technologies and multimedia, which combine entertainment and information, undermining the distinctions between these domains.

The constantly proliferating corporate mergers of the information and entertainment industries therefore call for an expansion of the concept of the knowledge, or information, society into concepts of technocapitalism and its networked infotainment society. In this conception, the synthesis of global corporate capitalism and information and entertainment technologies is constructing novel forms of society and culture, controlled by capital and with global reach. In this context, the concept of the *networked infotainment society* characterizes the emergent technocapitalist project in order to highlight the imbrications of information and entertainment in the wired and wireless multimedia and information/entertainment technologies of the present. Together, these corporate mergers, and the products and services that they are producing, constitute an emergent infotainment society that it is our challenge to theorize and attempt to shape to more humane and democratic purposes than the accumulation of capital and corporate/state hegemony.

The syntheses of entertainment and information in the creation of a networked infotainment society are part and parcel of a global restructuring of capital. Few theories of the information revolution and the new technologies contextualize the structuring, implementation, distribution, and use of information technologies and new media in the context of the vicissitudes of contemporary capitalism and the explosion of media spectacle and the domain of infotainment. The ideologues of the information society act as if technology were an autonomous force. They often neglect to theorize the interconnections of capital and technology, or they

---

14 See the chart in *The Nation* (January 7, 2002) and the accompanying article by Mark Crispin Miller, "What's wrong with this picture?" as well as the analysis of the impact of "media unlimited" in Gitlin (2002), who discusses oversaturation, intensifying speed, and an increasingly media-mediated existence in the contemporary era.

use the advancements of technology to legitimate market capitalism (i.e., Gilder 1989; 2000; Gates 1995; 1999). More conventional and older sociological theories, by contrast, fail to grasp the important role of entertainment and spectacle in contemporary society and culture. Likewise, other theories of the information society, such as those of Daniel Bell (1976), exaggerate the role of information and knowledge, and neglect the importance of entertainment and spectacle.

Thus, Guy Debord's concept of the "society of the spectacle" in which individuals are transfixed by the packaging, display, and consumption of commodities and the play of media events helpfully illuminates our present situation. Arguably, we are now at a stage of the spectacle at which it dominates the mediascape, politics, and more and more domains of everyday life. In a culture of the technospectacle, computers bring escalating information and multimedia extravaganzas into the home and workplace through the Internet, competing with television as the dominant medium of our time. The result is a spectacularization of politics, of culture, and of consciousness, as media multiply and new forms of culture colonize consciousness and everyday life, generating novel forms of struggle and resistance.

Questions

1. What are the economic forces behind any given performance?
2. What is the business arrangement driving the performance?
3. How does spectacle influence your choices of popular entertainment?
4. Research one of your favorite television channels or Internet delivery site. Who owns it? How big is the conglomerate and what other media interests does the company own? How easy was that information to find?
5. What does 'infotainment' mean to you and how does it compare with Kellner's ideas?

View

Web

Frontline: Merchants of Cool. (2001) http://www.pbs.org/wgbh/pages/frontline/shows/cool/

Film

This Film is Not Yet Rated (2006)
The Greatest Movie Ever Sold. (2011)

Read

Ang, Ien. "Audience as Market and Audience as Public." *Desperately Seeking the Audience.* London: Routledge, 1991. 26–32. Print.

King, Geoff. "Die Harder/Try Harder: Narrative, Spectacle and Beyond, from Hollywood to Videogame." *ScreenPlay: Cinema/Videogames/Interfaces.* Ed. Geoff King and Tanya Krzywinska. London: Wallflower Press, 2002. 50–65. Print.

Schirato, Tony, Angi Buettner, Thierry Jutel, and Geoff Stall, eds. "The Media as Spectacle." *Understanding Media Studies.* New York: Oxford University Press, 2010. 136–155. Print.

Siapera, Eugenia. "From Couch Potatoes to Cybernauts? The Expanding Notion of the Audience on TV Channels' Websites." *New Media and Society* 6 (2004): 155–172. Print.

US Department of Commerce Bureau of Economic Analysis. 2012. Web. 14 June 2012.

Popular Entertainment as Performance

Richard Schechner is one of the foremost performance studies scholars in the world. He founded the Department of Performance Studies at the Tisch School of the Arts at New York University, and the Performance Company, which later became the Wooster Group. He also founded the East Coast Artists group, a professional ensemble dedicated to re-inventing classic texts, debuting new international work, and challenging conventional notions of contemporary theatre and performer training. This essay outlines the basic concepts of the performance theories that serve as a foundational frame for our investigation of popular entertainment as performance.

All performances are what Schechner calls "restored behaviors." These are performances that people train for and/or rehearse (58). Restored behavior is marked, framed, or heightened by the form in which it appears. Performances of restored behavior are governed by the conventions, rules, and elements of the form, which are either followed or ignored by the producer/performer. Every performance is unique and depends on the interactivity between the production of the performance and the reception of the performance.

Schechner's articulation of the functions and elements of performance aid us in describing and analyzing how a particular performance is constructed and how those elements contribute to the interactivity between form and audience. Keep these in mind as you interact with different forms of entertainment and take note of how these elements are used to create the unique performance you are watching.

Ideas

Restored Behavior
Interactivity
Performance Elements: venue, function, audience involvement, structure, and the historical and cultural context
Projections
Make-Believe/Make-Belief

Functions and kinds of performance
Make Believe/Make Belief
Functions and kinds of performance

What Is Performance?

By Richard Schechner

What Is "To Perform"?

In business, sports, and sex, "to perform" is to do something up to a standard—to succeed, to excel. In the arts, "to perform" is to put on a show, a play, a dance, a concert. In everyday life, "to perform" is to show off, to go to extremes, to underline an action for those who are watching. In the twenty-first century, people as never before live by means of performance.

"To perform" can also be understood in relation to:

- Being
- Doing
- Showing doing
- Explaining "showing doing."

"Being" is existence itself. "Doing" is the activity of all that exists, from quarks to sentient beings to supergalactic strings. "Showing doing" is performing: pointing to, underlining, and displaying doing. "Explaining 'showing doing'" is performance studies.

It is very important to distinguish these categories from each other. "Being" may be active or static, linear or circular, expanding or contracting, material or spiritual. Being is a philosophical category pointing to whatever people theorize is the "ultimate reality." "Doing" and "showing doing" are actions. Doing and showing doing are always in flux, always changing—reality as the

> Heraclitus of Ephesus (c. 535–475 BCE): Greek philosopher credited with the creation of the doctrine of "flux." The theory of impermanence and change. You can't step into the same river twice because the flow of the river insures that new water continually replaces the old.

Guillermo Gómez-Peña (1955–): Mexican-born bi-national performance artist and author, leader of *La Pocha Nostra*. His works include both writings *Warrior for Gringostroika* (1993), *The New World Border* (1996), *Dangerous Border Crossers* (2000), *and Ethno-Techno Writings on Performance, Activism, and Pedagogy* (2005, with Elaine Peña)—and performances: *Border Brujo* (1990), *El Naftazeca* (1994), *Border Stasis* (1998), *Brownout: Border Pulp Stories* (2001), and *Mexterminator vs the Global Predator* (2005).

Coco Fusco (1960–): Cuban-born interdisciplinary artist based in New York City. Collaborated with Guillermo Gómez-Peña on the performance *Two Undiscovered Amerindians Visit the West* (1992). Other performances include: *Dolores from 10h to 22h* (2002, with Ricardo Dominguez) and *The Incredible Disappearing Woman* (2003, with Ricardo Dominguez). Fusco is the author of *English is Broken Here* (1995), *Corpus Delecti: Performance Art of the Americas* (2000), *The Bodies That Were Not Ours* (2001), and *Only Skin Deep* (2003, with Brian Wallis).

Reflexive: referring back to oneself or itself.

pre-Socratic Greek philosopher Heraclitus experienced it. Heraclitus aphorized this perpetual flux: "No one can step twice into the same river, nor touch mortal substance twice in the same condition". The fourth term, "explaining 'showing doing,'" is a reflexive effort to comprehend the world of performance and the world as performance. This comprehension is usually the work of critics and scholars. But sometimes, in Brechtian theatre where the actor steps outside the role to comment on what the character is doing, and in critically aware performance art such as Guillermo Gómez-Peña's and Coco Fusco's *Two Undiscovered Amerindians Visit the West* (1992), a performance is reflexive.

Performances

Performances mark identities, bend time, reshape and adorn the body, and tell stories. Performances—of art, rituals, or ordinary life—are "restored behaviors," "twice-behaved behaviors," performed actions that people train for and rehearse (see Goffman box). That making art involves training and rehearsing is clear. But everyday life also involves years of training and practice, of learning appropriate culturally specific bits of behavior, of adjusting and performing one's life roles in relation to social and personal circumstances. The long infancy and childhood specific to the human species is an extended period of training and rehearsal for the successful performance of adult life. "Graduation" into adulthood is marked in many cultures by initiation rites. But even before adulthood some persons more comfortably adapt to the life they live than others who resist or rebel. Most people live the tension between acceptance and rebellion. The activities of public life—sometimes calm, sometimes full of turmoil; sometimes visible, sometimes masked—are collective performances. These activities range from sanctioned politics through to street demonstrations and other forms of protest, and on to revolution. The performers of these actions intend to change things, to maintain the status quo, or, most commonly, to find or make some common ground. A revolution or civil war occurs when the players do not desist and there is no common ground. Any and all of the activities of human life can be studied "as" performance (I will discuss "as" later in this chapter). Every action from the smallest to the most encompassing is made of twice-behaved behaviors.

What about actions that are apparently "once-behaved"—the Happenings of Allan Kaprow, for example, or an everyday life occurrence (cooking, dressing, taking a walk, talking to a friend)? Even these are constructed from behaviors previously behaved. In fact, the everydayness of everyday life is precisely its familiarity, its being built from known bits of behavior rearranged and shaped in order to suit specific circumstances. But it is also true that many events and behaviors are one-time events. Their "onceness" is a function of context, reception, and the countless ways bits of behavior can be organized, performed, and displayed. The overall event may appear to be new or original, but its constituent parts—if broken down finely enough and analyzed—are revealed as restored behaviors. "Lifelike" art—as Kaprow calls much of his work—is close to everyday life. Kaprow's art slightly underlines, highlights, or makes one aware of ordinary behavior—paying close attention to how a meal is prepared, looking back at one's footsteps after walking in the desert. Paying attention to simple activities performed in the present moment is developing a Zen consciousness in relation to the daily, an honoring of the ordinary.

Honoring the ordinary is noticing how ritual-like daily life is, how much daily life consists of repetitions.

There is a paradox here. How can both Heraclitus and the theory of restored behavior be right? Performances are made from bits of restored behavior, but every performance is different from every

Allan Kaprow (1927–2006): American artist who coined the term "Happening" to describe his 1959 installation/performance *18 Happenings in 6 Parts*. Author of *Assemblage, Environments and Happenings* (1966), *Essays on the Blurring of Art and Life* (2003, with Jeff Kelley), and *Childsplay* (2004, with Jeff Kelley).

Restored behavior: physical, verbal, or virtual actions that are not-for-the-first time; that are prepared or rehearsed. A person may not be aware that she is performing a strip of restored behavior. Also referred to as twice-behaved behavior.

Erving Goffman
Defining Performance

A "performance" may be defined as all the activity of a given participant on a given occasion which serves to influence in any way any of the other participants. Taking a particular participant and his performance as a basic point of reference, we may refer to those who contribute to the other performances as the audience, observers, or co-participants. The pre-established pattern of action which is unfolded during a performance and which may be presented or played through on other occasions may be called a "part" or a "routine." These situational terms can easily be related to conventional structural ones. When an individual or performer plays the same part to the same audience on different occasions, a social relationship is likely to arise. Defining social role as the enactment of rights and duties attached to a given status, we can say that a social role will involve one or more parts and that each of these different parts may be presented by the performer on a series of occasions to the same kinds of audiences or to an audience of the same persons.

1959, *The Presentation of Self in Everyday Life*, 15–16.

---

other. First, fixed bits of behavior can be recombined in endless variations. Second, no event can exactly copy another event. Not only the behavior itself—nuances of mood, tone of voice, body language, and so on, but also the specific occasion and context make each instance unique. What about mechanically, digitally, or biologically reproduced replicants or clones? It may be that a film or a digitized performance art piece will be the same at each showing. But the context of every reception makes each instance different. Even though every "thing" is exactly the same, each event in which the "thing" participates is different. The uniqueness of an event does not depend on its materiality solely but also on its interactivity—and the interactivity is always in flux. If this is so with regard to film and digitized media, how much more so for live performance, where both production and reception vary from instance to instance. Or in daily life, where context cannot be perfectly controlled. Thus, ironically, performances resist that which produces them.

Which leads to the question, "Where do performances take place?" A painting "takes place" in the physical object; a novel takes place in the words. But a performance takes place as action, interaction, and relation. In this regard, a painting or a novel can be performative or can be analyzed "as" performance. Performance isn't "in" anything, but "between." Let me explain. A performer in ordinary life, in a ritual, at play, or in the performing arts does/shows something—performs an action. For example, a mother lifts a spoon to her own mouth and then to a baby's mouth to show the baby how to eat cereal. The performance is the action of lifting the spoon, bringing it to mother's mouth, and then to baby's mouth. The baby is at first the spectator of its mother's performance. At some point, the baby becomes a co-performer as she takes the spoon and tries the same action often at first missing her mouth and messing up her lips and chin with food. Father videotapes the whole show. Later, maybe many years later, the baby is a grown woman showing to her own baby a home video of the day when she began to learn how to use a spoon. Viewing this video is another performance existing in the complex relation between the original event, the video of the event, the memory of parents now old or maybe dead, and the present moment of delight as mother points to the screen and tells her baby, "That was mommy when I was your age!" The first performance "takes place" in between the action of showing baby how to use the spoon and baby's reaction to this action. The second performance takes place between the videotape of the first performance and the reception of that first performance by both the baby-now-mother and her own baby (or anyone else watching the videotape). What is true of this "home movie" performance is true of all performances. To treat any object, work, or product "as" performance—a painting, a novel, a shoe, or anything at all—means to investigate what the object does, how it interacts with other objects or beings, and how it relates to other objects or beings. Performances exist only as actions, interactions, and relationships.

Bill Parcells Wants You To Perform

A 1999 full-page advertisement in *The New York Times* selling the Cadillac Seville car features American legendary football coach Bill Parcells staring out at the reader. […] One of Parcells' eyes is in shadow, the darkness blending into the background for the stark large white-on-black text:

IF YOU WANT TO IMPRESS
BILL PARCELLS
YOU HAVE TO
PERFORM

Underneath a photograph of a Seville, the text continues in smaller type, "Great performers have always made a big impression on Bill Parcells. That explains his strong appreciation for Seville […].

The ad conflates performing in sports, business, sex, the arts, and technology. Parcells excels as a football coach. By making demands upon his players he motivates them and they respond on the field with winning performances. Parcells' excellence derives from his drive, his ability to organize, and his insistence on careful attention to each detail of the game. His stare has "sex appeal"—his penetrating gaze is that of a potent man able to control the giants who play football. He combines mastery, efficiency, and beauty. At the same time, Parcells displays an understated flash; he knows he is playing to the camera and to the crowds. All of this informs the ad, which tries to convince viewers that the Cadillac, like Parcells, is at the top of its game, sexy and powerful, well made down to the last detail, dependable, the leader in its field, and something that will stand out in a crowd.

> Bill Parcells (1941–): American football coach. Winner in 1987 and 1991 of two Superbowls with the New York Giants.

Eight Kinds of Performance

Performances occur in eight sometimes separate, sometimes overlapping situations:

1. In everyday life—cooking, socializing, "just living"
2. In the arts
3. In sports and other popular entertainments
4. In business
5. In technology
6. In sex
7. In ritual—sacred and secular
8. In play.

Even this list does not exhaust the possibilities (see Carlson box). If examined rigorously as theoretical categories, the eight situations are not commensurate. "Everyday life" can encompass most of the other situations. The arts take as their subjects materials from everywhat and everywhere. Ritual and play are not only "genres" of performance but present in all of the situations as qualities, inflections, or moods. I list these eight to indicate the large territory covered by performance. Some items—those occurring in business, technology, and sex—are not usually analyzed with the others, which have been the loci of arts-based performance theories. And the operation of making categories such as these eight is the result of a particular culture-specific kind of thinking.

It is impossible to come at a subject except from one's own cultural positions. But once I began writing this book, the best I could do is to be aware of, and share with the reader, my biases and limitations. That having been noted, designating

---

Marvin Carlson
What is Performance?

The term "performance" has become extremely popular in recent years in a wide range of activities in the arts, in literature, and in the social sciences. As its popularity and usage has grown, so has a complex body of writing about performance, attempting to analyze and understand just what sort of human activity it is. […] The recognition that our lives are structured according to repeated and socially sanctioned modes of behavior raises the possibility that all human activity could potentially be considered as "performance," or at least all activity carried out with a consciousness of itself. […] If we consider performance as an essentially contested concept, this will help us to understand the futility of seeking some overarching semantic field to cover such seemingly disparate usages as the performance of an actor, of a schoolchild, of an automobile.

1996, *Performance: A Critical Introduction*, 4–5.

---

music, dance, and theatre as the "performing arts" may seem relatively simple. But as categories even these are ambiguous. What is designated "art," if anything at all, varies historically and culturally. Objects and performances called "art" in some cultures are like what is made or done in other cultures without being so designated. Many cultures do not have a word for, or category called, "art" even though they create performances and objects demonstrating a highly-developed aesthetic sense realized with consummate skill.

Not only making but evaluating "art" occurs everywhere. People all around the world know how to distinguish "good" from "bad" dancing, singing, orating, storytelling, sculpting, fabric design, pottery, painting, and so on. But what makes something "good" or "bad" varies greatly from place to place, time to time, and even occasion to occasion. The ritual objects of one culture or one historical period become the artworks of other cultures or periods. Museums of art are full of paintings and objects that once were regarded as sacred (and still may be by pillaged peoples eager to regain their ritual objects and sacred remains). Furthermore, even if a performance has a strong aesthetic dimension, it is not necessarily "art." The moves of basketball players are as beautiful as those of ballet dancers, but one is termed sport, the other art. Figure skating and gymnastics exist in both realms. […] Deciding what is art depends on context, historical circumstance, use, and local conventions.

Separating "art" from "ritual" is particularly difficult. I have noted that ritual objects from many cultures are featured in art museums. But consider also religious services with music, singing, dancing, preaching, storytelling, speaking in tongues, and healing. At a Christian evangelical church service, for example, people go into trance, dance in the aisles, give testimony, receive anointment and baptism. The gospel music heard in African–American churches is closely related to blues, jazz, and rock and roll. Are such services art or ritual? Composers, visual artists, and performers have long made works of fine art for use in rituals. To what realm does Johann Sebastian Bach's *Mass in B Minor* and his many cantatas or Wolfgang Amadeus Mozart's *Mass in C Minor* belong? Church authorities in medieval Europe such as Amalarius, the Bishop of Metz, asserted that the Mass was theatre equivalent to ancient Greek tragedy (see Hardison box). More than a few people attend religious services as much for aesthetic pleasure and social interactivity as for reasons of belief. In many cultures, participatory performing is the core of ritual practices. In ancient Athens, the great theatre festivals were ritual, art, sports-like competition, and popular entertainment simultaneously. Today, sports are both live and media entertainment featuring competition, ritual, spectacle, and big business.

As noted, some sports are close to fine arts. Gymnastics, figure skating, and high diving are recognized by the Olympics. But there are no quantitative ways to determine winners as there are in racing, javelin throwing, or weight lifting. Instead, these "aesthetic athletes" are judged qualitatively on the basis of "form" and "difficulty." Their performances are more like dancing than competitions of speed or strength. But with the widespread use of slow-motion photography and replay, even "brute sports" like football, wrestling, and boxing yield an aesthetic dimension that is

> Johann Sebastian Bach (1685–1750): German composer, choir director, and organist. His polyphonic compositions of sacred music place him among Europe's most influential composers.

> Wolfgang Amadeus Mozart (1756–91): Austrian composer whose vast output and range of compositions including operas, symphonies, and liturgical music.

> Amalarius of Metz (780–850): Roman Catholic bishop and theologian, author of several major treatises on the performance of liturgical rites, including Eclogae de ordine romano (Pastoral Dialogues on the Roman Rite) (814) and Liber officialis (Book of the Service) (821).

O. B. Hardison
The Medieval Mass Was Drama

That there is a close relationship between allegorical interpretation of the liturgy and the history of drama becomes apparent the moment we turn to the Amalarian interpretations. Without exception, they present the Mass as an elaborate drama with definite roles assigned to the participants and a plot whose ultimate significance is nothing less than the "renewal of the whole plan of redemption" through the re-creation of the "life, death, and resurrection" of Christ. […] The church is regarded as a theatre. The drama enacted has a coherent plot based on conflict between a champion and an antagonist. The plot has a rising action, culminating in the passion and entombment. At its climax there is a dramatic reversal, the Resurrection, correlated with the emotional transition from the Canon of the Mass to the Communion. Something like dramatic catharsis is expressed in the gaudium [joy at the news of the Resurrection] of the Postcommunion. […]

Should church vestments then, with their elaborate symbolic meanings, be considered costumes? Should the paten, chalice, sindon, sudarium, candles, and thurible be considered stage properties? Should the nave, chancel, presbyterium, and altar of the church be considered a stage, and its windows, statues, images, and ornaments a "setting"? As long as there is clear recognition that these elements are hallowed, that they are the sacred phase of parallel elements turned to secular use on the profane stage, it is possible to answer yes. Just as the Mass is a sacred drama encompassing all history and embodying in its structure the central pattern of Christian life on which all Christian drama must draw, the celebration of the Mass contains all elements necessary to secular performances. The Mass as the general case for Christian culture, the archetype. Individual dramas are shaped in its mold.

1965, *Christian Rite and Christian Drama in the Middle Ages*, 39–40, 79.

---

more apparent in the re-viewing than in the swift, tumultuous action itself. An artful add-on is the taunting and victory displays of athletes who dance and prance their superiority.

For all that, everyone knows the difference between going to church, watching a football game, or attending one of the performing arts. The difference is based on function, the circumstance of the event within society, the venue, and the behavior expected of the players and spectators. There is even a big difference between various genres of the performing arts. Being tossed around a mosh pit at a rock concert is very different from applauding a performance of the American Ballet Theatre's Giselle at New York's Metropolitan Opera House. Dance emphasizes movement, theatre emphasizes narration and impersonation, sports emphasize competition, and ritual emphasizes participation and communication with transcendent forces or beings.

In business, to perform means doing a job efficiently with maximum productivity. In the corporate world, people, machines, systems, departments, and organizations are required to perform. At least since the advent of the factory in the nineteenth century, there has been a merging of the human, the technical, and the organizational. This has led to an increase in material wealth—and also the sense that individuals are just "part of the machine" […]. But also this melding of person and machine has an erotic quality. There is something sexual about high performance in business, just as there is a lot that's businesslike in sexual performance. Sexual performance also invokes meanings drawn from the arts and sports. Consider the range of meanings attached to the phrases "performing sex," "How did s/he perform in bed?" and being a "sexual performer." The first refers to the act in itself and the second to how well one "does it," while the third implies an element of either going to extremes or of pretending, of putting on a show and therefore maybe not really doing it at all.

Restoration of Behavior

Let us examine restored behavior more closely. We all perform more than we realize. The habits, rituals, and routines of life are restored behaviors. Restored behavior is living behavior treated as a film director treats a strip of film. These strips of behavior can be rearranged or reconstructed; they are independent of the causal systems (personal, social, political, technological, etc.) that brought them into existence. They have a life of their own. The original "truth" or "source" of the behavior may not be known, or may be lost, ignored, or contradicted—even while that truth or source is being honored. How the strips of behavior were made, found, or developed may be unknown or concealed; elaborated; distorted by myth and tradition. Restored behavior can be of long duration as in ritual performances or of short duration as in fleeting gestures such as waving goodbye.

Restored behavior is the key process of every kind of performing, in everyday life, in healing, in ritual, in play, and in the arts. Restored behavior is "out there," separate from "me." To put it in personal terms, restored behavior is "me behaving as if I were someone else," or "as I am told to do," or "as I have learned." Even if I feel myself wholly to be myself, acting independently, only a little investigating reveals that the units of behavior that comprise "me" were not invented by "me."

Or, quite the opposite, I may experience being "beside myself," "not myself," or "taken over" as in trance. The fact that there are multiple "me's" in every person is not a sign of derangement but the way things are. The ways one performs one's selves are connected to the ways people perform others in dramas, dances, and rituals. In fact, if people did not ordinarily come into contact with their multiple selves, the art of acting and the experience of possession trance would not be possible. Most performances, in daily life and otherwise, do not have a single author. Rituals, games, and the performances of everyday life are authored by the collective "Anonymous" or the "Tradition." Individuals given credit for inventing rituals or games usually turn out to be synthesizers, recombiners, compilers, or editors of already practiced actions.

Restored behavior includes a vast range of actions. In fact, all behavior is restored behavior—all behavior consists of recombining bits of previously behaved behaviors. Of course, most of the time people aren't aware that they are doing any such thing. People just "live life." Performances are marked, framed, or heightened behavior separated out from just "living life"—restored restored behavior, if you will. However, for my purpose here, it is not necessary to pursue this doubling. It is enough to define restored behavior as marked, framed, or heightened. Restored behavior can be "me" at another time or psychological state—for example, telling the story of or acting out a celebratory or traumatic event. Restored behavior can bring into play non-ordinary reality as in the Balinese trance dance enacting the struggle between the demoness Rangda and the Lion-god Barong [...]. Restored behavior can be actions marked off by aesthetic convention as in theatre, dance, and music. It can be actions reified into the "rules of the game," "etiquette," or diplomatic "protocol"—or any other of the myriad, known-beforehand actions of life. These vary enormously from culture to culture. Restored behavior can be a boy not shedding tears when jagged leaves slice the inside of his nostrils during a Papua New Guinea initiation; or the formality of a bride and groom during their wedding ceremony. Because it is marked, framed, and separate, restored behavior can be worked on, stored and recalled, played with, made into something else, transmitted, and transformed.

As I have said, daily life, ceremonial life, and artistic life consist largely of routines, habits, and rituals: the recombination of already behaved behaviors. Even the "latest," "original" "shocking," or "avant-garde" is mostly either a new combination of known behaviors or the displacement of a behavior from a known to an unexpected context or occasion. Thus, for example, nakedness caused a stir in the performing arts in the 1960s and early 1970s. But why the shock? Nude paintings

---

Robert Lanham
BurningAngel.com

Known informally as alt-porn, this genre attempts to embellish pornography with a hip veneer by offering soft- to hard-core erotica next to interviews with members of appropriately cool and underground bands. The form first surfaced in 2001, when the West Coast web site SuicideGirls began to offer erotic photos of young women online. Later the site added interviews of artists and celebrities (from Woody Allen to Natalie Portman to the current hot-band, Bloc Party) and then soft-core videos online. Imitators like fatalbeauty.com, brokendollz.com, and more than a dozen others soon followed.

Joanna Angel, 24, started BurningAngel in 2002 as a hard-core alternative to such sites. […] The first "BurningAngel.com: The Movie" was released for sale online on April 1 [2005] and sells for $20. Shot on a shoestring budget of $4,000, the film, which stars Ms. Angel (her stage name), is a series of hard-core sex scenes strung together without benefit of a plot. It burnishes its hipster credentials by incorporating music by the Brooklyn band Turing Machine and Tim Armstrong of Rancid. Interviews with bands like Dillinger Escape Plan and My Chemical Romance are interspersed with the sex.

"Some people make music, others paint, I make porn," she [Ms. Angel] said. Still, Ms. Angel is in no way a pioneer in her field; there seem to be plenty of women who, rather than struggle to get published in *The Paris Review* or written up in *ArtNews,* have instead channeled their creative ambitions into erotica.

2005, *Wearing Nothing but Attitude,* 15.

---

and sculptings were commonplace. At the other end of the "high art–low art" spectrum, striptease was also common—and erotic. But the naked art in museums were representations presumed to be non-erotic; and striptease was segregated and gender-specific: female strippers, male viewers. The "full frontal nudity" in productions such as *Dionysus in 69* (1968) or *Oh! Calcutta* (1972) caused a stir because actors of both genders were undressing in high-art/live-performance venues and these displays were sometimes erotic. This kind of nakedness was different from naked bodies at home or in gymnasium shower rooms.

At first, this art could not be comfortably categorized or "placed." But it didn't take long before high-art naked performers were accommodated in many genres and venues, from ballet to Broadway, on campuses and in storefront theatres. Even pornography has gone mainstream, further blurring genre boundaries (see Lanham box). Of course, in many cultures nakedness is the norm. In others, such as Japan, it has long been acceptable in certain public circumstances and forbidden in others.

Clifford Geertz

Human Behavior as Symbolic Action

Once human behavior is seen as […] symbolic action—action which, like phonation in speech, pigment in painting, line in writing, or sonance in music, signifies—the question as to whether culture is patterned conduct or a frame of mind, or even the two somehow mixed together, loses sense. […] Behavior must be attended to, and with some exactness, because it is through the flow of behavior—or more precisely, social action—that cultural forms find articulation. They find it as well, of course, in various sorts of artifacts, and various states of consciousness; but these draw their meaning from the role they play […] in an ongoing pattern of life […].

1973, *The Interpretation of Cultures*, 10, 17.

Today, no one in most global metropolitan cities can get a rise out of spectators or critics by performing naked. But don't try it in Kabul—or as part of kabuki. Restored behavior is symbolic and reflexive (see Geertz box). Its meanings need to be decoded by those in the know. This is not a question of "high" versus "low" culture. A sports fan knows the rules and strategies of the game, the statistics of key players, the standings, and many other historical and technical details. Ditto for the fans of rock bands. Sometimes the knowledge about restored behavior is esoteric, privy to only the initiated. Among Indigenous Australians, the outback itself is full of significant rocks, trails, water holes, and other markings that form a record of the actions of mythical beings. Only the initiated know the relationship between the ordinary geography and the sacred geography. To become conscious of restored behavior is to recognize the process by which social processes in all their multiple forms are transformed into theatre. Theatre, not in the limited sense of enactments of dramas on stages (which, after all, is a practice that, until it became very widespread as part of colonialism, belonged to relatively few cultures), but in the broader sense outlined in Chapter 1 [*of Performance Studies: An Introduction*]. Performance in the restored behavior sense means never for the first time, always for the second to nth time: twice-behaved behavior.

Caution! Beware of Generalizations

I want to emphasize: Performances can be generalized at the theoretical level of restoration of behavior, but as embodied practices each and every performance is specific and different from every other. The differences enact the conventions and traditions of a genre, the personal choices made by the performers, directors, and authors, various cultural patterns, historical circumstances, and the particularities of reception. Take wrestling, for example. In Japan, the moves of a sumo wrestler are well determined by long tradition. These moves include the athletes' swaggering circulation around the ring, adjusting their groin belts, throwing handfuls of salt, eyeballing the opponent, and the final, often very brief, grapple of the two enormous competitors […]. Knowing spectators see in these carefully ritualized displays a centuries-old tradition linked to Shinto, the indigenous Japanese religion. By contrast, American professional wrestling is a noisy sport for "outlaws" where each wrestler flaunts his own raucous and carefully constructed identity […]. During the matches referees are clobbered, wrestlers are thrown from the ring, and cheating is endemic. All this is spurred on by fans who hurl epithets and objects. However, everyone knows that the outcome of American wrestling is determined in advance, that the lawlessness is play-acting—it's pretty much "all a show." Fans of sumo and fans of World Wrestling Federation matches know their heroes and villains, can tell you the history of their sport, and react according to accepted conventions and traditions. Both sumo and what occurs under the banner of the World Wrestling Federation are "wrestling;" each enacts the values of its particular culture.

What's true of wrestling is also true of the performing arts, political demonstrations, the roles of everyday life (doctor, mother, cop, etc.), and all other performances. Each genre is divided into many sub-genres. What is American theatre? Broadway, off Broadway, off off Broadway, regional theatre, community theatre, community-based theatre, college theatre, and more. Each sub-genre has its own particularities—similar in some ways to related forms but also different. And the whole system could be looked at from other perspectives—in terms, for example, of comedy, tragedy, melodrama, musicals; or divided according to professional or amateur, issue-oriented or apolitical, and so on. Nor are categories fixed or static. New genres emerge, others fade away. Yesterday's avant-garde is today's mainstream is tomorrow's forgotten practice. Particular genres migrate from one category to another.

Take jazz, for example. During its formative years at the start of the twentieth century, jazz was not regarded as an art. It was akin to "folk performance" or "popular entertainment." But as performers moved out of red-light districts into respectable clubs and finally into concert halls, scholars increasingly paid attention to jazz. A substantial repertory of music was archived. Particular musicians' works achieved canonical status. By the 1950s jazz was regarded as "art." Today's popular music includes rock, rap, and reggae, but not "pure jazz." But that is not to say that rock and other forms of pop music will not some day be listened to and regarded in the same way that jazz or classical music is now. The categories of "folk," "pop," and "classical" have more to do with ideology, politics, and economic power than with the formal qualities of the music.

"Is" and "As" Performance

What is the difference between "is" performance and "as" performance? Certain events are performances and other events less so. There are limits to what "is" performance. But just about anything can be studied "as" performance. Something "is" a performance when historical and social context, convention, usage, and tradition say it is. Rituals, play and games, and the roles of everyday life are performances because convention, context, usage, and tradition say so. One cannot determine what "is" a performance without referring to specific cultural circumstances. There is nothing inherent in an action in itself that makes it a performance or disqualifies it from being a performance. From the vantage of the kind of performance theory I am propounding, every action is a performance. But from the vantage of cultural practice, some actions will be deemed performances and others not; and this will vary from culture to culture, historical period to historical period.

Let me use the European tradition as an example to explain in more detail how definitions operate within contexts. What "is" or "is not" performance does not depend on an event in itself but on how that event is received and placed. Today the enactment of dramas by actors "is" a theatrical performance. But it was not always so. What we today call "theatre" people in other times did not. The ancient Greeks used words similar to ours to describe the theatre (our words derive from theirs), but what the Greeks meant in practice was very different from what we mean. During the epoch of the tragedians Aeschylus, Sophocles, and Euripides, the enactment of tragic dramas was more a ritual infused with competitions for prizes for the best actor and the best play than it was theatre in our sense. The occasions for the playing of the tragedies were religious festivals. Highly sought-after prizes were awarded. These prizes were based on aesthetic excellence, but the events in which that excellence was demonstrated were not artistic but ritual. It was Aristotle, writing a century after the high point of Greek tragedy as embodied performance, who codified the aesthetic understanding of theatre in its entirety—in all of its "six parts," as the

> Aeschylus (c. 525–c. 456 BCE): Greek playwright and actor, regarded as the first great tragedian. Surviving works include *The Persians* (c. 472 BCE) and *The Oresteia* (458 BCE).

> Sophocles (c. 496–c. 406 BCE): Greek playwright, credited with introducing the third actor onto the stage of tragedy. Surviving plays include *Oedipus the King* (c. 429 BCE), *Electra* (date uncertain), and *Antigone* (c. 441 BCE).

> Euripides (c. 485–c. 405 BCE): Greek playwright whose surviving works include *Medea* (431 BCE), *Hippolytus* (428 BCE), *The Trojan Women* (415 BCE), and *The Bacchae* (c. 405 BCE).

philosopher parsed it. After Aristotle, in Hellenic and Roman times, the entertainment–aesthetic aspect of theatre became more dominant as the ritual–efficacious elements receded.

Skipping forward more than a millennium to medieval Europe, acting written dramas on public stages was "forgotten" or at least not practiced. But there was not a scarcity of performances. On the streets, in town squares, in churches, castles, and mansions a wide range of popular entertainments and religious ceremonies held people's attention. There were a multitude of mimes, magicians, animal acts, acrobats, puppet shows, and what would later become the *commedia dell'arte.* The Church offered a rich panoply of feasts, services, and rituals. By the fourteenth century the popular entertainments and religious observances joined to form the basis for the great cycle plays celebrating and enacting the history of the world from Creation through the Crucifixion and Resurrection to the Last Judgment. These we would now call "theatre," but they were not named that at the time. The anti-theatrical prejudice of the Church disallowed any such designation. But then, in the fifteenth and sixteenth centuries the revolution in thought and practice called the Renaissance began. Renaissance means "rebirth" because the humanists of the day thought they were bringing back to life the classical culture of Greece and Rome. When Andrea Palladio designed the Teatro Olimpico (Theatre of Olympus) in Vicenza, Italy, he believed he was reinventing a Greek theatre—the first production in the Olimpico was Sophocles' *Oedipus*—not pointing the way to the modern proscenium theatre which the Olimpico did.

Andrea Palladio (1508–80): Italian architect who worked in Vicenza and Venice designing villas and churches. Palladio's Teatro Olimpico, completed four years after his death, is the only remaining example of an indoor Renaissance theatre. Author of *I Quattro Libri dell' Architettura* (1570, *The Four Books on Architecture*, 1997).

Take another leap to the last third of the nineteenth century. The notion of theatre as an art was by then well-established. In fact, so well-founded that counter-movements called "avant-garde" erupted frequently as efforts among

---

Allan Kaprow
Artlike Art and Lifelike Art

Western art actually has two avantgarde histories: one of artlike art, and the other of lifelike art. […] Simplistically put, artlike art holds that art is separate from life and everything else, while lifelike art holds that art is connected to life and everything else. In other words, there's art at the service of art, and art at the service of life. The maker of artlike art tends to be a specialist; the maker of lifelike art, a generalist. […]

Avantgarde artlike art occupies the majority of attention from artists and public. It is usually seen as serious and a part of the mainstream Western art–historical tradition, in which mind is separate from body, individual is separate from people, civilization is separate from nature, and each art is separate from the other. […] Avantgarde artlike art basically believes in (or does not eliminate) the continuity of the traditionally separate genres of visual art, music, dance, literature, theatre, etc. […]

Avantgarde lifelike art, in contrast, concerns an intermittent minority (Futurists, Dadas, guatai, Happeners, fluxartists, Earthworkers, body artists, provos, postal artists, noise musicians, performance poets, shamanistic artists, conceptualists). Avantgarde lifelike art is not nearly as serious as avantgarde artlike art. Often it is quite humorous.

It isn't very interested in the great Western tradition either, since it tends to mix things up: body with mind, individual with people in general, civilization with nature, and so on. Thus it mixes up the traditional art genres, or avoids them entirely—for example, a mechanical fiddle playing around the clock to a cow in the barnyard. Or going to the laundromat.

Despite formalist and idealist interpretations of art, lifelike art makers' principal dialogue is not with art but with everything else, one event suggesting another. If you don't know much about life, you'll miss much of the meaning of the lifelike art that's born of it. Indeed, it's never certain if an artist who creates avantgarde lifelike art is an artist.

1983, *The Real Experiment*, 36, 38.

radical artists to disrupt the status quo. Onward into and throughout the twentieth century, each new wave attempted to dislodge what went before. Some of yesterday's avant-garde became today's establishment. The list of avant-garde movements is long, including realism, naturalism, symbolism, futurism, surrealism, constructivism, Dada, expressionism, cubism, theatre of the absurd, Happenings, Fluxus, environmental theatre, performance art … and more. Sometimes works in these styles were considered theatre, sometimes dance, sometimes music, sometimes visual art, sometimes multimedia, etc. Often enough, events were attacked or dismissed as not being art at all—as were Happenings, an antecedent to performance art. Allan Kaprow, creator of the first Happening, jumped at this chance to make a distinction between "artlike art" and "lifelike art" (see Kaprow box). The term "performance art" was coined in the 1970s as an umbrella for works that otherwise resisted categorization.

The outcome is that today many events that formerly would not be thought of as art are now so designated. These kinds of actions are performed everywhere, not just in the West. The feedback loop is very complicated. The work of a Japanese dancer may affect a German choreographer whose dances in turn are elaborated on by a Mexican performance artist … and so on without definite national or cultural limits. Beyond composed artworks is a blurry world of "accidental" or "incidental" performance. Webcams broadcast over the internet what people do at home. Television frames the news as entertainment. Public figures need to be media savvy. Is it by accident that an actor, Ronald Reagan, became president of the USA and that a playwright, Vaclav Havel, became president of the Czech

> **Ronald Reagan (1911–2004):** fortieth president of the United States (1981–89) and Governor of California (1967–75), Reagan was a broadcaster, movie actor, and public speaker before entering electoral politics. Known as the "Great Communicator," Reagan's self-deprecating quips and relaxed manner on camera endeared him to millions despite his conservative and often bellicose policies.

> **Vaclav Havel (1936–):** Czech playwright who was the last president of Czechoslovakia (1989–92) and the first of the Czech Republic (1993–2003). A fierce defender of free speech and leader of the "Velvet Revolution" of 1989 overturning Communist rule, Havel's often political plays include *The Memorandum* (1965), *Protest* (1978), and *Redevelopment* (1978).

> **Karol Jozef Wojtyla, Pope John Paul II (1920–2005):** Polish actor and playwright who in 1978 became pope. During World War II, Wojtyla was a member of the Rhapsodic Theatre, an underground resistance group. Ordained as a priest in 1945, Wojtyla continued to write for and about the theatre. His theatrical knowledge served him well as a globe-trotting, media-savvy pontiff. See his *Collected Plays and Writings on Theater* (1987).

Republic, while another actor and playwright, Karol Jozef Wojtyla, became pope? Performance theorists argue that everyday life is performance—courses are offered in the aesthetics of everyday life. At present, there is hardly any human activity that is not a performance for someone somewhere. Generally, the tendency over the past century has been to dissolve the boundaries separating performing from not-performing, art from not-art. At one end of the spectrum it's clear what a performance is, what an artwork is; at the other end of the spectrum no such clarity exists.

Maps "as" Performance

Any behavior, event, action, or thing can be studied "as" performance. Take maps, for example. Everyone knows the world is round and maps are flat. But you can't see the whole world at the same time on a globe. You can't fold a globe and tuck it in your pocket or backpack. Maps flatten the world the better to lay out territories on a table or tack them to a wall. On most maps, nations are separated from each other by colors and lines, and cities appear as circles, rivers as lines, and oceans as large, usually blue, areas. Nation-states drawn on maps seem so natural that when some people picture the world they imagine it divided into nation-states. Everything on a map is named—being "on the map" means achieving status. But the "real earth" does not look like its mapped representations—or even like a globe. People were astonished when they saw the first photographs taken from space of the white-flecked blue ball Earth […]. There was no sign of a human presence at all.

Nor are maps neutral. They perform a particular interpretation of the world. Every map is a "projection," a specific way of representing a sphere on a flat surface. On maps, nations do not overlap or share territories. Boundaries are definite. If more than one nation enforces its claim to the same space, war threatens, as between Pakistan and India over Kashmir, or Palestine and Israel over Jerusalem. The most common projection in use today is derived from the Mercator Projection, developed in the sixteenth century by the Flemish geographer–cartographer Gerardus Mercator [. .].

The Mercator Projection distorts the globe wildly in favor of the northern hemisphere. The further north, the relatively bigger the territory

Gerardus Mercator (1512–94): Flemish geographer–cartographer whose basic system of map-making is still practiced today. His actual name was Gerhard Kremer, but like many European scholars of his day, he Latinized his name.

appears. Spain is as large as Zimbabwe, North America dwarfs South America, and Europe is one-fourth the size of Africa. In other words, Mercator's map enacts the world as the colonial powers wished to view it. Although times have changed since the sixteenth century, the preponderance of world economic and military power remains in the hands of Europe and its North American inheritor, the USA. Perhaps it won't be this way in another century or two. If so, a different projection will be in common use. Indeed, satellite photography allows a detailed remapping of the globe. There are also maps showing the world "upside down," that is, with south on top; or drawn according to population, showing China and India more than four times the size of the USA. The Peters Projection developed in 1974 by Dr. Arno Peters is an "area accurate" map showing the world's areas sized correctly in relation to each other […]. No longer is Greenland the same size as Africa when in fact Africa is fourteen times larger than Greenland. But the Peters map has its own inaccuracies. It is not correct in terms of shape—the southern hemisphere is elongated, the northern squashed. Making a flat map of a round earth means that one must sacrifice either accurate shape or size. If the Peters map looks "unnatural," then you know how much the Mercator Projection—or any other map—is a performance.

One of the meanings of "to perform" is to get things done according to a particular plan or scenario. Mercator's maps proved very helpful for navigating the seas because straight lines on the projection kept to compass bearings. Mercator drew his maps to suit the scenarios of the mariners, merchants, and

> Arno Peters (1916–2002): German historian. Developed in 1974 an area-accurate world map, known as the Peters Projection.

military of an expansionist, colonizing Western Europe. Similarly, the authors of the new maps have scenarios of their own which their maps enact. Interpreting maps this way is to examine map-making "as" performance. Every map not only represents the Earth in a specific way, but also enacts power relationships.

It's not just maps. Everything and anything can be studied "as" any discipline of study—physics, economics, law, etc. What the "as" says is that the object of study will be regarded "from the perspective of," "in terms of," "interrogated by" a particular discipline of study. For example, I am composing this book on a Dell Dimension 4100 desktop computer. If I regard it "as physics," I would examine its size, weight, and other physical qualities, perhaps even its atomic and subatomic qualities. If I regard it "as mathematics," I would delve into the binary codes of its programs. Regarding it "as law" would mean interpreting networks of patents, copyrights, and contracts. If I were to treat the computer "as performance," I would evaluate the speed of its processor, the clarity of its display, the usefulness of the pre-packaged software, its size and portability, and so on. I can envision Bill Parcells staring out at me telling me how well my computer performs.

Make Belief and Make-Believe

Performances can be either "make belief" or "make-believe." The many performances in everyday life such as professional roles, gender and race roles, and shaping ones identity are not make-believe actions (as playing a role on stage or in a film most probably is). The performances of everyday life […], make belief—create the very social realities they enact. In "make-believe" performances, the distinction between what's real and what's pretended is kept clear. Children playing "doctor" or "dress-up" know that they are pretending. On stage, various conventions—the stage itself

> Make-believe performances maintain a clearly marked boundary between the world of the performance and everyday reality. Make-belief performances intentionally blur or sabotage that boundary.

as a distinct domain, opening and closing a curtain or dimming the lights, the curtain call, etc.—mark the boundaries between pretending and "being real." People watching a movie or a play know that the social and personal worlds enacted are not those of the actors but those of the characters. Or do they? This distinction was first challenged by the avant-garde and later further eroded by the media and the internet.

Public figures are often making belief—enacting the effects they want the receivers of their performances to accept "for real." When an American president signs an important piece of legislation, or makes a grave announcement of national importance, his handlers often stage the event in the Oval Office of the White House where the president can perform his authority. Behind him is an array of VIPs, including the vice-president. A large presidential seal provides an appropriately patriotic foreground […]. At other times, the national leader may wish to appear as a friend or a good neighbor talking informally with "fellow citizens" […].

By now, everyone knows these kinds of activities are meticulously staged. Today's American presidency—at least its public face—is a totally scripted performance. The president's words are written by professional speech-writers, the backdrops and settings carefully designed for maximum effect, the chief executive himself well rehearsed. Teleprompters insure that the president will appear to be speaking off the cuff while he is actually reading every word. Each detail is choreographed, from how the president makes eye contact (with the camera, with the selected audience at a town meeting), to how he uses his hands, dresses, and is made up. The goal of all this is to "make belief"—first, to build the public's confidence in the president, and second, to sustain the president's belief in himself. His performances convince himself even as he strives to convince others.

Arguably, the president is an important personage by virtue of his position of authority. But with the exponential growth of media, hordes of citizens have jumped into the make-belief business. Some are hucksters selling everything from cooking utensils and firm buttocks to everlasting salvation. Others are venerable network "anchors"—"familiar voices and faces holding the public in place amidst the swift currents of the news." Still others are "pundits," experts—economists, lawyers, retired generals, etc.—whose authority is reaffirmed if not created by their frequent appearances. Then come the "spin doctors," employed by politicians and corporations to turn bad news into good. As for the producers behind the scenes, their job is to make certain that whatever is going on is dramatic enough to attract viewers. The greater the number watching, the higher the revenues from sponsors. Some news is inherently exciting—disasters, wars, crimes, and trials. But media masters have learned how to dramatize the stock market and the weather. How to build the "human interest" angle into every story. The producers know that the same information is available from many different sources, so their job is to develop attractive sideshows. Paradoxically, the result is a public less easy to fool. With so many kinds of performances on view, many people have become increasingly sophisticated and suspicious deconstructors of the theatrical techniques deployed to lure them.

Blurry Boundaries

Let's return to Mercator's map. The world represented there is one of neatly demarcated sovereign nation-states. That world no longer exists, if it ever did (in Mercator's day the European nations were frequently at war with each other over who controlled what). Today national boundaries are extremely porous, not only to people but even more so to information and ideas. The newest maps can't be drawn because what needs to be represented are not territories but networks of relationships. Mapping these takes fractals or streams of numbers continually changing their shapes and values. The notion of fixity has been under attack at least since 1927, when Werner Heisenberg proposed his "uncertainty principle" and its accompanying "Heisenberg effect." Few people outside of a select group of quantum physicists really understood Heisenberg's theory. But "uncertainty" or "indeterminacy" rang a bell. It has proven to be a very appropriate, durable, and powerful metaphor affecting thought in many disciplines including the arts. Music theorist and composer John Cage often used indeterminacy as the basis for his music, influencing a generation of artists and performance theorists.

Boundaries are blurry in different ways. On the internet, people participate effortlessly in a system that transgresses national boundaries. Even languages present less of a barrier than before. Already you can log in, write in your own language, and know that your message will be translated into the language of whomever you are addressing. At present, this facility is available in only a limited number of languages. But the repertory of translatables will increase. It will be routine for Chinese-speakers to address Kikuyu-speakers or for someone in a remote village to address a message to any number of people globally. Furthermore, for better or worse, English has become a global rather than national language. At the United Nations, 120 countries representing more than 97 percent of the world's populations choose English as their medium for international communication.

The dissolution of national boundaries is occurring in relation to manufactured objects as well as with regard to politics and information. If, for example, you drive an American or Japanese or Swedish or German or Korean car, you may believe it came from the country whose label it displays. But where were the parts manufactured? Where was the car assembled, where designed? The brand name refers to itself, not to a place of origin. Japanese cars are made in Tennessee and Fords roll

---

Werner Heisenberg (1901–76): German physicist, winner of the Nobel Prize for Physics in 1932 for his formulation of quantum mechanics which is closely related to his uncertainty principle.

Uncertainty principle: a tenet of quantum mechanics proposed by Werner Heisenberg in 1927 which states that the measurement of a particle's position produces uncertainty in the measurement of the particle's momentum, or vice versa. While each quantity may be measured accurately on its own, both cannot be totally accurately measured at the same time. The uncertainty principle is closely related to the Heisenberg effect which asserts that the measurement of an event changes the event.

John Cage (1912–92): American composer and music theorist whose interests spanned using indeterminacy to make art, Zen Buddhism, and mushrooms. Author of *Silence: Selected Lectures and Writings* (1961) and *A Year from Monday* (1967). His many musical compositions include *Fontana Mix* (1960) and *Roaratorio* (1982).

off assembly lines in Canada, Europe, and elsewhere. Mexico is a major assembly point for many cars. And what about your clothes? Look at the labels of the clothes you are wearing right now. Do your dress, pants, shoes, and blouse come from the same country? Do you even know where they were stitched or by whom and at what wage or under what working conditions?

But more than cars and clothes are transnational. Cultures are also blurring. Globalization is accelerating. Airports are the same wherever you travel; standardized fast food is available in just about every major city in the world. American television and movies are broadcast everywhere. But the USA itself is increasingly intercultural in both its populations and its living styles. The profusion of international arts festivals and the hosts of artists touring all parts of the world are a major means of circulating styles of performing. "World beat" music combines elements of African, Asian, Latin American, and Euro-American sounds. New hybrids are emerging all the time. People are arguing whether or not all this mixing is good or bad. Is globalization the equivalent of Americanization? […].

The Functions of Performance

I have touched on what performance is and what can be studied as performance. But what do performances accomplish? It is difficult to stipulate the functions of performance. Over time, and in different cultures, there have been a number of proposals. One of the most inclusive is that of the Indian sage Bharata, who felt that performance was a comprehensive repository of knowledge and a very powerful vehicle for the expression of emotions (see Bharata box). The Roman poet–scholar Horace in his *Ars poetica* argued that theatre ought to entertain and educate, an idea taken up by many Renaissance thinkers and later by the German playwright and director Bertolt Brecht.

Putting together ideas drawn from various sources, I find seven functions of performance:

1. To entertain
2. To make something that is beautiful
3. To mark or change identity
4. To make or foster community
5. To heal

Bharata
The Functions of Natya (Dance-Music-Theatre)

I [The god Brahma] have created the Natyaveda to show good and bad actions and feelings of both the gods and yourselves: It is a representation of the entire three worlds and not only of the gods or of yourselves. Now dharma [duty], now artha [strategies], now kama [love], now humor, now fights, now greed, now killing. Natya teaches right to people going wrong; it gives enjoyment for those who are pleasure seekers; it chastises those who are ill-behaved and promotes tolerance in the well-behaved. It gives courage to cowards, energy to the brave. It enlightens people of little intellect and gives wisdom to the wise. Natya provides entertainment to kings, fortitude to those grief-stricken, money to those who want to make a living, and stability to disturbed minds. Natya is a representation of the ways of the world involving various emotions and differing circumstances. It relates the actions of good, bad, and middling people, giving peace, entertainment, and happiness, as well as beneficial advice, to all. It brings rest and peace to persons afflicted by sorrow, fatigue, grief, or helplessness. There is no art, no knowledge, no learning, no action that is not found in natya.

1996 [second century bce–second century ce], *The Natyasastra*, chapter 1.

---

6. To teach, persuade, or convince
7. To deal with the sacred and/or the demonic.

These are not listed in order of importance. For some people one or a few of these will be more important than others. But the hierarchy changes according to who you are and what you want to get done. Few if any performances accomplish all of these functions, but many performances emphasize more than one.

For example, a street demonstration or propaganda play may be mostly about teaching, persuading, and convincing—but such a show also has to entertain and may foster community. Shamans heal, but they entertain also, foster community, and deal with the sacred and/or demonic. A doctor's "bedside manner" is a performance of encouragement, teaching, and healing. A charismatic Christian church service heals, entertains, maintains community solidarity, invokes both the sacred and the demonic, and, if the sermon is effective, teaches. If someone at the service declares for Jesus and is reborn, that person's identity is marked and changed. A state leader addressing the nation wants to convince and foster community—but she had better entertain also if she wants people to listen. Rituals tend to have the greatest number of functions, commercial productions the fewest. A Broadway musical will entertain, but little else. The seven functions are best represented as

Bharata (c. second century bce–c. second century ce): Indian sage, the putative author of *The Natyasastra,* the earliest and still very influential South Asian theoretical and practical treatise on all aspects of traditional Indian theatre, dance, play-writing, and to a lesser extent, music.

Horace (65–68 BC): Roman poet whose *Ars poetica (The Art of Poetry,* 1974) offers advice on the construction of drama. His basic instruction that art should both "entertain and educate" is very close to Brecht's ideas on the function of theatre.

Bertolt Brecht (1898–1956): German playwright, director, and performance theorist. In 1949 he and actress Helene Weigel (1900–71), his wife, founded the Berliner Ensemble. Major works include The *Threepenny Opera* (1928), *The Rise and Fall of the City of Mahagonny* (1930), *Mother Courage and her Children* (1941), *Galileo* (1943), *The Good Woman of Szechwan* (1943), and *The Caucasian Chalk Circle* (1948 Eng; 1954 Ger.) The dates refer to stage premieres. Many of his theoretical writings are anthologized in English, in *Brecht on Theatre* (1964).

overlapping and interacting spheres, a network […].

Whole works, even genres, can be shaped to very specific functions. Examples of political or propaganda performances are found all over the world. El Teatro Campesino of California, formed in the 1960s in order to support Mexican migrant farm workers in the midst of a bitter strike, built solidarity among the strikers, educated them to the issues involved, attacked the bosses, and entertained. Groups such as Greenpeace and ACTUP use performance militantly in support of a healthy ecology and to gain money for AIDS research and treatment.

"Theatre for development" as practiced widely since the 1960s in Africa, Latin America, and Asia educates people in a wide range of subjects and activities, from birth control and cholera prevention to irrigation and the protection of endangered species. Augusto Boal's Theatre of the Oppressed empowers "spectators" to enact, analyze, and change their situations.

Boal's Theatre of the Oppressed is based to some degree on Brecht's work, especially his *Lehrstücke* or "learning plays" of the 1930s such as *The Measures Taken* or *The Exception and the Rule* […]. During China's Cultural Revolution (1966–75), which she helped orchestrate, Jiang Qing produced a series of "model operas" carefully shaped to teach, entertain, and put forward a new kind of community based on the values of Chinese Communism as Jiang interpreted them. These theatre and ballet pieces employed both traditional Chinese performance styles modified to

Augusto Boal (1931–[2009]): Brazilian director and theorist, founder of Theatre of the Oppressed. His books include *Theatre of the Oppressed* (1985), *Games for Actors and Non-Actors* (1980, Eng. 1992), *Legislative Theatre* (1998), and his autobiography, *Hamlet and the Baker's Son* (2001).

Sheila Melvin and Cai Jindong
The Model Operas

"The Communist Party of China is like the bright sun," sang Granny Sha, her face glowing through wrinkles of sorrow as she told of abuse at the hands of a "poisonous snake, bloodsucker" landlord in Kuomintang-ruled China. Her words, soaring and elongated in the lyrical gymnastics of Beijing Opera, were punctuated by a roar of applause from the audience in the Yifu theatre here. […] While the scene on stage closely resembled Cultural Revolution-era performance, the audience members—mostly middle-aged and stylishly dressed, casually taking cell phone calls, slurping Cokes and licking ice cream bars as the opera proceeded—were decidedly Shanghai 2000. […] As the number of performances increases, so do attempts to analyze the artistic value of this genre created expressly to serve politics. "Naturally, this is sensitive," said Wang Renyuan, a Nanjing-based professor who wrote a book on the music in model operas. "We oppose the Cultural Revolution now, so of course products from then are also criticized. But model operas were very special, and we can't just ignore them. If we say that the Cultural Revolution was politics raping art, then we shouldn't still be doing this today. Criticize the Cultural Revolution, criticize Jiang Qing, but why can't we analyze model operas artistically?" […]

Most intellectuals, even those who detest the genre, are willing to concede that if people want to watch model operas, they should have that right. "I don't want to watch them" said Mr. Luo Zhengrong, the composer.

"I don't want to hear them. But they were created well, and if they didn't have a political purpose, they wouldn't exist. The fact is there's a market for them. If there wasn't a market, they wouldn't be performed."

2000, *Why this Nostalgia for Fruits of Chaos?* 1, 31.

---

suit the ideological purposes of the Cultural Revolution and elements of Western music and staging […]. The Utopian vision of the model operas contradicted the terrible fact of the millions who were killed, tortured, and displaced by the Cultural Revolution. But by the turn of the twenty-first century, the model operas were again being performed, studied, and enjoyed for their entertainment value, technical excellence, and artistic innovations (see Melvin and Cai box).

Entertainment means something produced in order to please a public. But what may please one audience may not please another. So one cannot specify exactly what constitutes entertainment—except to say that almost all performances strive, to some degree or other, to entertain. I include in this regard both fine and popular arts, as well as rituals and the performances of everyday "life." What about performances of avant-garde artists and political activists designed to offend? Guerrilla theatre events disrupt and may even destroy. These are not entertaining. However, "offensive" art usually is aimed at two publics simultaneously: those who do not find the work pleasant, and those who are entertained by the discomfort the work evokes in others.

Beauty is hard to define. Beauty is not equivalent to being "pretty." The ghastly, terrifying events of kabuki, Greek tragedy, Elizabethan theatre, and some performance art are not pretty. Nor are the demons invoked by shamans. But

> Jiang Qing (1914–91): Chinese Communist leader, wife of Chairman Mao Zedong (1893–3 976). As Deputy Director of China's Cultural Revolution (1966–76), Jiang Qing sought to redefine all forms of artistic expression in strict adherence to revolutionary ideals. She oversaw the development of "model operas" and "model ballets," versions of Chinese traditional performance genres that made heroes of peasants and workers instead of aristocrats. After the Cultural Revolution, she was tried as one of "The Gang of Four." She died in prison.

> Francisco de Goya y Lucientes (1746–1828): Spanish artist. Often referred to simply as "Goya." His series of etchings titled *The Disasters of War* chronicled the Peninsular Wars (1808–14) among Spain, Portugal, and France.

> Susanne K. Langer (1895–1985): American philosopher and aesthetician. Her major works include *Philosophy in a New Key* (1942), *Feeling and Form* (1953), and *Problems of Art* (1957).

the skilled enactment of horrors can be beautiful and yield aesthetic pleasure. Is this true of such absolute horrors as slavery, the Shoah, or the extermination of Native Americans? Francisco de Goya y Lucientes' *The Disasters of War* shows that nothing is beyond the purview of artistic treatment […]. Philosopher Susanne K. Langer argued that in life people may endure terrible experiences, but in art these experiences are transformed into "expressive form" (see Langer box). One of the differences between "art" and "life" is that in art, we do not experience the event itself but its representation. Langer's classical notions of aesthetics are challenged today, an epoch of simulation, digitization, performance artists, and webcam performers who "do" the thing itself in front of our very eyes. A considerable amount of postmodern art does not offer viewers objects or actions for contemplation.

Susanne K. Langer
Every Good Art Work is Beautiful

A work of art is intrinsically expressive; it is designed to abstract and preset forms for perception—forms of life and feeling, activity, suffering, selfhood—whereby we conceive these realities, which otherwise we can but blindly undergo. Every good work of art is beautiful; as soon as we find it so, we have grasped its expressiveness, and until we do we have not seen it as good art, though we may have ample intellectual reason to believe that it is so. Beautiful works may contain elements that, taken in isolation, are hideous. […] The emergent form, the whole, is alive and therefore beautiful, as awful things may be—as gargoyles, and fearful African masks, and the Greek tragedies of incest and murder are beautiful. Beauty is not identical with the normal, and certainly not with charm and sense appeal, though all such properties may go to the making of it. Beauty is expressive form.

1953, *Feeling and Form*, 395–96.

Conclusion

There are many ways to understand performance. Any event, action, or behavior may be examined "as" performance. Using the category "as" performance has advantages. One can consider things provisionally, in process, and as they change over time. In every human activity there are usually many players with different and even opposing points of view, goals, and feelings. Using "as" performance as a tool, one can look into things otherwise closed off to inquiry. One asks performance questions of events: How is an event deployed in space and disclosed in time? What special clothes or objects are put to use? What roles are played and how are these different, if at all, from who the performers usually are? How are the events controlled, distributed, received, and evaluated?

"Is" performance refers to more definite, bounded events marked by context, convention, usage, and tradition. However, in the twenty-first century, clear distinctions between "as" performance and "is" performance are vanishing. This is part of a general trend toward the dissolution of boundaries. The internet, globalization, and the ever-increasing presence of media is saturating human behavior at all levels. More and more people experience their lives as a connected series of performances that often overlap: dressing up for a party, interviewing for a job, experimenting with sexual orientations and gender roles, playing a life role such as mother or son, or a professional role such as doctor or teacher. The sense that "performance is everywhere" is heightened by an increasingly mediatized environment where people communicate by fax, phone, and the internet, where an unlimited quantity of information and entertainment comes through the air.

One way of ordering this complex situation is to arrange the performance genres, performative behaviors, and performance activities into a continuum [...]. These genres, behaviors, and activities do not each stand alone. As in the spectrum of visible light, they blend into one another; their boundaries are indistinct. They interact with each other. The continuum is drawn as a straight line to accommodate the printed page. If I could work in three dimensions, I would shape the relationships as more of an overlapping and interlacing spheroid network. For example, though they stand at opposite ends of the straight-line continuum, playing and ritualizing are closely related to each other. In some ways, they underlie all the rest as a foundation.

[... G]ames, sports, pop entertainments, and performing arts include many genres each with their own conventions, rules, history, and traditions. An enormous range of activities comes under these banners. Even the same activity—cricket, for example—varies widely. Cricket at a test match is not the same as that played on a neighborhood oval. And cricket in the Trobriand Islands, where it was changed into a ritual encounter between towns featuring dancing as much as hitting and fielding, and with the home team always winning, is something else again. The fact that the ritualized cricket match shown in Jerry W. Leach's and Gary Kildea's *Trobriand Cricket* (1973) was staged for the cameras adds another layer of performative complexity. Despite all complicating factors, certain generalizations can be made. Even though genres are distinct, and no one would confuse the Superbowl with *Les Sylphides,* both ballet and football are about movement, contact, lifting, carrying, falling, and rushing to and fro. In many cultures, theatre, dance, and music are so wholly integrated that it is not possible to place a given event into one or the other category. Kathakali in India, a Makishi performance in Zambia, and the Deer Dance of the Yaquis are but three examples among many that integrate music, dance, and theatre [...].

[...] Even the most apparently casual social interaction is rule-guided and culture-specific. Politeness, manners, body language, and the like all operate according to known scenarios. The specifics of the rules differ from society to society, circumstance to circumstance. But there is no human social interaction that is not "lawful," that is not rule-bound.

Talk About

1. Pick an action not usually thought to be a performance. For example, waiting in line at a supermarket checkout counter, crossing the street at a busy intersection, visiting a sick friend. In what ways can each of these be analyzed "as" a performance?
2. Select a sports match, a religious ritual, an everyday life occurrence, and a performing art. Discuss their similarities and differences "as" performances with regard to venue, function, audience involvement, event structure, and historical-cultural context.

Perform

1. Observe an everyday encounter of people you do not know. Intervene in the encounter yourself with a definite goal in mind. Afterwards, discuss how your intervention changed the performances of the others. Did they welcome or resent your intervention? Why?
2. In small groups, take turns reproducing for your group a bit of behavior that you ordinarily do only in private. How did the behavior change when you were self-consciously performing for others?

Read

Carlson, Marvin. (2004). "What is Performance?" *The Performance Studies Reader,* Henry Bial, ed.: (pp. 68–73). London and New York: Routledge.

Gabler, Neal. (2004). "Life the Movie." *The Performance Studies Reader*, Henry Bial, ed.: (pp. 74–75). London and New York: Routledge.

Geertz, Clifford. (2004). "Blurred Genres: The Refiguration of Social Thought." *The Performance Studies Reader*, Henry Bial, ed.: (pp. 64–67). London and New York: Routledge.

Goffman, Erving. (2004). "Performances: Belief in the Part One Is Playing." *The Performance Studies Reader*, Henry Bial, ed.: (pp. 59–63). London and New York: Routledge.

Kaprow, Allan. (2003). "Art which Can't Be Art (1986)." *Essays on the Blurring of Art and Life,* Allan Kaprow and Jeff Kelley: (pp. 219–22). Berkeley, Calif.: University of California Press.

Phelan, Peggy. (2004). "Marina Abramovic: Witnessing Shadows." *Theatre Journal* 56, 4: 569–77.

Schechner, Richard. (1985)."Restoration of Behavior." *Between Theater and Anthropology:* (pp. 35–116). Philadelphia, Pa.: University of Pennsylvania Press.

Taylor, Diana. (2002). "Translating Performance." *Profession* 2002, 1: 44–50.

Questions

1. How does the medium mark, frame and/or heighten the "restored behavior" in the performance?
2. How would you define the action and the interaction and/or relationship between the maker and the receiver?
3. How are performances controlled, distributed by producer/maker/audience?
4. How are performances received and evaluated by producer/maker/audience?

View

YouTube

"Bharata Natyam" (2006)
"Sumo" (2007)
"John Cage: 'Dream'" (2008)
"Kaprow Happening" (2008)
"Highlights from workshop of *The Measures Taken*" (2009)
"Makishi of the Upper Zambezi Peoples" (2010)

Web

IndiaVideo.org. "Kathakali Training Classical Dance Drama Kerala" (2010)
China.org.cn. "Modern Peking Opera: The Red Lantern" (2011)
wwe.com. World Wrestling Entertainment, Inc. (2012)

Film/Video

Modern Times (1936)

Read

"Map Projections." *National Atlas of the United States*. U.S. Department of the Interior. 26 January 2011. Web. 14 June 2012.

Berger, Arthur Asa. "The Nature of Narratives." *Narratives in Popular Culture, Media and Everyday Life*. Arthur Asa Berger. Thousand Oaks, CA: Sage Publications, 1997. 1–16. Print.

Schechner, Richard. *Performance Theory*. New York: Routledge, 2010.

Turner, Victor Witter. *From Ritual to Theatre*. New York: Performing Arts Journal
     Publications, 1982.

Performance and Adaptation

This reading extends our understanding of performance by looking at narrative structure and key story ingredients present in all entertainment media. As restored behaviors, all performances are adaptations of one form or another. Adaptations are attractive to audiences and financially appealing to makers/producers by virtue of their references to the familiar. Hutcheon's theories present adaptation as both a process and a product. As process and product, adaptations are acknowledged transpositions of recognizable other work or works. This definition allows us to discard notions of outright plagiarism, which does not acknowledge the appropriation of adapted text at all. While Hutcheon's theories are based on the idea of an extended relationship with the adapted text, combining her ideas with Schechner's performance as restored behavior considers allusions to or echoes of recognized work as adaptations as well.

The product that results from adaptations is uniquely connected to the process of engaging with the original work as well as the adapted product. Hutcheon discusses the processes of reception and how a work engages the audience's imagination. The form that a popular entertainment product takes influences the modes of engagement.

Ideas

Adaptation as product
Adaptation as a process of creation
Adaptation as a process of reception
Heterocosm
Multi-laminated
Modes of engagement
Remediation

Translation/Transcoding
Paraphrase
Intertextuality
Palimpsestuous

Beginning to Theorize Adaptation

What? Who? Why? How? Where? When?

By 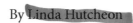Linda Hutcheon

---

[C]inema is still playing second fiddle to literature.

—**Rabindranath Tagore (1929)**

Writing a screenplay based on a great novel [George Eliot's *Daniel Deronda*] is foremost a labor of simplification. I don't mean only the plot, although particularly in the case of a Victorian novel teeming with secondary characters and subplots, severe pruning is required, but also the intellectual content. A film has to convey its message by images and relatively few words; it has little tolerance for complexity or irony or tergiversations. I found the work exceedingly difficult, beyond anything I had anticipated. And, I should add, depressing: I care about words more than images, and yet I was constantly sacrificing words and their connotations. You might tell me that through images film conveys a vast amount of information that words can only attempt to approximate, and you would be right, but approximation is precious in itself, because it bears the author's stamp. All in all, it seemed to me that my screenplay was worth much less than the book, and that the same would be true of the film.

—**Novelist John North in Louis Begley's novel, *Shipwreck* (2003)**

Familiarity and Contempt

A daptations are everywhere today: on the television and movie screen, on the musical and dramatic stage, on the Internet, in novels and comic books, in your nearest theme park and video arcade. A certain level of self-consciousness about—and perhaps even acceptance of—their ubiquity is suggested by the fact that films have been made about the process itself, such as Spike Jonze's *Adaptation* or Terry Gilliam's *Lost in La Mancha,* both in 2002. Television series have also explored the act of adaptation, like the eleven-part BRAVO documentary "Pageto Screen." Adaptations are obviously not new to our time, however; Shakespeare transferred his culture's stories from page to stage and made them available to a whole new audience. Aeschylus and Racine and Goethe and da Ponte also retold familiar stories in new forms. Adaptations are so much a part of Western culture that they appear to affirm Walter Benjamin's insight that "storytelling is always the art of repeating stories" (1992: 90). The critical pronouncements of T. S. Eliot or Northrop Frye were certainly not needed to convince avid adapters across the centuries of what, for them, has always been a truism: art is derived from other art; stories are born of other stories.

Nevertheless, in both academic criticism and journalistic reviewing, contemporary popular adaptations are most often put down as secondary, derivative, "belated, middlebrow, or culturally inferior" (as noted by Naremore 2002b: 6). This is what Louis Begley's novelist-adapter is expressing in the epigraph; but there are more strong and decidedly moralistic words used to attack film adaptations of literature: "tampering," "interference," "violation" (listed in McFarlane 1996: 12), "betrayal," "deformation," "perversion," "infidelity," and "desecration" (found by Stam 2000: 54). The move from the literary to the filmic or televisual has even been called a move to "a willfully inferior form of cognition" (Newman 1985: 129). Although adaptation's detractors argue that "all the directorial Scheherazades of the world cannot add up to one Dostoevsky" (Peary and Shatzkin 1977: 2), it does seem to be more or less acceptable to adapt *Romeo and Juliet* into a respected high art form, like an opera or a ballet, but not to make it into a movie, especially an updated one like Baz Luhrmann's (1996) *William Shakespeare's Romeo + Juliet.* If an adaptation is perceived as "lowering" a story (according to some imagined hierarchy of medium or genre), response is likely to be negative. Residual suspicion remains even in the admiration expressed for something like Julie Taymor's *Titus* (1999), her critically successful film version of Shakespeare's *Titus Andronicus.* Even in our postmodern age of cultural recycling, something—perhaps the commercial success of adaptations—would appear to make us uneasy.

As early as 1926, Virginia Woolf, commenting on the fledgling art of cinema, deplored the simplification of the literary work that inevitably occurred in its transposition to the new visual medium and called film a "parasite" and literature its "prey" and "victim" (1926: 309). Yet she also foresaw that film had the potential to develop its own independent idiom: "cinema has within its grasp innumerable symbols for emotions that have so far failed to find expression" in words (309). And so it does. In the view of film semiotician Christian Metz, cinema "tells us continuous stories; it 'says' things that could be conveyed also in the language of words; yet it says them differently. There is a reason for the possibility as well as for the necessity of adaptations" (1974: 44). However, the same could be said of adaptations in the form of musicals, operas, ballets, or songs. All these adapters relate stories in their different ways. They use the same tools that storytellers have always used: they actualize or concretize ideas; they make simplifying selections, but also amplify and extrapolate; they make analogies; they critique or show their respect, and so on. But the stories they relate are taken from elsewhere, not invented anew. Like parodies, adaptations have an overt and defining relationship to prior texts, usually revealingly called "sources." Unlike parodies, however, adaptations usually openly announce this relationship. It is the (post-) Romantic valuing of the original creation and of the originating creative genius that is clearly one source of the denigration of adapters and adaptations. Yet this negative view is actually a late addition to Western culture's long and happy history of borrowing and stealing or, more accurately, sharing stories.

For some, as Robert Stam argues, literature will always have axiomatic superiority over any adaptation of it because of its seniority as an art form. But this hierarchy also involves what he calls iconophobia (a suspicion of the visual) and logophilia (love of the word as sacred) (2000: 58). Of course, a negative view of adaptation might simply be the product of thwarted expectations on the part of a fan desiring fidelity to a beloved adapted text or on the part of someone teaching literature and therefore needing proximity to the text and perhaps some entertainment value to do so.

If adaptations are, by this definition, such inferior and secondary creations, why then are they so omnipresent in our culture and, indeed, increasing steadily in numbers? Why, even according to 1992 statistics, are 85 percent of all Oscar-winning Best Pictures adaptations? Why do adaptations make up 95 percent of all the miniseries and 70 percent of all the TV movies of the week that win Emmy Awards? Part of the answer no doubt has to do with the constant appearance of new media and new channels of mass diffusion (Groensteen 1998b: 9). These have clearly fueled an enormous demand for all kinds of stories. Nonetheless, there must be something particularly appealing about adaptations *as adaptations.*

Part of this pleasure, I want to argue, comes simply from repetition with variation, from the comfort of ritual combined with the piquancy of surprise. Recognition and remembrance are part of the pleasure (and risk) of experiencing an adaptation; so too is change. Thematic and narrative persistence combines with material variation (Ropars-Wuilleumier 1998: 131), with the result that adaptations are never simply reproductions that lose the Benjaminian aura. Rather, they carry that aura with them. But as John Ellis suggests, there is something counterintuitive about this desire for persistence within a post-Romantic and capitalist world that values novelty primarily: the "process of adaptation should thus be seen as a massive investment (financial and psychic) in the desire to repeat particular acts of consumption within a form of representation [film, in this case] that discourages such a repetition" (1982: 4–5).

As Ellis' commercial rhetoric suggests, there is an obvious financial appeal to adaptation as well. It is not just at times of economic downturn that adapters turn to safe bets: nineteenth-century Italian composers of that notoriously expensive art form, opera, usually chose to adapt reliable—that is, already financially successful—stage plays or novels in order to avoid financial risks, as well as trouble with the censors (see Trowell 1992: 1198, 1219). Hollywood films of the classical period relied on adaptations from popular novels, what Ellis calls the "tried and tested" (1982: 3), while British television has specialized in adapting the culturally accredited eighteenth- and nineteenth-century novel, or Ellis' "tried and trusted." However, it is not simply a matter of risk-avoidance; there is money to be made. A best-selling book may reach a million readers; a successful Broadway play will be seen by 1 to 8 million people; but a movie or television adaptation will find an audience of many million more (Seger 1992: 5).

The recent phenomenon of films being "musicalized" for the stage is obviously economically driven. The movies of *The Lion King* or *The Producers* offer ready-made name recognition for audiences, thereby relieving some of the anxiety for Broadway producers of expensive musicals. Like sequels and prequels, "director's cut" DVDs and spin-offs, videogame adaptations based on films are yet another way of taking one "property" in a "franchise" and reusing it in another medium. Not only will audiences already familiar with the "franchise" be attracted to the new "repurposing" (Bolter and Grusin 1999: 45), but new consumers will also be created. The multinationals who own film studios today often already own the rights to stories in other media, so they can be recycled for videogames, for example, and then marketed by the television stations they also own (Thompson 2003: 81–82).

Does the manifest commercial success of adaptations help us understand why the 2002 film *The Royal Tenenbaums* (directed by Wes Anderson with a script by Owen Wilson) opens with a book being checked out of a library—the book upon which the film implicitly claims to be based? Echoing movies like David Lean's *Great Expectations* (1946), which begins with a shot of the Dickens novel opened to Chapter 1, scene changes in Anderson's movie are marked by a shot of the Tenenbaums' "book" opened to the next chapter, the first lines of which describe what we then see on screen. Because, to my knowledge, this film is *not* adapted from any literary text, the use of this device is a direct and even parodic recall of its use in earlier films, but with a difference: the authority of literature as an institution and thus also of the act of adapting it seems to be what is being invoked and emphasized. But why would a film want to be seen as an adaptation? And what do we mean by a work being seen *as an adaptation*?

Treating Adaptations *as Adaptations*

To deal with adaptations *as adaptations* is to think of them as, to use Scottish poet and scholar Michael Alexander's great term (Ermarth 2001: 47), inherently "palimpsestuous" works, haunted at all times by their adapted texts. If we know that prior text, we always feel its presence shadowing the one we are experiencing directly. When we call a work *an adaptation*, we openly announce its overt relationship to another work or works. It is what Gérard Genette would call a text in the "second degree" (1982: 5), created and then received in relation to a prior text. This is why adaptation studies are so often comparative studies (cf. Cardwell 2002: 9). This is not to say that adaptations are not also autonomous works that can be interpreted and valued as such; as many theorists have insisted, they obviously are (see, for example, Bluestone 1957/1971; Ropars 1970). This is one reason why an adaptation has its own aura, its own "presence in time and space, its unique existence at the place where it happens to be" (Benjamin 1968: 214). I take such a position as axiomatic, but not as my theoretical focus. To interpret an adaptation *as an adaptation* is, in a sense, to treat it as what Roland Barthes called, not a "work," but a "text," a plural "stereophony of echoes, citations, references" (1977: 160). Although adaptations are also aesthetic objects in their own right, it is only as inherently double- or multi-laminated works that they can be theorized *as adaptations*.

An adaptation's double nature does not mean, however, that proximity or fidelity to the adapted text should be the criterion of judgment or the focus of analysis. For a long time, "fidelity criticism," as it came to be known, was the critical orthodoxy in adaptation studies, especially when dealing with canonical works such as those of Pushkin or Dante. Today that dominance has been challenged from a variety of perspectives (e.g., McFarlane 1996: 194; Cardwell 2002: 19) and with a range of results. And, as George Bluestone pointed out early on, when a film becomes a financial or critical success, the question of its faithfulness is given hardly any thought (1957/1971: 114). My decision not to concentrate on this particular aspect of the relationship between adapted text and adaptation means that there appears to be little need to engage directly in the constant debate over degrees of proximity to the "original" that has generated those many typologies of adaptation processes: borrowing versus intersection versus transformation (Andrew 1980:10–12); analogy versus commentary versus transposition (Wagner 1975: 222–31); using the source as raw material versus reinterpretation of only the core narrative structure versus a literal translation (Kleinand Parker 1981: 10).

Of more interest to me is the fact that the morally loaded discourse of fidelity is based on the implied assumption that adapters aim simply to reproduce the adapted text (e.g., Orr 1984: 73). Adaptation is repetition, but repetition without replication. And there are manifestly many different possible intentions behind the act of adaptation: the urge to consume and erase the memory of the adapted text or to call it into question is as likely as the desire to pay tribute by copying. Adaptations such as film remakes can even be seen as mixed in intent: "contested homage" (Greenberg 1998: 115), Oedipally envious and worshipful at the same time (Horton and McDougal 1998b: 8).

If the idea of fidelity should not frame any theorizing of adaptation today, what should? According to its dictionary meaning, "to adapt" is to adjust, to alter, to make suitable. This can be done in any number of ways. As the next section will explore in more depth, the phenomenon of adaptation can be defined from three distinct but interrelated perspectives, for I take it as no accident that we use the same word—adaptation—to refer to the process and the product.

First, seen as a *formal entity or product*, an adaptation is an announced and extensive transposition of a particular work or works. This "transcoding" can involve a shift of medium (a poem to a film) or genre (an epic to a novel), or a change of frame and therefore context: telling the same story from a different point of view, for instance, can create a manifestly different interpretation. Transposition can also mean a shift in ontology from the real to the fictional, from a historical account or biography to a fictionalized narrative or drama. Sister Helen Prejean's 1994 book, *Dead Man Walking: An Eyewitness Account of the Death Penalty in the United States*, became first a fictionalized film (directed by Tim Robbins, 1995) and then, a few years later, an opera (written by Terrence McNally and Jake Heggie).

Second, as *a process of creation*, the act of adaptation always involves both (re-)interpretation and then (re-)creation; this has been called both appropriation and salvaging, depending on your perspective. For every aggressive appropriator outed by a political opponent, there is a patient salvager. Priscilla Galloway, an adapter of mythic and historical narratives for children and young adults, has said that she is motivated by a desire to preserve stories that are worth knowing but will not necessarily speak to a new audience without creative "reanimation" (2004), and *that* is her task. African film adaptations of traditional oral legends are also seen as a way of preserving a rich heritage in an aural and visual mode (Cham 2005: 300).

Third, seen from the perspective of its *process of reception*, adaptation is a form of intertextuality: we experience adaptations (*as adaptations*) as palimpsests through our memory of other works that resonate through repetition with variation. For the right audience, then, the novelization by Yvonne Navarro of a film like *Hellboy* (2004) may echo not only with Guillermo del Toro's film but also with the Dark Horse Comics series from which the latter was adapted. Paul Anderson's 2002 film *Resident Evil* will be experienced differently by those who have played the videogame of the same name, from which the movie was adapted, than by those who have not.

In short, adaptation can be described as the following:

- An acknowledged transposition of a recognizable other work or works.
- A creative *and* an interpretive act of appropriation/salvaging.
- An extended intertextual engagement with the adapted work.

Therefore, an adaptation is a derivation that is not derivative—a work that is second without being secondary. It is its own palimpsestic thing.

There is some apparent validity to the general statement that adaptation "as a concept can expand or contract. Writ large, adaptation includes almost any act of alteration performed upon specific cultural works of the past and dovetails with a general process of cultural recreation" (Fischlin and Fortier 2000: 4). But, from a pragmatic point of view, such a vast definition would clearly make adaptation rather difficult to theorize. My more restricted double definition of adaptation as process and product is closer to the common usage of the word and is broad enough to allow me to treat not just films and stage productions, but also musical arrangements and song covers, visual art revisitations of prior works and comic book versions of history, poems put to music and remakes of films, and videogames and interactive art. It also permits me to draw distinctions; for instance, allusions to and brief echoes of other works would not qualify as extended engagements, nor do most examples of musical sampling, because they recontextualize only short fragments of music. Plagiarisms are not acknowledged appropriations, and sequels and prequels are not really adaptations either, nor is fan fiction. There is a difference between never wanting a story to end—the reason behind sequels and prequels, according to Marjorie Garber (2003: 73–74)—and wanting to retell the same story over and over in different ways. With adaptations, we seem to desire the repetition as much as the change. Maybe this is why, in the eyes of the law, adaptation is a "derivative work"—that is, one based on one or more pre-existing works, but "recast, transformed" (17 USC §101). That seemingly simple definition, however, is also a theoretical can of worms.

Exactly What Gets Adapted? How?

What precisely is "recast" and "transformed"? In law, ideas themselves cannot be copyrighted; only their expression can be defended in court. And herein lies the whole problem. As Kamilla Elliott has astutely noted, adaptation commits the heresy of showing that form (expression) can be separated from content (ideas)—something both mainstream aesthetic and semiotic theories have resisted or denied (2003: 133), even as legal theory has embraced it. The form changes with adaptation (thus evading most legal prosecution); the content persists. But what exactly constitutes that transferred and transmuted "content"?

Many professional reviewers and audience members alike resort to the elusive notion of the "spirit" of a work or an artist that has to be captured and conveyed in the adaptation for it to be a success. The "spirit" of Dickens or Wagner is invoked, often to justify radical changes in the "letter" or form. Sometimes it is "tone" that is deemed central, though rarely defined (e.g., Linden 1971: 158, 163); at other times it is "style" (Seger 1992: 157). But all three are arguably equally subjective and, it would appear, difficult to discuss, much less theorize.

Most theories of adaptation assume, however, that the story is the common denominator, the core of what is transposed across different media and genres, each of which deals with that story in formally different ways and, I would add, through different modes of engagement—narrating, performing, or interacting. In adapting, the story-argument goes, "equivalences" are sought in different sign systems for the various elements of the story: its themes, events, world, characters, motivations, points of view, consequences, contexts, symbols, imagery, and so on. As Millicent Marcus has explained, however, there are two opposing theoretical schools of thought on this point: either a story can exist independently of any embodiment in any particular signifying system or, on the contrary, it cannot be considered separately from its material mode of mediation (1993: 14). What the phenomenon of adaptation suggests, however, is that, although the latter is obviously true for the audience, whose members experience the story in a particular material form, the various elements of the story can and are considered separately by adapters and by theorists, if only because technical constraints of different media will inevitably highlight different aspects of that story (Gaudreault and Marion 1998: 45).

Themes are perhaps the easiest story elements to see as adaptable across media and even genres or framing contexts. As author Louis Begley said about the themes of his 1996 novel *About Schmidt* when the work was transcribed to the screen by Alexander Payne and Jim Taylor: "I was able to hear them rather like melodies transposed into a different key" (2003: 1). Many Romantic ballets were derived from Hans Christian Andersen's stories simply, some say, because of their traditional and easily accessible themes, such as quests, magical tasks, disguise and revelation, and innocence versus evil (Mackrell 2004). Composer Alexander Zemlinsky wrote a "symphonic fantasy" adaptation of Andersen's famous "The Little Mermaid" (1836) called *Die Seejungfrau* (1905) that includes musical programmatic descriptions of such elements as the storm and musical leitmotifs that tell the story and its themes of love, pain, and nature, as well as music that evokes emotions and atmosphere befitting the story. A modern manual for adapters explains, however, that themes are, in fact, of most importance to novels and plays; in TV and films, themes must always serve the story action and "reinforce or dimensionalize" it, for in these forms, story-line is supreme—except in European "art" films (Seger 1992: 14).

Characters, too, can obviously be transported from one text to another, and indeed, as Murray Smith has argued, characters are crucial to the rhetorical and aesthetic effects of both narrative and performance texts because they engage receivers' imaginations through what he calls recognition, alignment, and allegiance (1995: 4–6). The theater and the novel are usually considered the forms in which the human subject is central. Psychological development (and thus receiver empathy) is part of the narrative and dramatic arc when characters are the focus of adaptations. Yet, in playing videogame adaptations of films, we can actually "become" one of the characters and act in their fictional world.

The separate units of the story (or the *fabula*) can also be transmediated—just as they can be summarized in digest versions or translated into another language (Hamon 1977: 264). But they may well change—often radically—in the process of adaptation, and not only (but most obviously) in terms of their plot ordering. Pacing can be transformed, time compressed or expanded. Shifts in the focalization or point of view of the adapted story may lead to major differences. When David Lean wrote, directed, and edited the film version of E. M. Forster's 1924 novel *Passage to India* in 1984, he altered the novel's focalization on the two men, Fielding and Aziz, and their cross-cultural interrelations. Instead, the film tells Adela's story, adding scenes to establish her character and make it more complex and interesting than it arguably is in the novel. More radically, *Miss Havisham's Fire* (1979/revised 1996), Dominick Argento and John Olon-Scrymgeour's operatic adaptation of Dickens' *Great Expectations* (1860/1861), all but ignored the story of the protagonist Pip to tell that of the eccentric Miss Havisham.

In other cases, it might be the point of departure or conclusion that is totally transfigured in adaptation. For instance, in offering a different ending in the film version of Michael Ondaatje's novel *The English Patient*, Anthony Minghella, in his film script and in his directing, removed the postcolonial politics of the Indian Kip's response to the bombing of Hiroshima, substituting instead another smaller, earlier bomb that kills his co-worker and friend. In other words, a personal crisis is made to replace a political one. As the movie's editor Walter Murch articulated the decision: "The film [unlike the novel] was so much about those five individual people: the Patient, Hana, Kip, Katharine, Caravaggio—that to suddenly open it up near the end and ask the audience to imagine the death of hundreds of thousands of unknown people … It was too abstract. So the bomb of Hiroshima became the bomb that killed Hardy, someone you knew" (qtd. in Ondaatje 2002: 213). And, in the movie version (but not in the novel), the nurse Hana actually gives her patient the fatal morphine shot at the end, undoubtedly so that she can be seen to merge with his lover Katharine in the patient's memory, as in ours. On the soundtrack, their voices merge as well. The focus of the film is on the doomed love affair alone. This change of ending may not be quite the same as Nahum Tate's making Cordelia survive and marry Edgar in his infamous 1681 version of *King Lear*, but it is a major shift of emphasis nonetheless.

If we move from considering only the medium in this way to considering changes in the more general manner of story presentation, however, other differences in what gets adapted begin to appear. This is because each manner involves a different mode of engagement on the part of both audience and adapter. As we shall see in more detail shortly, being shown a story is not the same as being told it—and neither is it the same as participating in it or interacting with it, that is, experiencing a story directly and kinesthetically. With each mode, different things get adapted and in different ways. As my examples so far suggest, to tell a story, as in novels, short stories, and even historical accounts, is to describe, explain, summarize, expand; the narrator has a point of view and great power to leap through time and space and sometimes to venture inside the minds of characters. To show a story, as in movies, ballets, radio and stage plays, musicals and operas, involves a direct aural and usually visual performance experienced in real time.

Although neither telling nor showing renders its audience passive in the least, they also do not engage people as immediately and viscerally as do virtual environments, videogames (played on any platform), or even theme-park rides that are, in their own ways, adaptations or "remediations" (Bolter and Grusin 1999). The interactive, physical nature of this kind of engagement entails changes both in the story and even in the importance of story itself. If a film can be said to have a three-act structure—a beginning in which a conflict is established; a middle in which the implications of the conflict are played out; an end where the conflict is resolved—then a videogame adaptation of a film can be argued to have a different three-act structure. The introductory material, often presented in what are called "movie cut-scenes," is the first act; the second is the core gameplay experience; the third is the climax, again often in filmed cut-scenes (Lindley 2002: 206). Acts one and three obviously do the narrative work—through showing—and set up the story frame, but both are in fact peripheral to the core: the second-act gameplay, with its intensity of cognitive and physical engagement, moves the narrative along through visual spectacle and audio effects (including music) and through problem-solving challenges. As Marie-Laure Ryan has pointed out: "The secret to the narrative success of games is their ability to exploit the most fundamental of the forces that move a plot forward: the solving of problems" (2004c: 349). Story, in this case, is no longer central or at least no longer an end in itself, although it is still present as a means toward a goal (King 2002: 51).

Although there has been a long debate recently about whether interactivity and storytelling are at odds with one another (see Ryan 2001: 244; Ryan 2004c: 337), what is more relevant in a game adaptation is the fact that players can inhabit a known fictional, often striking, visual world of digital animation. Nintendo's 3-D world of Zelda, for instance, has been described as "a highly intricate environment, with a complicated economics, an awesome cast of creatures, a broad range of landscapes and indoor scenarios, and an elaborated chemistry, biology, geology and ecology so that its world can almost be studied like an alternative version of nature" (Weinbren 2002: 180). Though *Zelda* is not an adaptation, this description of its world fits so many games that are adaptations. Similarly, Disney World visitors who go on the Aladdin ride can enter and physically navigate a universe originally presented as a linear experience through film.

What gets adapted here is a heterocosm, literally an "other world" or cosmos, complete, of course, with the stuff of a story—settings, characters, events, and situations. To be more precise, it is the "*res extensa*"—to use Descartes' terminology—of that world, its material, physical dimension, which is transposed and then experienced through multisensorial interactivity (Grau 2003: 3). This heterocosm possesses what theorists call "truth-of-coherence" (Ruthven 1979: 11)—here, plausibility and consistency of movement and graphics within the context of the game (Ward 2002: 129)—just as do narrated and performed worlds, but this world also has a particular kind of "truth-of-correspondence"—not to any "real world" but to the universe of a particular adapted text. The videogame of *The Godfather* uses the voices and physical images of some of the film's actors, including Marlon Brando, but the linear structure of the movie is transmuted into that of a flexible game model in which the player becomes a nameless mafia henchman, trying to win the respect of the main characters by taking over businesses, killing people, and so on. In other words, the point of view has been changed from that of the mafia bosses to that of the underlings, who allow us to see familiar scenes from the film's world from a different perspective and possibly create a different resolution.

What videogames, like virtual reality experiments, cannot easily adapt is what novels can portray so well: the "*res cogitans*," the space of the mind. Even screen and stage media have difficulty with this dimension, because when psychic reality is shown rather than told about, it has to be made manifest in the material realm to be perceived by the audience. However, expanding the idea of what can be adapted to include this idea of a heterocosm or visual world as well as other aspects of the story opens up the possibility of considering, for instance, Aubrey Beardsley's famous illustrations for Oscar Wilde's play *Salomé* as a possible adaptation or even Picasso's cubist recodings of some of the canonical paintings of Velásquez.

Are some kinds of stories and their worlds more easily adaptable than others? Susan Orlean's book, *The Orchid Thief*, proved intractable to screenwriter "Charlie Kaufman" in the movie *Adaptation*. Or did it? Linear realist novels, it would appear, are more easily adapted for the screen than experimental ones, or so we might assume from the evidence: the works of Charles Dickens, Ian Fleming, and Agatha Christie are more often adapted than those of Samuel Beckett, James Joyce, or Robert Coover. "Radical" texts, it is said, are "reduced to a kind of cinematic homogenization" (Axelrod 1996: 204) when they are adapted. But Dickens' novels have been called "theatrical" in their lively dialogue and their individualized, if broadly drawn, characters, complete with idiosyncratic speech patterns. Their strongly pictorial descriptions and potential for scenes of spectacle also make them readily adaptable or at least "adaptogenic" (Groensteen 1998a: 270) to the stage and screen. Historically, it is melodramatic worlds and stories that have lent themselves to adaptation in the form of opera and musical dramas, where music can reinforce the stark emotional oppositions and tensions created by the requisite generic compression (because it takes longer to sing than to speak a line). Today, spectacular special effects films like the various *The Matrix* or *Star Wars* movies are the ones likely to spawn popular videogames whose players can enjoy entering and manipulating the cinematic fantasy world.

Double Vision: Defining Adaptation

Given this complexity of what can be adapted and of the means of adaptation, people keep trying to coin new words to replace the confusing simplicity of the word "adaptation" (e.g., Gaudreault 1998: 268). But most end up admitting defeat: the word has stuck for a reason. Yet, however straightforward the idea of adaptation may appear on the surface, it is actually very difficult to define, in part, as we have seen, because we use the same word for the process and the product. As a product, an adaptation can be given a formal definition, but as a process—of creation and of reception—other aspects have to be considered. This is why those different perspectives touched on earlier are needed to discuss and define adaptation.

Adaptation as Product: Announced, Extensive, Specific Transcoding

As openly acknowledged and extended reworkings of particular other texts, adaptations are often compared to translations. Just as there is no such thing as a literal translation, there can be no literal adaptation. Nevertheless, the study of both has suffered from domination by "normative and source-oriented approaches" (Hermans 1985: 9). Transposition to another medium, or even moving within the same one, always means change or, in the language of the new media, "reformatting." And there will always be both gains and losses (Stam 2000: 62). Although this seems commonsensical enough, it is important to remember that, in most concepts of translation, the source text is granted an axiomatic primacy and authority, and the rhetoric of comparison has most often been that of faithfulness and equivalence. Walter Benjamin did alter this frame of reference when he argued, in "The Task of the Translator," that translation is not a rendering of some fixed nontextual meaning to be copied or paraphrased or reproduced; rather, it is an engagement with the original text that makes us see that text in different ways (1992: 77). Recent translation theory argues that translation involves a transaction between texts and between languages and is thus "an act of both inter-cultural and inter-temporal communication" (Bassnett 2002: 9).

This newer sense of translation comes closer to defining adaptation as well. In many cases, because adaptations are to a different medium, they are re-mediations, that is, specifically translations in the form of intersemiotic transpositions from one sign system (for example, words) to another (for example, images). This is translation but in a very specific sense: as transmutation or transcoding, that is, as necessarily a recoding into a new set of conventions as well as signs. For example, Harold Pinter's screenplay for Karel Reisz's film *The French Lieutenant's Woman* (1981) transposed the narrative of John Fowles' novel (1969) into a totally cinematic code. The novel juxtaposed a modern narrator and a Victorian story; in the equally self-reflexive movie, we have, instead, a Victorian scenario within a modern film that is itself a movie about the filming of the nineteenth-century story. The self-consciousness of the novel's narrator was translated into cinematic mirroring, as the actors who play the Victorian characters live out the scripted romance in their own lives. The role-playing motif of film acting effectively echoed the hypocrisy and the schizoid morality of the Victorian world of the novel (see Sinyard 1986: 135–40).

The idea of paraphrase (Bluestone 1957/1971: 62) is an alternative frequently offered to this translation analogy. Etymologically, a paraphrase is a mode of telling "beside" (para) and, according to the *Oxford English Dictionary*, one of its first meanings is "a free rendering or amplification of a passage" that is verbal but, by extension, musical as well. John Dryden is quoted as defining paraphrase as "translation with latitude, where the author is kept in view … , but his words are not so strictly followed as his sense; and that too is admitted to be amplified." Perhaps this describes best what scriptwriter Robert Nelson Jacobs and director Lasse Hallstrom did in their 2001 cinematic adaptation of E. Annie Proulx's novel *The Shipping News* (1993). The novel protagonist's psychic world, which is amply explored, thanks to the omniscient narration, is freely rendered in the film by having him think in visualized headlines—a realistic device for a newspaperman. In a sense, even the novel's metaphoric writing style is paraphrased in the recurring visual imagery derived from his fear of drowning. Similarly, Virginia Woolf's densely rich associative language in *Mrs. Dalloway* is rendered or paraphrased in "associative visual imagery" in the 1998 film directed by Marleen Gorris (see Cuddy-Keane 1998: 173–74).

Paraphrase and translation analogies can also be useful in considering what I earlier called the ontological shift that can happen in adaptations of an historical event or an actual person's life into a reimagined, fictional form. The adapted text may be an authoritative historical rendering or a more indefinite archive (see Andrew 2004: 200), and the form can range from "biopics" to "heritage" films, from television docudramas to videogames, such as *JFK Reloaded* (by Traffic Games in Scotland), based on the Kennedy assassination. Sometimes the text being paraphrased or translated is very immediate and available. For example, the German television movie called *Wannseekonferenz* (*The Wannsee Conference*) was an 85-minute film adaptation scripted from the actual minutes of the 85-minute meeting held in 1942 and chaired by Reinhard Heydrich, the Chief of the German State Police, in which the "Final Solution to the Jewish Question" was decided. In 2001, Loring Mandel did a further adaptation in English for BBC and HBO called *Conspiracy*.

At other times, the adapted text is more complex or even multiple: Sidney Lumet's 1975 film *Dog Day Afternoon* was a fictionalized adaptation of an actual 1972 bank robbery and hostage situation in Brooklyn that was covered live on television and was much discussed in the media. In fact, a *Life* magazine article by P.F. Kluge was the basis of the film's screenplay. But in 2002 artist Pierre Huyghe asked the real robber, John Wojtowicz, to reenact and narrate—in effect, to translate or paraphrase—the original event for his camera. In the process, a second-level adaptation occurred: as the perpetrator relived his own past, what became clear was that he could not do so except through the lenses of the subsequent movie version. In effect, the film became, for him, as much the text to be adapted as was the lived event preserved in either his memory or the media coverage. In ontological shifts, it makes little sense to talk about adaptations as "historically accurate" or "historically inaccurate" in the usual sense. *Schindler's List* is not *Shoah* (see Hansen 2001) in part because it is an adaptation of a novel by Thomas Keneally, which is itself based on survivor testimony. In other words, it is a paraphrase or translation of a *particular* other text, a particular interpretation of history. The seeming simplicity of the familiar label, "based on a true story," is a ruse: in reality, such historical adaptations are as complex as historiography itself.

Adaptation as Process

The Adapter's Creative Interpretation/Interpretive Creation: Early in the film *Adaptation*, screenwriter "Charlie Kaufman" faces an anguished dilemma: he worries about his responsibility as an adapter to an author and a book he respects. As he senses, what is involved in adapting can be a process of appropriation, of taking possession of another's story, and filtering it, in a sense, through one's own sensibility, interests, and talents. Therefore, adapters are first interpreters and then creators. This is one reason why *Morte a Venezia*, Luchino Visconti's 1971 Italian film version of Thomas Mann's 1911 novella *Der Tod in Venedig*, is so different in focus and impact from Benjamin Britten and Myfanwy Piper's English opera *Death in Venice*, which premiered only a few years later in 1973. The other reason, of course, is the adapter's choice of medium.

E. H. Gombrich offers a useful analogy when he suggests that if an artist stands before a landscape with a pencil in hand, he or she will "look for those aspects which can be rendered in lines"; if it is a paintbrush that the hand holds, the artist's vision of the very same landscape will be in terms of masses, not lines (1961: 65). Therefore, an adapter coming to a story with the idea of adapting it for a film would be attracted to different aspects of it than an opera librettist would be.

Usually adaptations, especially from long novels, mean that the adapter's job is one of subtraction or contraction; this is called "a surgical art" (Abbott 2002: 108) for a good reason. In adapting Philip Pullman's trilogy of novels, *His Dark Materials*, from 1,300 print pages to two three-hour plays, Nicholas Wright had to cut major characters (for example, the Oxford scientist Mary Malone) and therefore whole worlds they inhabit (for example, the land of the mulefas); he had to speed up the action and involve the Church right from the start. Of course, he also had to find two major narrative climaxes to replace the three of the trilogy. He also found he had to explain certain themes and even plot details, for there was not as much time for the play's audience to piece things together as there was for those reading the novels.

Obviously, not all adaptations involve simply cutting. Short stories, in particular, have often inspired movies; for example, John M. Cunningham's 1947 "The Tin Star" became Fred Zinneman and Carl Forman's 1952 film *High Noon*. Short story adaptations have had to expand their source material considerably. When filmmaker Neil Jordan and Angela Carter adapted Carter's story "The Company of Wolves" in 1984, they added details from two other related tales in Carter's *The Bloody Chamber* (1979): "The Werewolf" and "Wolf-Alice." They took a contemporary prologue from Carter's own earlier radio play adaptation to set up the dream logic of the piece. Screenwriter Noel Baker similarly described his attempt to take "a whisper of a movie idea" and make it into a feature film. He had been asked to adapt not a short story but, in fact, Michael Turner's book *Hard Core Logo* (1993), but this book is a fragmentary narrative about the reunion of a 1980s punk band that is made up of letters, songs, answering machine messages, invoices, photos, handwritten notes, diary entries, contracts, and so on. Baker said that he first felt the challenge of the fragmentation itself and then of the fact that it was "lean and spare, full of gaps and silences, the eloquence of things left unsaid" (1997: 10). In the end, he noted in his diary that this latter point was what made the task more fun, more creative: "Must thank Turner for writing so little yet suggesting so much" (14).

Of course, there is a wide range of reasons why adapters might choose a particular story and then transcode it into a particular medium or genre. As noted earlier, their aim might well be to economically and artistically supplant the prior works. They are just as likely to want to contest the aesthetic or political values of the adapted text as to pay homage. This, of course, is one of the reasons why the rhetoric of "fidelity" is less than adequate to discuss the process of adaptation. Whatever the motive, from the adapter's perspective, adaptation is an act of appropriating or salvaging, and this is always a double process of interpreting and then creating something new.

If this sounds somewhat familiar, there is good reason, given the long history in the West of *imitatio* or *mimesis*—imitation—as what Aristotle saw as part of the instinctive behavior of humans and the source of their pleasure in art (Wittkower 1965: 143). Imitation of great works of art, in particular, was not intended only to capitalize on the prestige and authority of the ancients or even to offer a pedagogical model (as the *Rhetorica ad Herennium* argued [I.ii.3 and IV.i.2]), though it did both. It was also a form of creativity: "*Imitatio* is neither plagiarism nor a flaw in the constitution of Latin literature. It is a dynamic law of its existence" (West and Woodman 1979: ix). Like classical imitation, adaptation also is not slavish copying; it is a process of making the adapted material one's own. In both, the novelty is in what one *does with* the other text. Indeed, for "Longinus," *imitatio* went together with *aemulatio*, linking imitation and creativity (Russell 1979: 10). Perhaps one way to think about unsuccessful adaptations is not in terms of infidelity to a prior text, but in terms of a lack of the creativity and skill to make the text one's own and thus autonomous.

For the reader, spectator, or listener, adaptation *as adaptation* is unavoidably a kind of intertextuality *if the receiver is acquainted with the adapted text*. It is an ongoing dialogical process, as Mikhail Bakhtin would have said, in which we compare the work we already know with the one we are experiencing (Stam 2000: 64). By stressing the relation of individual works to other works and to an entire cultural system, French semiotic and post-structuralist theorizing of intertextuality (e.g., by Barthes 1971/1977; Kristeva 1969/1986) has been important in its challenges to dominant post-Romantic notions of originality, uniqueness, and autonomy. Instead, texts are said to be mosaics of citations that are visible and invisible, heard and silent; they are always already written and read. So, too, are adaptations, but with the added proviso that they are also acknowledged as adaptations *of specific texts*. Often, the audience will recognize that a work is an adaptation of more than one specific text. For instance, when later writers reworked—for radio, stage, and even screen—John Buchan's 1914 novel, *The Thirty-Nine Steps*, they often adapted Alfred Hitchcock's dark and cynical 1935 film adaptation along with the novel (Glancy 2003: 99–100). And films about Dracula today are as often seen as adaptations of other earlier films as they are of Bram Stoker's novel.

The Audience's "Palimpsestuous" Intertextuality: For audiences, such adaptations are obviously "multi-laminated"; they are directly and openly connected to recognizable other works, and that connection is part of their formal identity, but also of what we might call their hermeneutic identity. This is what keeps under control the "background noise" (Hinds 1998: 19) of all the other intertextual parallels to the work the audience might make that are due to similar artistic and social conventions, rather than specific works. In all cases, the engagement with these other works in adaptations are extended ones, not passing allusions.

Part of both the pleasure and the frustration of experiencing an adaptation is the familiarity bred through repetition and memory. Depending on our relationship with any of the traditionally choreographed versions of Tchaikovsky's 1877 ballet, *Swan Lake* (and there are many of these, from the Petipa/Ivanov one to its reworkings by Ashton and Dowell), we will be either delighted or irritated by Matthew Bourne's adaptation, with its updating and queer ironizing of the popular classical ballet. His muscular male swans and their homoerotic, violent, and sexually charged choreography allows, among many other things, the traditional *pas de deux* between the prince and the swan to be a dance of equals—perhaps for the first time. This prince is no athletic assistant to a ballerina star. Not everyone in the audience will enjoy this transgression of and critical commentary upon the sexual politics of the balletic tradition. But no matter what our response, our inter-textual expectations about medium and genre, as well as about this specific work, are brought to the forefront of our attention. The same will be true of experiencing the Australian Dance Theatre's version, entitled *Birdbrain* (2001), with its hyperspeed edgy choreography, film clips, and mechanized music. As audience members, we need memory in order to experience difference as well as similarity.

Modes of Engagement

A doubled definition of adaptation as a product (as extensive, particular transcoding) and as a process (as creative reinterpretation and palimpsestic inter-textuality) is one way to address the various dimensions of the broader phenomenon of adaptation. An emphasis on process allows us to expand the traditional focus of adaptation studies on medium-specificity and individual comparative case studies in order to consider as well relations among the major modes of engagement: that is, it permits us to think about how adaptations allow people to tell, show, or interact with stories. We can be told or shown a story, each in a range of different media. However, the perspective, and thus the grammar, changes with the third mode of engagement; as audience members, we interact *with* stories in, for instance, the new media, from virtual reality to machinima. All three modes are arguably "immersive," though to different degrees and in different ways: for example, the telling mode (a novel) immerses us through imagination in a fictional world; the showing mode (plays and films) immerses us through the perception of the aural and the visual—the latter in a way related to that Renaissance perspective painting and Baroque *trompe l'oeil* (Ryan 2001: 3); the participatory mode (videogames) immerses us physically and kinesthetically. But if all are, in some sense of the word, "immersive," only the last of them is usually called "interactive." Neither the act of looking at and interpreting black marks—words or notes—on a white page nor that of perceiving and interpreting a direct representation of a story on the stage or screen is in any way passive; both are imaginatively, cognitively, and emotionally active. But the move to participatory modes in which we also engage physically with the story and its world—whether it be in a violent action game or a role-playing or puzzle/skill testing one—is not more active but certainly active in a different way.

In the telling mode—in narrative literature, for example—our engagement begins in the realm of imagination, which is simultaneously controlled by the selected, directing words of the text and liberated—that is, unconstrained by the limits of the visual or aural. We can stop reading at any point; we can re-read or skip ahead; we hold the book in our hands and feel, as well as see, how much of the story remains to be read. But with the move to the mode of showing, as in film and stage adaptations, we are caught in an unrelenting, forward-driving story. And we have moved from the imagination to the realm of direct perception—with its mix of both detail and broad focus. The performance mode teaches us that language is not the only way to express meaning or to relate stories. Visual and gestural representations are rich in complex associations; music offers aural "equivalents" for characters' emotions and, in turn, provokes affective responses in the audience; sound, in general, can enhance, reinforce, or even contradict the visual and verbal aspects. On the other hand, however, a *shown* dramatization cannot approximate the complicated verbal play of *told* poetry or the interlinking of description, narration, and explanation that is so easy for prose narrative to accomplish. Telling a story in words, either orally or on paper, is never the same as showing it visually and aurally in any of the many performance media available.

Some theorists argue that, at a basic level, there is no significant difference between a verbal text and visual images, that, as W. J. T. Mitchell outlines this position, "communicative, expressive acts, narration, argument, description, exposition and other so-called 'speech acts' are not medium-specific, are not 'proper' to some medium or another" (1994: 160). (See also Cohen 1991b.) A consideration of the differences between the modes of engagement of telling and showing, however, suggests quite the contrary: each mode, like each medium, *has* its own specificity, if not its own essence. In other words, no one mode is inherently good at doing one thing and not another; but each has at its disposal different means of expression—media and genres—and so can aim at and achieve certain things better than others.

Consider, for example, the interesting technical task the British novelist E. M. Forster set himself at one point in his 1910 novel *Howards End*: how to represent *in told words* the effect and the meaning of *performed music*—music that his readers would have to imagine, of course, and not hear. He begins the novel's fifth chapter with these words: "It will be generally admitted that Beethoven's Fifth Symphony is the most sublime noise that has ever penetrated into the ear of man" (Forster 1910/1941: 31). Forster goes on to describe the effect on each member of the Schlegel family, whose ears this "sublime noise" penetrates. In a telling mode, a novel can do this: it can take us into the minds and feelings of characters at will. However, the focus of this episode, in which the family attends a symphony concert in Queen's Hall in London together, is specifically on one character, Helen Schlegel—young, newly hurt in love, and therefore someone whose response to the music is intensely personal and deeply tied to her emotional troubles at the time.

As the orchestra plays the third movement, we are told that she hears "a goblin walking quietly over the universe, from end to end" (32). In the first movement, she had heard "heroes and shipwrecks," but here it is terrible goblins she hears, and an "interlude of elephants dancing" (32). These creatures are frightening because of what Helen sees as their casualness: they "observed in passing that there was no such thing as splendour or heroism in the world" (32). Forster continues, telling us that: "Helen could not contradict them, for, once at all events, she had felt the same, and had seen the reliable walls of youth collapse. Panic and emptiness! Panic and emptiness! The goblins were right" (33). Totally moved, not to mention upset, by the end of the piece, she finds she has to leave her family and be alone. As the novel puts it: "The music had summed up to her all that had happened or could happen in her career. She read it as a tangible statement, which could never be superceded" (34). She leaves the hall, taking by mistake the umbrella of a stranger, one Leonard Bast, who will play an important part in the rest of her life and, indeed, in the rest of the novel.

What happens when this told scene is transposed to the showing mode—in this case, to film—in the Merchant/Ivory production adapted by Ruth Prawer Jhabvala? The concert, in a sense, remains, but Helen attends alone. It is not a full orchestral concert this time, but a four-handed piano performance, accompanying a lecture on Beethoven's Fifth Symphony. A few of Forster's own words remain, but very few. Because we can only *see* Helen on film and not get into her head, we can only guess at her thoughts. So in the shown version, it is not she who experiences the "panic and emptiness" of the goblins; it is simply the lecturer who uses this as an image in his explanation of the piece in response to a question from a member of the audience. In fact, Helen, from what we can see, seems rather more bored than upset by the whole experience. We do get to hear the full orchestral version of the symphony on the soundtrack (non-diegetically), but only after she leaves the hall, pursued by the young man whose umbrella she has taken by mistake.

Although Forster uses this scene to tell us about the imaginative and emotional world of Helen Schlegel, the film makes it the occasion to show us Helen meeting Leonard Bast in an appropriately culturally loaded context. In terms of plot action, that is indeed what happens in this scene, and so this is what the film aims to achieve. Interestingly, what the showing mode can do that the telling one cannot is to let us actually *hear* Beethoven's music. We cannot, however, get at the interior of the characters' minds as they listen; they must visibly, physically embody their responses for the camera to record, or they must talk about their reactions. Of course, this film contains lots of performed talk about music, art, and many other things, and not only in this rather overt lecture form.

Interacting with a story is different again from being shown or told it—and not only because of the more immediate kind of immersion it allows. As in a play or film, in virtual reality or a videogame, language alone does not have to conjure up a world; that world is present before our eyes and ears. But in the showing mode we do not physically enter that world and proceed to act within it. Because of its visceral impact, a scripted paintball war game would be considered by some to be a different kind of adaptation of a war story than, say, even the graphic violence of a film like *Saving Private Ryan* (1998). Civil War battle re-enactments may involve role-playing, and new narrative media works may require database "combinatorics," but, in both cases, the audience's engagement is different in kind than when we are told or shown the same story.

Stories, however, do not consist only of the material means of their transmission (media) or the rules that structure them (genres). Those means and those rules permit and then channel narrative expectations and communicate narrative meaning *to someone* in *some context*, and they are created *by someone* with that intent. There is, in short, a wider communicative context that any theory of adaptation would do well to consider. That context will change with the mode of presentation or engagement: the telling mode can use a variety of material media, as can the live or mediated showing mode, just as each medium can support a variety of genres. But media distinctions alone will not necessarily allow the kind of differentiations that adaptations call to our attention. For instance, "machinima" is a form of filmmaking that uses computer game technology to make films within the virtual reality of a game engine. As such, it's a hybrid form, but basically the *medium* is electronic. The machinima adaptation of Percy Bysshe Shelley's 1817 poem "Ozymandias" (by Hugh Hancock for Strange Company) is indeed a digitalized visualization of the poem's "story" about a man walking across a solitary desert and finding a ruined statue of a king inscribed with a chillingly ironic message about worldly glory and the power of time. Even if the figure of the man on screen creates suspense by having to wipe the sand off the final line of the inscription ("Look upon my works, ye Mighty, and despair"), we experience little in the digital version of the frisson we feel reading the poem's devastating irony. Considering medium alone would not be useful to getting at the success (or failure) of this adaptation: although this machinima is in a digital medium, it is not interactive. If anything, the act of interpreting what is really a shown story here is even less actively engaging than reading the told version.

This is not to say that we do not engage differently with different media, but the lines of differentiation are not as clear as we might expect. The private and individual experience of reading is, in fact, closer to the private visual and domestic spaces of television, radio, DVD, video, and computer than it is to the public and communal viewing experience in a dark theater of any kind. And when we sit in the dark, quiet and still, being shown real live bodies speaking or singing on stage, our level and kind of engagement are different than when we sit in front of a screen and technology mediates "reality" for us. When we play a first-person shooter videogame and become an active character in a narrative world and viscerally experience the action, our response is different again. Medium alone cannot explain what happens when an interactive videogame is adapted into a museum-displayed digital work of art, for it becomes a way to show, rather than interact with, a story. For instance, in a piece by Israeli American video artist Eddo Stern called *Vietnam Romance* (2003), the viewer finds that the game's enemies have already been taken out by the artist-shooter, leaving us to watch—in other words, to be shown—only a series of empty sets that have been manipulated to recall classic shots from war films, from *M*A*S*H* to *Apocalypse Now*. In reversing the intended outcome by breaking all the rules of game action, the artist has ensured that the audience cannot and does not engage in the same manner as it would with the interactive game. Likewise, Stern's *Fort Paladin: America's Army* presents a scale model of a medieval castle within which a video screen reveals—again—the final results of the artist's mastery of the U.S. military's game used for recruiting, also called *America's Army*. The work and the pleasure of the observing audience here are different from the kinetic and cognitive involvement of the interactive gamer.

Framing Adaptation

Keeping these three modes of engagement—telling, showing, and interacting with stories—in the forefront can allow for certain precisions and distinctions that a focus on medium alone cannot. It also allows for linkages across media that a concentration on medium-specificity can efface, and thus moves us away from just the formal definitions of adaptation to consider the process. These ways of engaging with stories do not, of course, ever take place in a vacuum. We engage in time and space, within a particular society and a general culture. The contexts of creation and reception are material, public, and economic as much as they are cultural, personal, and aesthetic. This explains why, even in today's globalized world, major shifts in a story's context—that is, for example, in a national setting or time period—can change radically how the transposed story is interpreted, ideologically and literally. How do we react today, for instance, when a male director adapts a woman's novel or when an American director adapts a British novel, or both—as in Neil LaBute's film version of A. S. Byatt's 1991 novel, *Possession*? In shifting cultures and therefore sometimes shifting languages, adaptations make alterations that reveal much about the larger contexts of reception and production. Adapters often "indigenize" stories, to use an anthropological term (Friedman 2004). In Germany, for instance, Shakespeare's works were appropriated through Romantic translations and, through an assertion of the Bard's Germanic affinity, used to generate a German national literature. However strange it may seem, this is why the plays of an enemy-culture's major dramatist continued to be performed—with major variations that could be called adaptations—throughout the two World Wars. The National Socialists, in fact, made these works both political, with private values stressed as being subordinated to public ones in the tragedies, and heroic, with leadership themes dominating (Habicht 1989: 110–15).

Even a shift of time frame can reveal much about when a work is created and received. Robert Louis Stevenson's 1886 novel, *The Strange Case of Dr. Jekyll and Mr. Hyde*, has been adapted many times for the stage and for the movie and television screens. (To get a sense of the whole range, see Geduld 1983.) The showing mode entails embodying and enacting, and thereby often ends up spelling out important ambiguities that are central to the told version—especially, in this case, Hyde's undefined and unspecified evil. Because of mode change, these various versions have had to show—and thus to "figure"—that evil physically, and the means they have chosen to do so are revealing of the historical and political moments of their production. In 1920, at the start of Prohibition, we witness a sexual fall through alcohol in John Robertson's silent film; in the 1971 Hammer film, *Dr. Jekyll and Sister Hyde* (directed by Roy Ward Baker), we see instead Britain's confused responses to feminism after the 1960s (see McCracken-Flesher 1994: 183–94). For economic reasons, adapters often rely on selecting works to adapt that are well known and that have proved popular over time; for legal reasons, they often choose works that are no longer copyrighted.

Technology, too, has probably always framed, not to mention driven, adaptation, in that new media have constantly opened the door for new possibilities for all three modes of engagement. Lately, new electronic technologies have made what we might call fidelity to the *imagination*—rather than a more obvious fidelity to *reality*—possible in new ways, well beyond earlier animation techniques and special effects. We can now enter and act within those worlds, through 3-D digital technology. One of the central beliefs of film adaptation theory is that audiences are more demanding of fidelity when dealing with classics, such as the work of Dickens or Austen. But a whole new set of cult popular classics, especially the work of J. R. R. Tolkien, Philip Pullman, and J. K. Rowling, are now being made visible and audible on stage, in the movie theater, on the video and computer screens, and in multiple gaming formats, and their readers are proving to be just as demanding.

Although our imaginative visualizations of literary worlds are always highly individual, the variance among readers is likely even greater in fantasy fiction than in realist fiction. What does this mean when these fans see one particular version on screen that comes from the director's imagination rather their own (see Boyum 1985)? The answer(s), of course, can be found in the reviews and the audience reactions to the recent adaptations of *The Lord of the Rings* stories and the Harry Potter novels. Now that I know what an enemy orc or a game of Quidditch (can) look like (from the movies), I suspect I will never be able to recapture my first imagined versions again. Palimpsests make for permanent change.

Nicholas Wright's dramatic adaptation of Pullman's *His Dark Materials* trilogy had to cope with the fact that the books had sold three million copies and had been translated into thirty-six languages. The adapter had to find a way to visualize and then bring to physical life on stage—without the technological advantages of film—important elements that the fans would demand be done well: things like the novels' multiple parallel worlds, the windows cut to move characters into each world, and especially the wondrous creatures known as "daemons"—animals of the opposite sex that embody the inner soul of characters. These were technical issues as well as imaginative ones, because Wright knew the novels' fans would be a demanding audience. The two plays that were finally seen in London at the National Theatre in 2003 and revised in 2004 were set within an elaborate "paratextual" context in order to prepare the audience and perhaps forestall any objections: the program was larger and much more informative than most, offering photos, interviews with the novelist and the adapter, maps, a glossary of places, people, things, and "other beings," and a list of literary intertexts.

As this suggests, a further framing of adaptation across all modes of engagement is economic. Broadway adapts from Hollywood; novelizations are timed to coincide with the release of a film. November 2001 saw the infamous simultaneous international release of the film and multiplatform videogame versions of the first installment of the story of Harry Potter. Book publishers produce new editions of adapted literary works to coincide with the film version and invariably put photos of the movie's actors or scenes on the cover. General economic issues, such as the financing and distribution of different media and art forms, must be considered in any general theorizing of adaptation. To appeal to a global market or even a very particular one, a television series or a stage musical may have to alter the cultural, regional, or historical specifics of the text being adapted. A bitingly satiric novel of social pretense and pressure may be transformed into a benign comedy of manners in which the focus of attention is on the triumph of the individual, as has happened in most American television and film versions of Thackeray's *Vanity Fair* (1848). Videogames derived from popular films and vice versa are clearly ways to capitalize on a "franchise" and extend its market. But how different is this from Shakespeare's decision to write a play for his theater based on that familiar story about two teenage lovers or, for that matter, from Charles Gounod's choice to compose what he hoped would be a hit opera about them? In their different ways, Giuseppe Verdi and Richard Wagner were both deeply involved in the financial aspects of their operatic adaptations, yet we tend to reserve our negatively judgmental rhetoric for popular culture, as if it is more tainted with capitalism than is high art.

In beginning to explore this wide range of theoretical issues surrounding adaptation, I have been struck by the unproductive nature of both that negative evaluation of popular cultural adaptations as derivative and secondary and that morally loaded rhetoric of fidelity and infidelity used in comparing adaptations to "source" texts. Like others, I have found myself asking whether we could use any less compromised image to think about adaptation as both process and product. Robert Stam, too, has seen one intriguing possibility in the film *Adaptation,* despite all its ironies; because his focus is specifically on novel to film adaptation, he finds an analogy between these two media and the film's dichotomous screenwriting twins (or split personality). He is also attracted to the metaphor of adaptations as hybrid forms, as "meeting places of different 'species,'" like the orchid (Stam 2005b: 2). For Stam, mutations—filmic adaptations—can help their "source novel 'survive'" (3).

Because my focus is on modes of engagement rather than on two specific media or on "sources," different things have caught my attention. I was struck by the other obvious analogy to adaptation suggested in the film by Darwin's theory of evolution, where genetic adaptation is presented as the biological process by which something is fitted to a given environment. To think of narrative adaptation in terms of a story's fit and its process of mutation or adjustment, through adaptation, to a particular cultural environment is something I find suggestive. Stories also evolve by adaptation and are not immutable over time. Sometimes, like biological adaptation, cultural adaptation involves migration to favorable conditions: stories travel to different cultures and different media. In short, stories adapt just as they are adapted.

In his 1976 book on Darwinian theory called *The Selfish Gene*, Richard Dawkins bravely suggested the existence of a cultural parallel to Darwin's biological theory: "Cultural transmission is analogous to genetic transmission in that, although basically conservative, it can give rise to a form of evolution" (1976/1989: 189). Language, fashions, technology, and the arts, he argued, "all evolve in historical time in a way that looks like highly speeded up genetic evolution, but has really nothing to do with genetic evolution" (190). Nonetheless, he posits the parallel existence of what he calls "memes"—units of cultural transmission or units of imitation—that, like genes, are "replicators" (191–92). But unlike genetic transmission, when memes are transmitted, they always change, for they are subject to "continuous mutation, and also to blending" (195), in part to adapt for survival in the "meme pool." Although Dawkins is thinking about ideas when he writes of memes, stories also are ideas and could be said to function in this same way. Some have great fitness through survival (persistence in a culture) or reproduction (number of adaptations). Adaptation, like evolution, is a transgenerational phenomenon. Some stories obviously have more "stability and penetrance in the cultural environment," as Dawkins would put it (193). Stories do get retold in different ways in new material and cultural environments; like genes, they adapt to those new environments *by virtue of* mutation—in their "offspring" or their adaptations. And the fittest do more than survive; they flourish.

Bibliography

Abbott, H. Porter. 2002. *The Cambridge introduction to narrative*. Cambridge: Cambridge University
Press.
Andrew, Dudley J. 1980. The well-worn muse: adaptation in film and theory. In *Narrative Strategies*.
Macomb: Western Illinois Press, 9–17.
___. 2004. "Adapting cinema to history: A revolution in the making." In Stam and Raengo 2004,189–204.
Axelrod, Mark. 1996. "Once upon a time in Hollywood; or the commodification of form in the adaptation
of fictional" texts to the Hollywood cinema." *Literature/Film Quarterly* 24 (2): 201–8.
Baker, Noel. 1997. *Hard core road show: A screenwriter's diary*. Toronto: Anansi.
Barthes, Roland. 1971/1977. "From Work to Text." Trans. Stephen Heath. In Barthes 1977,155–164.
___. *Image—Music—Text*. Trans. Stephen Heath. New York: Hill & Wang.
Bassnett, Susan. 2002. *Translation studies*, 3rd Edition, London: Routledge.
Begley, Louis. 2003. "About Schmidt" was changed, but not its core. *New York Times*. 19 Jan., Arts and Leisure: 1, 22.
Benjamin, Walter. 1968 *Illiuminations*. Trans. Harry Zohn, intro. Hannah Arendt. New York: Harcourt, Brace and World.
___. 1992. The task of the translator. In Schulte and Biguenet 1992, 71–92.
Bluestone, George. 1957/1971. *Novels into film*. Berkeley: University of California Press.
Bolter, Jay David, and Grusin, Richard. 1999. *Remediation: Understanding new media*. Cambridge, MA: MIT Press.
Boyum, Joy Gould. 1985. *Double exposure: Fiction into film*. New York: Universe Books.

Cardwell, Sarah. 2002. *Adaptation revisited: Television and the classic novel*. Manchester: Manchester University Press.

Cham, Mbye. 2005. *Oral traditions, literature, and cinema in Africa*. In Stam and Raengo 2005, 295–312.

Cohen, Keith. 1991b. Introduction. In Cohen, ed. *Writing in a film age: Essays by contemporary novelists*. Niwot, CO: University Press of Colorado.

Cuddy-Keane, Melba. 1998. *Mrs. Dalloway*: Film, times, and trauma. In Laura Davis and Jeanette McVicker, *Virginia Woolf and her influences: Selected papers from the seventh annual Virginia Woolf conference*. New York: Pace University Press, 171–175.

Dawkins, Richard. 1976/1989. *The selfish game*. New York and Oxford: Oxford University Press.

Elliott, Kamilla. 2003. *Rethinking the novel/film debate*. Cambridge: Cambridge University Press.

Ellis, John. 1982. The literary adaptation. *Screen* 23 (May–June): 3–5.

Ermarth, Elizabeth Deeds. 2001. Agency in the discursive condition. *History and Theory* 40: 34–59.

Fischlin, Daniel and Fortier, Mark, eds. 2000. *Adaptations of Shakespeare: A critical anthology of plays from the seventeenth century to the present*. London and New York: Routledge.

Forster, E. M. 1910/1941. *Howards End*. Harmondsworth: Penguin.

Friedman, Susan Stanford. 2004. Whose modernity? The global landscape of modernism. Humanities Institute Lecture, University of Texas, Austin. 18 February.

Garber, Marjorie. 2003. *Quotation marks*. London and New York: Routledge.

Gaudreault, André. 1998. Variations sure une problematique. In Groensteen 1998a, 267–271.

Geduld, Harry M. 1983. *The definitive Dr. Jekyll and Mr. Hyde companion*. New York: Gardan.

Genette, Gerard. 1982. *Palimpsestes: La litterature au second degré*. Paris: Seuil.

Glancy, Mark. 2003. *The 39 Steps*. London and New York: I.B. Tauris.

Gombrich, E.H. 1961. *Art and illusion: A study in the psychology of pictorial representation*. New York: Panther.

Grau, Oliver. 2003. *Virtual art: From illusion to immersion*. Trans. Gloria Custance. Cambridge: MIT Press.

Greenberg, Harvey R. 1998. Raiders of the lost text: Remaking as contested homage in *Always*. In Horton and McDougal 1998a, 115–30.

Groensteen, Thierry, ed. 1998a. *La transécriture: Pour une théorie de ladaptation*. Colloque de Cerisy, 14–21 Aug. 1993, Quebec: Editions Nota Bene.

___. 1998b. Fictions sans frontieres. In Groensteen 1998a, 9–29.

Habicht, Werner. 1989. Shakespeare and theatre politics in the Third Reich. In Scolnicov and Holland 1989,110–120.

Hamon, Philippe. 1977. Texte littéraire et métalanguage. *Poétique* 31: 263–284.

Hansen, Mirian Bratu. 2001. *Schindler's List* is not *Shoah*: The second commandment, popular modernism, and public memory. In Landy 2001a, 201–17.

Hermans, Theo. 1985. Introduction: Translation studies and a new paradigm. In Theo Harmans, ed., *The manipulation of literature: Studies in literary translation*. London: Croom Helm, 7–15.

Hinds, Stephen. 1998 *Aullusion and intertext: Dynamics of appropriation in Roman Poetry*. Cambridge: Cambridge University Press.

Horton, Andrew and McDougal, Stuart Y., eds. 1998b. Introduction. In Horton and McDougal, *Play it again, Sam: Retakes on remakes*. Berkeley: University of California Press.

___. 202. Die hard/try harder: Narrative spectacle and beyond, from Hollywood to videogame. In King and Krzywinska 2002a, 50–65.

Klein, Michael, and Parker, Gillian, eds. 1981. *The English novel and the movies*. New York: Frederick Ungar, 1–13.

Kristeva, Julia. 1969/1986. *Sémiótiké: Recherches pour une sémanalyse*. Paris: Seuil.

Linden, George. 1971. The storied world. In F. Marcus 1971,157–63.

Lindley, Craig. 2002. The gameplay gestalt, narrative, and interactive storytelling. In Mäyrä 2002, 203–15.

Mackrell, Judith. 2004. Born in the wrong body. *The Guardian*. 1 Nov. http://www.gaurdian.co.uk. 2 Nov 2004.

Marcus, Millicent. 1993. *Filmmaking by the book: Italian cinema and literary adaptation*. Baltimore: Johns Hopkins University Press.

McCracken-Flesher, Caroline. 1994. Cultural projections: The "strange case" of Dr. Jekyll, Mr. Hyde, and cinematic response. In Carlisle and Schwarz 1994,179–199.

McFarlane, Brian. 1996. *Novel to film: An introduction to the theory of adaptation*. Oxford: Clarendon Press.

Metz, Christian. 1974. *Film language: A semiotics of the cinema*. Trans. Michael Taylor. New York: Oxford University Press.

Naremore, James. Introduction: Film and the reign of adaptation. In Naremore, 2000a, 1–16.

Newman, Charles. 1985. *The postmodern aura*. Evanston, IL: Northwestern University Press.

Ondaatje, Michael. 1997. Forward to Minghella 1997: vii–x.

Orr, C. 1984. The discourse on adaptation. *Wide Angle* 6 (2): 72–76.

Peary, Gerald, and Shatzkin, Roger, eds. 1977. *The classic American novel and the movies*. New York: Frederick Ungar.

Ropars, Marie-Clair. 1970. *De la littérature au cinema*. Paris: Armand Colin.

Ropars-Wuilleumier, Marie-Clair. 1998. L'oeuvre au double: Sur les paradoxes de l'adaptation. In Groensteen 1998a, 131–49.

Russell, D.A. 1979. De Imitatione. In West and Woodman 1979,1–16.

Ruthven, K.K. 1979. *Critical assumptions*. Cambridge and New York: Cambridge University Press.

Ryan, Marie-Laure. 2001. *Narrative as virtual reality: Immersion and interactivity in literature and electronic media*. Baltimore: Johns Hopkins University Press.

___. 2004c. Will new media produce new narratives? In Ryan 2004a, 337–59.

Seger, Linda. 1992. *The art of adaptation: Turning fact and fiction into film*. New York: Henry Holt and Co.

Sinyard, Neil. 1986. *Filming literature: The art of screen adaptation*. London: Croom Helm.

Smith, Murray. 1995. *Engaging characters: Fiction, emotion, and the cinema*. Oxford: Clarendon Press.

Stam, Robert. 2000. The dialogics of adaptation. In Naremore 2000a, 54–76.

___. 2005b Introduction: The theory and practice of adaptation. In Stam and Raengo, 2005,1–52.

Thompson, Kristin. 2003. *Storytelling in film and television*. Cambridge, MA: Harvard University Press.

Trowell, Brian. 1992. Libretto. In Sadie 1992,1185-1252.

Wagner, Geoffrey. 1975. *The novel and the cinema*. Rutherford, NJ: Fairleigh Dickinson Press.

Ward, Paul. 2002. Videogames as remediated animation. In King and Krzywinksa 2002a, 122–35.

West, David, and Woodman, Tony. 1979. *Creative imitation and Latin literature*. Cambridge and New York: Cambridge University Press.

Wittkower, Rudolf. 1965. Imitation, eclecticism, and genius. In Earl R. Wasserman, ed., *Aspects of the eighteenth century*. Baltimore: Johns Hopkins University Press, 143–61.

Woolf, Virginia. 1926. The movies and reality. *New Republic* 47 (4 Aug.): 308–10.

Questions

1. What are some of the reasons adaptations are seen as "inferior and secondary creations"?
2. How can adaptation be viewed as both a process and a product?
3. Besides form or medium, what else gets adapted?
4. According to Hutcheon, what is the difference between translation, paraphrasing, and adaptation?
5. What do we gain by thinking of adaptation as a process of creation and a process of reception?
6. What are the three basic modes of engagement discussed here?

View

Film
Lost in La Mancha (2003)
Hamlet 2 (2008)
Adaptation (2010)

Television
Page to Screen (2002)

Read

Berger, Arthur Asa. "The Nature of Narratives." *Narratives in Popular Culture, Media and Everyday Life*. Arthur Asa Berger. Thousand Oaks, CA: Sage Publications, 1997. 1–16. Print.

Costa, Amanda Lin. "What Directing Documentaries Taught Me About Adaptation, Drama and Truth." *Film Courage*. 7 June 2011. Web. 14 June 2012.

Malone, Toby. "Behind the Red Curtain of Verona Beach: Baz Luhrmann's William Shakespeare's Romeo + Juliet." *Shakespeare Survey* (December 2012): 398–412.

1. Compare and contrast responses you have to commercials and responses to a live performance. Which is more active?

2. Record all of the different kinds of media you consume during the course of twenty-four hours. Note when you are consuming more than one simultaneously.

3. Watch a favorite television show and consider the primary elements of venue, function, audience interaction, and historical/social contexts. How are these elements expressed within the given program?

4. Find a TV show that you think illustrates each of Schechner's eight kinds of performance.

5. Think of a popular adaptation you know. Consider the media for both the source and the adapted version. How did the media affect the performance?

Part 2

Spectacle and the

Spectacular

Part Two begins with Jenkins' introductory essay on the phenomenon of cultural convergence. This theory builds on Kellner's triumph of spectacle and Hutcheon's concept of a multi-laminated experience. From there, we apply our understandings of spectacle and convergence to three mediums of popular entertainment: the circus, the theatre, and the cinema. The readings on these three media trace the historical foundations while focusing on the contemporary iterations within popular entertainment and the many uses of spectacle.

Spectacle is the totality of the visual, aural, and emotional elements of performed entertainment. Kellner's article in Part One highlights the concept of spectacle that "unifies and explains a great diversity of apparent phenomena" (36). Spectacle involves the audience in all three of Hutcheon's modes of engagement (showing, telling, and interacting). Spectacle can also refer to a society dominated by electronic media, consumption, and surveillance, reducing citizens to spectators by political neutralization. Kellner draws our attention to how the "seductive spectacles" of our multimedia culture "are becoming more technologically dazzling and are playing an ever-escalating role in everyday life" (37). Recently the word has become associated with the many ways in which a capitalist economy creates play-like celebrations of its products for leisure-time consumption.

Convergence
Bread and Circus
The Mouse and the Musical
Film and the Hollywood Blockbuster

Convergence

Henry Jenkins' book, *Convergence Culture: Where Old and New Media Collide* (2008), brought attention to the enormous experimentation and interactions between the wide variety of media and the effect on audiences living in an ever-connected society. "Worship at the Altar of Convergence" highlights this age of media transition in which everyone is constantly looking for stories to tell and a variety of commercial and grassroots media outlets to spread the word. Media industries find themselves in a continual struggle to keep current audiences searching for new platforms and intersections. The ability to move back and forth/in and out of multiple stories and multiple mediums impacts the relationship between audiences, producers/makers, and content. This leads to what Jenkins refers to as a "participatory culture" of consumers.

Participatory culture creates a kind of collective intelligence that can account for the buzz of what is popular or what is soon to be popular. Jenkins' theory of convergence combines with performance and adaptation theories to provide another tool for analyzing popular entertainment. Convergence carries the potential of placing more critical power in the hands of consumers. Given the mammoth power of corporate marketing and the conglomerate approach to entertainment industries, this power of the people is needed now more than ever.

Ideas

Convergence
Media Platforms
Participatory Culture
Collective Intelligence

Introduction: "Worship at the Altar of Convergence"

A New Paradigm for Understanding Media Change

By Henry Jenkins

Worship at the Altar of Convergence
> —slogan, the New Orleans Media Experience (2003)

The story circulated in the fall of 2001: Dino Ignacio, a Filipino–American high school student created a Photoshop collage of *Sesame Street's* (1970) Bert interacting with terrorist leader Osama Bin Laden as part of a series of "Bert Is Evil" images he posted on his homepage. Others depicted Bert as a Klansman, cavorting with Adolf Hitler, dressed as the Unabomber, or having sex with Pamela Anderson. It was all in good fun.

In the wake of September 11, a Bangladesh-based publisher scanned the Web for Bin Laden images to print on anti-American signs, posters, and T-shirts. *Sesame Street* is available in Pakistan in a localized format; the Arab world, thus, had no exposure to Bert and Ernie. The publisher may not have recognized Bert, but he must have thought the image was a good likeness of the al-Qaeda leader. The image ended up in a collage of similar images that was printed on thousands of posters and distributed across the Middle East.

CNN reporters recorded the unlikely sight of a mob of angry protestors marching through the streets chanting anti-American slogans and waving signs depicting Bert and Bin Laden. Representatives from the Children's Television Workshop, creators of the *Sesame Street* series, spotted the CNN footage and threatened to take legal action: "We're outraged that our characters would be used in this unfortunate and distasteful manner. The people responsible for this should be ashamed of themselves. We are exploring all legal options to stop this abuse and any similar abuses in the future. It was not altogether clear who they planned to [direct their intellectual property attorneys towards]—the young man who had initially appropriated their images, or the terrorist supporters who deployed them. Coming full circle, amused fans produced a number of new sites, linking various *Sesame Street* characters with terrorists.

From his bedroom, Ignacio sparked an international controversy. His images criss-crossed the world, sometimes on the backs of commercial media, sometimes via grassroots media. And, in the end, he inspired his own cult following. As the publicity grew, Ignacio became more concerned and ultimately decided to dismantle his site: "I feel this has gotten too close to reality, … "Bert Is Evil" and its following has always been contained and distanced from big media. This issue throws it out in the open."[1] Welcome to convergence culture, where old and new media collide, where grassroots and corporate media intersect, where the power of the media producer and the power of the media consumer interact in unpredictable ways.

[*Convergence culture: where old and new media collide,* by Henry Jenkins] is about the relationship between three concepts—media convergence, participatory culture, and collective intelligence.

By convergence, I mean the flow of content across multiple media platforms, the cooperation between multiple media industries, and the migratory behavior of media audiences who will go almost anywhere in search of the kinds of entertainment experiences they want. Convergence is a word that manages to describe technological, industrial, cultural, and social changes depending on who's speaking and what they think they are talking about. …

In the world of media convergence, every important story gets told, every brand gets sold, and every consumer gets courted across multiple media platforms. Think about the circuits that the Bert Is Evil images traveled—from *Sesame Street* through Photoshop to the World Wide Web, from Ignacio's bedroom to a print shop in Bangladesh, from the posters held by anti-American protestors that are captured by CNN and into the living rooms of people around the world. Some of its circulation depended on corporate strategies, such as the localization of *Sesame Street* or the global coverage of CNN. Some of its circulation depended on tactics of grassroots appropriation, whether in North America or in the Middle East.

This circulation of media content—across different media systems, competing media economies, and national borders—depends heavily on consumers' active participation. I will argue here against the idea that convergence should be understood primarily as a technological process bringing together multiple media functions within the same devices. Instead, convergence represents a cultural shift as consumers are encouraged to seek out new information and make connections among dispersed media content. This book is about the work—and play—spectators perform in the new media system.

The term *participatory culture* contrasts with older notions of passive media spectatorship. Rather than talking about media producers and consumers as occupying separate roles, we might now see them as participants who interact with each other according to a new set of rules that none of us fully understands. Not all participants are created equal. Corporations—and even individuals within corporate media—still exert greater power than any individual consumer or even the aggregate of consumers. And some consumers have greater abilities to participate in this emerging culture than others.

Convergence does not occur through media appliances, however sophisticated they may become. Convergence occurs within the brains of individual consumers and through their social interactions with others. Each of us constructs our own personal mythology from bits and fragments of information extracted from the media flow and transformed into resources through which we make sense of our everyday lives. Because there is more information on any given topic than anyone can store in their head, there is an added incentive for us to talk among ourselves about the media we consume. This conversation creates buzz that is increasingly valued by the media industry. Consumption has become a collective process—and that's what this book means by collective intelligence, a term coined by French cybertheorist Pierre Levy. None of us can know everything; each of us knows something; and we can put the pieces together if we pool our resources and combine our skills. Collective intelligence can be seen as an alternative source of media power. We are learning how to use that power through our day-to-day interactions within convergence culture. Right now, we are mostly using this collective power through our recreational life, but soon we will be deploying those skills for more "serious" purposes. In [*Convergence culture: where old and new media collide*] I explore how collective meaning-making within popular culture is starting to change the ways religion, education, law, politics, advertising, and even the military operate.

Convergence Talk

Another snapshot of convergence culture at work: In December 2004, a hotly anticipated Bollywood film, *Rok Sako To Rok Lo* (2004), was screened in its entirety to movie buffs in Delhi, Bangalore, Hyderabad, Mumbai, and other parts of India through EDGE-enabled mobile phones with live video streaming facility This is believed to be the first time that a feature film had been fully accessible via mobile phones.[2] It remains to be seen how this kind of distribution fits into people's lives. Will it [act as a] substitute for going to the movies or will people simply use it to sample movies they may want to see at other venues? Who knows?

Over the past several years, many of us have watched as cell phones have become increasingly central to the release strategies of commercial motion pictures around the world, as amateur and professional cell phone movies have competed for prizes in international film festivals, as mobile users have been able to listen in to major concerts, as Japanese novelists serialize their work via instant messenger, and as game players have used mobile devices to compete in augmented and alternate reality games. Some functions will take root; others will fail.

Call me old-fashioned. The other week I wanted to buy a cell phone—you know, to make phone calls. I didn't want a video camera, a still camera, a Web access device, an MP3 player, or a game system. I also wasn't interested in something that could show me movie previews, would have customizable ring tones, or would allow me to read novels. I didn't want the electronic equivalent of a Swiss army knife. When the phone rings, I don't want to have to figure out which button to push. I just wanted a phone. The sales clerks sneered at me; they laughed at me behind my back. I was told by company after mobile company that they don't make single-function phones anymore. Nobody wants them. This was a powerful demonstration of how central mobiles have become to the process of media convergence.

You've probably been hearing a lot about convergence lately. You are going to be hearing even more.

The media industries are undergoing another paradigm shift. It happens from time to time. In the 1990s, rhetoric about a coming digital revolution contained an implicit and often explicit assumption that new media was going to push aside old media, that the Internet was going to displace broadcasting, and that all of this would enable consumers to more easily access media content that was personally meaningful to them. A best-seller in 1990, Nicholas Negroponte's *Being Digital*, drew a sharp contrast between "passive old media" and "interactive new media," predicting the collapse of broadcast networks in favor of an era of narrowcasting and niche media on demand: "What will happen to broadcast television over the next five years is so phenomenal that it's difficult to comprehend."[3] At one point, he suggests that no government regulation will be necessary to shatter the media conglomerates: "The monolithic empires of mass media are dissolving into an array of cottage industries. … Media barons of today will be grasping to hold onto their centralized empires tomorrow. … The combined forces of technology and human nature will ultimately take a stronger hand in plurality than any laws Congress can invent."[4] Sometimes, the new media companies spoke about convergence, but by this term, they seemed to mean that old media would be absorbed fully and completely into the orbit of the emerging technologies. George Gilder, another digital revolutionary, dismissed such claims: "The computer industry is converging with the television industry in the same sense that the automobile converged with the horse, the TV converged with the nickelodeon, the word-processing program converged with the typewriter, the CAD program converged with the drafting board, and digital desktop publishing converged with the linotype machine and the letterpress."[5] For Gilder, the computer had come not to transform mass culture but to "destroy it."

The popping of the dot-com bubble threw cold water on this talk of a digital revolution. Now, convergence has reemerged as an important reference point as old and new media companies try to imagine the future of the entertainment industry. If the digital revolution paradigm presumed that new media would displace old media, the emerging convergence paradigm assumes that old and new media will interact in ever more complex ways. The digital revolution paradigm claimed that new media was going to change everything. After the dot-com crash, the tendency was to imagine that new media had changed nothing. As with so many things about the current media environment, the truth lay somewhere in between. More and more, industry leaders are returning to convergence as a way of making sense of a moment of disorienting change. Convergence is, in that sense, an old concept taking on new meanings.

There was lots of convergence talk to be heard at the New Orleans Media Experience in October 2003. The New Orleans Media Experience was organized by HSI Productions, Inc., a New York-based company that produces music videos and commercials. HSI has committed to spend $100 million over the next five years, to make New Orleans the mecca for media convergence that Slamdance has become for independent cinema. The New Orleans Media Experience is more than a film festival; it is also a showcase for game releases, a venue for commercials and music videos, an array of concerts and theatrical performances, and a three-day series of panels and discussions with industry leaders.

Inside the auditorium, massive posters featuring images of eyes, ears, mouths, and hands urged attendees to "worship at the Altar of Convergence" but it was far from clear what kind of deity they were genuflecting before. Was it a New

Testament God who promised them salvation? An Old Testament God threatening destruction unless they followed His rules? A multifaced deity that spoke like an oracle and demanded blood sacrifices? Perhaps, in keeping with the location, convergence was a voodoo goddess who would give them the power to inflict pain on their competitors?

Like me, the participants had come to New Orleans hoping to glimpse tomorrow before it was too late. Many were nonbelievers who had been burned in the dot-com meltdown and were there to scoff at any new vision. Others, were freshly … minted from America's top business schools and there to find ways to make their first million. Still others were there because their bosses had sent them, hoping for enlightenment, but willing to settle for one good night in the French Quarter.

The mood was tempered by a sober realization of the dangers of moving too quickly, as embodied by the ghost-town campuses in the Bay Area and the office furniture being sold at bulk prices on eBay; and the dangers of moving too slowly, as represented by the recording industry's desperate flailing as it tries to close the door on file-sharing after the cows have already come stampeding out of the barn. The participants had come to New Orleans in search of the "just right"—the right investments, predictions, and business models. No longer expecting to surf the waves of change, they would be content with staying afloat. The old paradigms were breaking down faster than the new ones were emerging, producing panic among those most invested in the status quo and curiosity in those who saw change as opportunity.

Advertising guys in pinstriped shirts mingled with recording industry flacks with backward baseball caps, Hollywood agents in Hawaiian shirts, pointy-bearded technologists, and shaggy-haired gamers. The only thing they all knew how to do was to exchange business cards.

As represented on the panels at the New Orleans Media Experience, convergence was a "come as you are" party, and some of the participants were less ready for what was planned than others. It was also a swap meet where each of the entertainment industries traded problems and solutions, finding through the interplay among media what they can't achieve working in isolation. In every discussion, there emerged different models of convergence followed by the acknowledgment that none of them knew for sure what the outcomes were going to be. Then, everyone adjourned for a quick round of Red Bulls (a conference sponsor) as if funky high-energy drinks were going to blast them over all of those hurdles.

Political economists and business gurus make convergence sound so easy; they look at the charts that show the concentration of media ownership as if they ensure that all of the parts will work together to pursue maximum profits. But from the ground, many of the big media giants look like great big dysfunctional families, whose members aren't speaking with each other and pursue their own short-term agendas even at the expense of other divisions of the same companies. In New Orleans, however, the representatives for different industries seemed tentatively ready to lower their guard and speak openly about common visions.

This event was billed as a chance for the general public to learn firsthand about the coming changes in news and entertainment. In accepting an invitation to be on panels, in displaying a willingness to "go public" with their doubts and anxieties, perhaps industry leaders were acknowledging the importance of the role that ordinary consumers can play not just in accepting convergence, but actually in *driving* the process. If the media industry in recent years has seemed at war with its consumers, in that it is trying to force consumers back into old relationships and into obedience to well-established norms, companies hoped to use this New Orleans event to justify their decisions to consumers and stockholders alike.

Unfortunately, although this was not a closed-door event, it might as well have been. Those few members of the public who did show up were ill-informed. After an intense panel discussion about the challenges of broadening the uses of game consoles, the first member of the audience to raise his hand wanted to know when *Grand Theft Auto III* was coming out on the Xbox. You can scarcely blame consumers for not knowing how to speak this new language or even what questions to ask when so little previous effort has been made to educate them about convergence thinking.

At a panel on game consoles, the big tension was between Sony (a hardware company) and Microsoft (a software company); both had ambitious plans but fundamentally different business models and visions. All agreed that the core challenge was to expand the potential uses of this cheap and readily accessible technology so that it became *the* "black box," the "Trojan horse" that smuggled convergence culture right into people's living rooms. What was mom going to do with the console when her kids were at school? What would get a family to give a game console to grandpa for Christmas? They had the technology to bring about convergence, but they hadn't figured out why anyone would want it.

Another panel focused on the relationship between video games and traditional media. Increasingly, movie moguls saw games not simply as a means of stamping the franchise logo on some ancillary product but as a means of expanding the storytelling experience. These filmmakers had come of age as gamers and had their own ideas about the creative intersections between the media; they knew who the most creative designers were, and they worked the collaboration into their contract. They wanted to use games to explore ideas that couldn't fit within two-hour films.

Such collaborations meant taking everyone out of their "comfort zones," as one movieland agent explained. These relationships were difficult to sustain, since all parties worried about losing creative control, and since the time spans for development and distribution in the media were radically different. Should the game company try to align its timing to the often unpredictable production cycle of a movie with the hopes of hitting Wal-Mart the same weekend the film opens? Should the movie producers wait for the often equally unpredictable game development cycle to run its course, sitting out the clock while some competitor steals their thunder? Will the game get released weeks or months later, after the buzz of the movie has dried up or, worse yet, after the movie has bombed? Should the game become part of the publicity buildup toward a major release, even though that means starting development before the film project has been "green lighted" by a studio? Working with a television production company is even more nerve wracking, since the turnaround time is much shorter and the risk much higher that the series will never reach the air.

If the game industry folks had the smirking belief that they controlled the future, the record industry types were sweating bullets; their days were numbered unless they figured out how to turn around current trends (such as dwindling audiences, declining sales, and expanding piracy). The panel on "monetizing music" was one of the most heavily attended. Everyone tried to speak at once, yet none of them were sure their "answers" would work. Will the future revenue come from rights management, from billing people for the music they download, or from creating a fee the servers had to pay out to the record industry as a whole? And what about cell phone rings—which some felt represented an unexplored market for new music as well as a grassroots promotional channel? Perhaps the money will lie in the intersection between the various media with new artists promoted via music videos that are paid for by advertisers who want to use their sounds and images for branding, with new artists tracked via the Web, which allows the public to register its preferences in hours rather than weeks.

And so it went, in panel after panel. The New Orleans Media Experience pressed us into the future. Every path forward had roadblocks, most of which felt insurmountable, but somehow, they would either have to be routed around or broken down in the coming decade.

The messages were plain:

- Convergence is coming and you had better be ready.
- Convergence is harder than it sounds.
- Everyone will survive if everyone works together. (Unfortunately, that was the one thing nobody knew how to do.)

The Prophet of Convergence

If *Wired* magazine declared Marshall McLuhan the patron saint of the digital revolution, we might well describe the late MIT political scientist Ithiel de Sola Pool as the prophet of media convergence. Pool's *Technologies of Freedom* (1983) was probably the first book to lay out the concept or convergence as a force or change within the media industries:

> A process called the "convergence of modes" is blurring the lines between media, even between point-to-point communications, such as the post, telephone, and telegraph, and mass communications, such as the post, radio, and television. A single physical means—be it wires, cables or airwaves—may carry services that in the past were provided in separate ways. Conversely, a service that was provided in the past by any one medium—be it broadcasting, the press, or telephony—can now be provided in several different physical ways. So the one-to-one relationship that used to exist between a medium and its use is eroding.[6]

Some people today talk about divergence rather than convergence, but Pool understood that they were two sides of the same phenomenon.

"Once upon a time," Pool explained, "companies that published newspapers, magazines, and books did very little else; their involvement with other media was slight."[7] Each medium had its own distinctive functions and markets, and each was regulated under different regimes, depending on whether its character was centralized or decentralized, marked by scarcity or plentitude, dominated by news or entertainment, and owned by governmental or private interests. Pool felt that these differences were largely the product of political choices and preserved through habit rather than any essential characteristic of the various technologies. But he did see some communications technologies as supporting more diversity and a greater degree of participation than others: "Freedom is fostered when the means of communication are dispersed, decentralized, and easily available, as are printing presses or microcomputers. Central control is more likely when the means of communication are concentrated, monopolized, and scarce, as are great networks."[8]

Several forces, however, have begun breaking down the walls separating these different media. New media technologies enabled the same content to flow through many different channels and assume many different forms at the point of reception. Pool was describing what Nicholas Negroponte calls the transformation of "atoms into bytes" or digitization.[9] At the same time, new patterns of cross-media ownership that began in the mid-1980s, during what we can now see as the first phase of a longer process of media concentration, were making it more desirable for companies to distribute content across those various channels rather than within a single media platform. Digitization set the conditions for convergence; corporate conglomerates created its imperative.

Much writing about the so-called digital revolution presumed that the outcome of technological change was more or less inevitable. Pool, on the other hand, predicted a period of prolonged transition, during which the various media systems competed and collaborated, searching for the stability that would always elude them: "Convergence does not mean ultimate stability or unity. It operates as a constant force for unification but always in dynamic tension with change. … There is no immutable law of growing convergence; the process of change is more complicated than that."[10]

As Pool predicted, we are in an age of media transition, one marked by tactical decisions and unintended consequences, mixed signals and competing interests, and most of all, unclear directions and unpredictable outcomes.[11] Two decades later, I find myself re-examining some of the core questions Pool raised—about how we maintain the potential of participatory culture in the wake of growing media concentration, about whether the changes brought about by convergence open new opportunities for expression or expand the power of big media.

Pool was interested in the impact of convergence on political culture; I am more interested in its impact on popular culture, … the lines between the two have now blurred.

It is beyond my abilities to describe or fully document all of the changes that are occurring. My aim is more modest. I want to describe some of the ways that convergence thinking is reshaping American popular culture and, in particular, the ways it is impacting the relationship between media audiences, producers, and content. Although this chapter will outline the big picture (insofar as any of us can see it clearly yet), subsequent chapters [of *Convergence culture: where old and new media collide*] ... examine these changes through a series of case studies focused on specific media franchises and their audiences. My goal is to help ordinary people grasp how convergence is impacting the media they consume and, at the same time, to help industry leaders and policymakers understand consumer perspectives on these changes. Writing this book has been challenging because everything seems to be changing at once and there is no vantage point that takes me above the fray. Rather than trying to write from an objective vantage point, I describe in this book what this process looks like from various localized perspectives—advertising executives struggling to reach a changing market, creative artists discovering new ways to tell stories, educators tapping informal learning communities, activists deploying new resources to shape the political future, religious groups contesting the quality of their cultural environs, and, of course, various fan communities who are early adopters and creative users of emerging media.

I can't claim to be a neutral observer in any of this. For one thing, I am not simply a consumer of many of these media products; I am also an active fan. The world of media fandom has been a central theme of my work for almost two decades—an interest that emerges from my own participation within various fan communities as much as it does from my intellectual interests as a media scholar. During that time, I have watched fans move from the invisible margins of popular culture and into the center of current thinking about media production and consumption. For another, through my role as director of the MIT Comparative Media Studies Program, I have been an active participant in discussions among industry insiders and policymakers; I have consulted with some of the companies discussed in this book; my earlier writings on fan communities and participatory culture have been embraced by business schools and are starting to have some modest impact on the way media companies are relating to their consumers; many of the creative artists and media executives I interviewed are people I would consider friends. At a time when the roles between producers and consumers are shifting, my job allows me to move among different vantage points. I hope this book allows readers to benefit from my adventures into spaces where few humanists have gone before. Yet, readers should also keep in mind that my engagement with fans and producers alike necessarily colors what I say. My goal here is to document conflicting perspectives on media change rather than to critique them. I don't think we can meaningfully critique convergence until it is more fully understood; yet if the public doesn't get some insights into the discussions that are taking place, they will have little to no input into decisions that will dramatically change their relationship to media.

The Black Box Fallacy

Almost a decade ago, science fiction writer Bruce Sterling established what he calls the Dead Media Project. As his Web site (http://www.deadmedia.org) explains, "The centralized, dinosaurian one-to-many media that roared and trampled through the twentieth century are poorly adapted to the postmodern technological environment."[12] Anticipating that some of these "dinosaurs" were heading to the tar pits, he constructed a shrine to "the media that have died on the barbed wire of technological change." His collection is astounding, including relics like "the phenakistoscope, the telharmonium, the Edison wax cylinder, the stereopticon … various species of magic lantern."[13]

Yet, history teaches us that old media never die—and they don't even necessarily fade away. What dies are simply the tools we use to access media content—the 8-track, the Beta tape. These are what media scholars call *delivery technologies*. Most of what Sterling's project lists falls under this category. Delivery technologies become obsolete and get replaced; media, on the other hand, evolve. Recorded sound is the medium. CDs, MP3 files, and 8-track cassettes are delivery technologies.

To define media, let's turn to historian Lisa Gitelman, who offers a model of media that works on two levels: on the first, a medium is a technology that enables communication; on the second, a medium is a set of associated "protocols" or social and cultural practices that have grown up around that technology.[14] Delivery systems are simply and only technologies; media are also cultural systems. Delivery technologies come and go all the time, but media persist as layers within an ever more complicated information and entertainment stratum.

A medium's content may shift (as occurred when television displaced radio as a story-telling medium, freeing radio to become the primary showcase for rock and roll), its audience may change (as occurs when comics move from a mainstream medium in the 1950s to a niche medium today), and its social status may rise or fall (as occurs when theater moves from a popular form to an elite one), but once a medium establishes itself as satisfying some core human demand, it continues to function within the larger system of communication options. Once recorded sound becomes a possibility, we have continued to develop new and improved means of recording and playing back sound. Printed words did not kill spoken words. Cinema did not kill theater. Television did not kill radio.[15] Each old medium was forced to coexist with the emerging media. That's why convergence seems more plausible as a way of understanding the past several decades of media change than the old digital revolution paradigm was. Old media are not being displaced. Rather, their functions and status are shifted by the introduction of new technologies.

The implications of this distinction between media and delivery systems become clearer as Gitelman elaborates on what she means by "protocols." She writes: "Protocols express a huge variety of social, economic, and material relationships. So telephony includes the salutation 'Hello?' (for English speakers, at least) and includes the monthly billing cycle and includes the wires and cables that materially connect our phones. … Cinema includes everything from the sprocket holes that run along the sides of film to the widely shared sense of being able to wait and see 'films' at home on video. And protocols are far from static."[16] This book will have less to say about the technological dimensions of media change than about the shifts in the protocols by which we are producing and consuming media.

Much contemporary discourse about convergence starts and ends with what I call the Black Box Fallacy. Sooner or later, the argument goes, all media content is going to flow through a single black box into our living rooms (or, in the mobile scenario, through black boxes we carry around with us everywhere we go). If the folks at the New Orleans Media Experience could just figure out which black box will reign supreme, then everyone can make reasonable investments for the future. Part of what makes the black box concept a fallacy is that it reduces media change to technological change and strips aside the cultural levels we are considering here.

I don't know about you, but in my living room, I am seeing more and more black boxes. There are my VCR, my digital cable box, my DVD player, my digital recorder, my sound system, and my two game systems, not to mention a huge mound of videotapes, DVDs and CDs, game cartridges and controllers, sitting atop, laying alongside/toppling over the edge of my television system. (I would definitely qualify as an early adopter, but most American homes now have, or soon will have, their own pile of black boxes.) The perpetual tangle of cords that stands between me and my "home entertainment" center reflects the degree of incompatibility and dysfunction that exist between the various media technologies. And many of my MIT students are lugging around multiple black boxes—their laptops, their cells, their iPods, their Game Boys, their BlackBerrys, you name it.

As Cheskin Research explained in a 2002 report, "The old idea of convergence was that all devices would converge into one central device that did everything for you (*a la* the universal remote). What we are now seeing is the hardware diverging while the content converges. … Your e-mail needs and expectations are different whether you're at home, work, school, commuting, the airport, etc., and these different devices are designed to suit your needs for accessing content depending on where you are—your situated context."[17] This pull toward more specialized media appliances coexists with a push toward more generic devices. We can see the proliferation of black boxes as symptomatic of a moment of convergence: because no one is sure what kinds of functions should be combined, we are forced to buy a range of specialized and incompatible appliances. On the other end of the spectrum, we may also be forced to deal with an escalation of functions within the same media appliance, functions that decrease the ability of that appliance to serve its original function, and so I can't get a cell phone that is just a phone.

Media convergence is more than simply a technological shift. Convergence alters the relationship between existing technologies, industries, markets, genres, and audiences. Convergence alters the logic by which media industries operate and by which media consumers process news and entertainment. Keep this in mind: convergence refers to a process, not an endpoint. There will be no single black box that controls the flow of media into our homes. Thanks to the proliferation of channels and the portability of new computing and telecommunications technologies, we are entering an era when media will be everywhere. Convergence isn't something that is going to happen one day when we have enough bandwidth or figure out the correct configuration of appliances. Ready or not, we are already living within a convergence culture.

Our cell phones are not simply telecommunications devices; they also allow us to play games, download information from the Internet, and take and send photographs or text messages. Increasingly they allow us to watch previews of new films, download installments of serialized novels, or attend concerts from remote locations. All of this is already happening in northern Europe and Asia. Any of these functions can also be performed using other media appliances. You can listen to the Dixie Chicks through your DVD player, your car radio, your Walkman, your iPod, a Web radio station, or a music cable channel.

Fueling this technological convergence is a shift in patterns of media ownership. Whereas old Hollywood focused on cinema, the new media conglomerates have controlling interests across the entire entertainment industry. Warner Bros, produces film, television/popular music, computer games, Web sites, toys, amusement park rides, books, newspapers, magazines, and comics.

In turn, media convergence impacts the way we consume media. A teenager doing homework may juggle four or five windows, scan the Web, listen to and download MP3 files, chat with friends, word-process a paper, and respond to e-mail, shifting rapidly among tasks. And fans of a popular television series may sample dialogue, summarize episodes, debate subtexts, create original fan fiction, record their own soundtracks, make their own movies—and distribute all of this worldwide via the Internet.

Convergence is taking place within the same appliances, within the same franchise, within the same company, within the brain of the consumer, and within the same fandom. Convergence involves both a change in the way media is produced and a change in the way media is consumed.

The Cultural Logic of Media Convergence

Another snapshot of the future: Anthropologist Mizuko Ito has documented the growing place of mobile communications among Japanese youth, describing young couples who remain in constant contact with each other throughout the day, thanks to their access to various mobile technologies.[18] They wake up together, work together, eat together, and go to bed together even though they live miles apart and may have face-to-face contact only a few times a month. We might call it tele-cocooning.

Convergence doesn't just involve commercially produced materials and services traveling along well-regulated and predictable circuits. It doesn't just involve the mobile companies getting together with the film companies to decide when and where we watch a newly released film. It also occurs when people take media in their own hands. Entertainment content isn't the only thing that flows across multiple media platforms. Our lives, relationships, memories, fantasies, desires also flow across media channels. Being a lover or a mommy or a teacher occurs on multiple platforms.[19] Sometimes we tuck our kids into bed at night and other times we Instant Message them from the other side of the globe.

And yet another snapshot: Intoxicated students at a local high school use their cell phones spontaneously to produce their own soft-core porn movie involving topless cheerleaders making out in the locker room. Within hours, the movie is circulating across the school, being downloaded by students and teachers alike and watched between classes on personal media devices. When people take media into their own hands, the results can be wonderfully creative; they can also be bad news for all involved.

For the foreseeable future, convergence will be a kind of kludge—a jerry-rigged relationship among different media technologies—rather than a fully integrated system. Right now, the cultural shifts, the legal battles, and the economic consolidations that are fueling media convergence are preceding shifts in the technological infrastructure. How those various transitions unfold will determine the balance of power in the next media era.

The American media environment is now being shaped by two seemingly contradictory trends: on the one hand, new media technologies have lowered production and distribution costs, expanded the range of available delivery channels, and enabled consumers to archive, annotate, appropriate, and recirculate media content in powerful new ways. At the same time, there has been an alarming concentration of the ownership of mainstream commercial media, with a small handful of multinational media conglomerates dominating all sectors of the entertainment industry. No one seems capable of describing both sets of changes at the same time, let alone showing how they impact each other. Some fear that media is out of control, others that it is too controlled. Some see a world without gatekeepers, others a world where gatekeepers have unprecedented power. Again, the truth lies somewhere in between.

Another snapshot: People around the world are affixing stickers showing Yellow Arrows (http://global.yellowarrow.net) alongside public monuments and factories, beneath highway overpasses, onto lamp posts. The arrows provide numbers others can call to access recorded voice messages—personal annotations on our shared urban landscape. They use it to share a beautiful vista or criticize an irresponsible company. And increasingly, companies are co-opting the system to leave their own advertising pitches.

Convergence, as we can see, is both a top-down corporate-driven process and a bottom-up consumer-driven process. Corporate convergence coexists with grassroots convergence. Media companies are learning how to accelerate the flow of media content across delivery channels to expand revenue opportunities, broaden markets, and reinforce viewer commitments. Consumers are learning how to use these different media technologies to bring the flow of media more fully under their control and to interact with other consumers. The promises of this new media environment raise expectations of a freer flow of ideas and content. Inspired by those ideals, consumers are fighting for the right to participate more fully in their culture. Sometimes, corporate and grassroots convergence reinforce each other, creating closer, more rewarding relations between media producers and consumers. Sometimes, these two forces are at war, and those struggles will redefine the face of American popular culture.

Convergence requires media companies to rethink old assumptions about what it means to consume media, assumptions that shape both programming and marketing decisions. If old consumers were assumed to be passive, the new consumers are active. If old consumers were predictable and stayed where you told them to stay, then new consumers are migratory, showing a declining loyalty to networks or media. If old consumers were isolated individuals, the new consumers are more socially connected. If the work of media consumers was once silent and invisible, the new consumers are now noisy and public

Media producers are responding to these newly empowered consumers in contradictory ways, sometimes encouraging change, sometimes resisting what they see as renegade behavior. And consumers, in turn, are perplexed by what they see as mixed signals about how much and what kinds of participation they can enjoy.

As they undergo this transition, the media companies are not behaving in a monolithic fashion; often, different divisions of the same company are pursuing radically different strategies, reflecting their uncertainty about how to proceed. On the one hand, convergence represents an expanded opportunity for media conglomerates, since content that succeeds in one sector can spread across other platforms. On the other, convergence represents a risk since most of these media fear a fragmentation or erosion of their markets. Each time they move a viewer from television to the Internet, say, there is a risk that the consumer may not return.

Industry insiders use the term "extension" to refer to their efforts to expand the potential markets by moving content across different delivery systems, "synergy" to refer to the economic opportunities represented by their ability to own and control all of those manifestations, and "franchise" to refer to their coordinated effort to brand and market fictional content under these new conditions. Extension, synergy, and franchising are pushing media industries to embrace convergence. For that reason, the case studies I selected for this book deal with some of the most successful franchises in recent media history. Some *(American Idol, 2002, and Survivor,* 2000) originate on television, some *(The Matrix,* 1999, *Star Wars,* 1977) on the big screen, some as books *(Harry Potter,* 1998), and some as games *(The Sims,* 2000), but each extends outward from its originating medium to influence many other sites of cultural production. Each of these franchises offers a different vantage point from which to understand how media convergence is reshaping the relationship between media producers and consumers. [...]

You are now entering convergence culture. It is not a surprise that we are not yet ready to cope with its complexities and contradictions. We need to find ways to negotiate the changes taking place. No one group can set the terms. No one group can control access and participation.

Don't expect the uncertainties surrounding convergence to be resolved anytime soon. We are entering an era of prolonged transition and transformation in the way media operates. Convergence describes the process by which we will sort through those options. There will be no magical black box that puts everything in order again. Media producers will find their way through their current problems only by renegotiating their relationship with their consumers. Audiences, empowered by these new technologies, occupying a space at the intersection between old and new media, are demanding the right to participate within the culture. Producers who fail to make their peace with this new participatory culture will face declining goodwill and diminished revenues. The resulting struggles and compromises will define the public culture of the future.

Notes

1. Grossberg, Josh. (October 10, 2001). *"The Bert–Bin Laden Connection?"* E-Online, (http://www.eonline.com/News/Items/0,1,8950,00.html). For a different perspective on Bert and Bin Laden, see Roy Rosenzweig. (June 2003). "Scarcity or Abundance? Preserving the Past in a Digital Era," *American Historical Review,* 108.

2. IndiaFM News Bureau. (December 6, 2004). *"RSTRL to Premier on Cell Phone,"* (http://www.indiafm.com/scoop/04/dec/0612rstrlcell/index.shtml).

3. Negroponte, Nicholas. (1995). *Being Digital.* (p. 54). New York: Alfred A. Knopf.

4. Ibid., (pp. 57–58).

5. Gilder, George. (1994). "Afterword: The Computer Juggernaut: Life after Life after Television," added to the 1994 edition of *Life after Television: The Coming Transformation of Media and American Life.* (p. 189). New York: W. W. Norton. The book was originally published in 1990.

6. Pool, Ithiel de Sola. (1983). *Technologies of Freedom: On Free Speech in an Electronic Age.* (p. 23). Cambridge, Mass.: Harvard University Press.

7. Ibid.

8. Ibid., (p. 5).

9. Negroponte, Nicholas. (1995). *Being Digital.* New York: Alfred A. Knopf.

10. Pool, Ithiel de Sola. (1983). *Technologies of Freedom.* (pp. 53–54).

11. For a fuller discussion of the concept of media in transition, see David Thorburn and Henry Jenkins. (2003). "Towards an Aesthetics of Transition," in Thorburn, David and Jenkins, Henry (eds.), *Rethinking Media Change: The Aesthetics of Transition.* Cambridge, Mass.: MIT Press.

12. Sterling, Bruce. *"The Dead Media Project: A Modest Proposal and a Public Appeal,"* (http://www.deadmedia.org/modest-proposal.html).

13. Ibid.

14. Gitelman, Lisa. "Introduction: Media as Historical Subjects," in *Always Already New: Media, History and the Data of Culture* (work in progress).

15. For a useful discussion of the recurring idea that new media kill off old media, see Coit Murphy, Priscilla. (2003). "Books Are Dead, Long Live Books," in David Thorburn and Henry Jenkins (eds.), *Rethinking Media Change: The Aesthetics of Transition.* Cambridge, Mass.: MIT Press.

16. Gitelman, Lisa. "Introduction: Media as Historical Subjects," in *Always Already New: Media, History and the Data of Culture* (work in progress).

17. Cheskin Research. (Fall 2002). "Designing Digital Experiences for Youth," *Market Insights Series.* (pp. 8–9).

18. Ito, Mizuko. "Mobile Phones, Japanese Youth and the Replacement of the Social Contract," in Rich Ling and Per Petersen (eds.), *Mobile Communications: ReNegotiation of the Social Sphere* (forthcoming), (http://www.itofisher.com/mito/archives/mobileyouth.pdf).

19. For a useful illustration of this point, see Jenkins, Henry. (2005). "Love Online," in Jenkins, Henry (ed.), *Fans, Gamers, and Bloggers*. New York: New York University Press.

Questions

1. Conduct a small survey. Do you or your friends have land-line telephones? Do you watch performances on your mobile phone? How many own a television set versus those who watch television only on the computer through the Internet? How many watch or interact with more than one medium simultaneously?
2. Consider Jenkins' idea of the "Black Box Fallacy." He says there will be no single black box that controls the flow of media into our homes. Is this true today?
3. How does Jenkins' theory of cultural convergence relate to Hutcheon's concept of multi-laminated experience?

View

YouTube
"History of Batman" (Parts 1-4) (2011)

Web
"Confessions of an Aca-Fan: The Official weblog of Henry Jenkins" (henryjenkins. org)

Film/Video
Glee (2009-)
The Glee Project (2011)

Read

Bakir, Vian and David M. Barlow. *Communication in the Age of Suspicion: Trust and the Media*. Basingstoke, England: Palgrave Macmillan, 2007. Print.

King, Geoff. "Die Harder/Try Harder: Narrative, Spectacle and Beyond, from Hollywood to Videogame." *ScreenPlay: Cinema/Videogames/Interfaces*. Ed. Geoff King and Tanya Krzywinska. London: Wallflower Press, 2002. 50–65. Print.

Pearson, Roberta E. and William Uricchio. *The Many Lives of the Batman: Critical Approaches to a Superhero and His Media*. New York: Routledge, 1991. Print.

Bread and Circus

When the Roman poet Juvenal stated "the public has long since cast off its cares… meddles no more and longs eagerly for just two things: bread and circuses…" he was satirizing the Roman elite's practice of maintaining civil order in the face of underlying social and economic problems (qtd. in Kohne and Ewigleben 8). These elite gave a monthly allotment of grain for bread to all the adult men of Rome. Many spent time in the circuses, which were lavish displays of spectacle in the form of chariot races, horse races, and contests of wrestling. Later in the third century BCE, festivals featuring contests between animals and man, javelin and discus throwing, and the spectacle of the gladiators became enormously popular.

The circuses and pantomimes of ancient Rome are the roots of modern circus, combining the pageantry, the athletic skills of acrobats and trapeze artists, the animal acts, and the clowns with the theatrical and the dramatic. The modern concept of a circus as a circular arena surrounded by tiers of seats, for the exhibition of equestrian, acrobatic, and other performances, seems to have existed since the late 1700s and mirrors the architecture of the coliseums of ancient Rome.

Albrecht's essay introduces the beginnings of the modern circus with considerable discussion on the contemporary circus. These companies have transformed the traditional circus through a commitment to the theatrical and dramatic. They use modern technology to create circus as a unique art form—what he calls the art of the spectacular. Albrecht uses Cirque du Soliel as the primary example of a contemporary circus successfully feeding audiences' voracious appetites for the spectacular. The Canadian company employs approximately four thousand employees from over forty countries worldwide. They generate an estimated $810 million annually and more than ninety million people have witnessed their shows.

Ideas

Spectacle
Circus
Ensemble work
Clowning
Pantomime

Introduction: The Circus
as an Art Form

By Ernest Albrecht

In 1974 Alexis Gruss and his *Cirque National a l'ancienne* reintroduced western audiences to the sanctity of the single ring and the possibilities of the circus as an art form. This is the circus that inspired both Paul Binder of the Big Apple Circus and Guy Caron of Cirque du Soleil, and it was the first to feature many of the elements that came to be the hallmarks of the contemporary circus.

The Grusses' annual productions are still performed by no more than twelve people, nine of whom are members of Alexis's immediate family. Everyone pitches in wherever needed, whether making crêpes in the reception tent before the performance, ushering, or moving props. Yet there is never the sense of anyone having to rush from one chore to the next or having arrived at his moment in the spotlight even slightly winded. Here is the ensemble work that has come to be one of the hallmarks of the contemporary circus, presented in a style that is both joyous and graceful, suggesting in its supreme effortlessness that circus is a natural extension of mankind's love of challenge taken to the level of art.

The Gruss circus also invokes and honors the equestrian spirit of the originators of the art form that came to be known as *circus*, and Alexis Gruss is himself nothing less than its high priest, imperviously serene, elegant, and in control, reacting to his horses as if they were precocious children.

The other eye-opening aspect of the Gruss performance is its ten-piece orchestra. "What is so remarkable about it, apart from the sound they are able to produce, is the degree to which the orchestra and music are integrated into the overall performance. Each of the male members of the family joins the orchestra at various times during the performance on an assortment of instruments, and their accomplishments here are every bit as virtuosic as their exploits in the sawdust ring. Very often the musical interludes provide the transition from one ring display to another.

The family's women are hardly relegated to supporting roles. Gipsy, Alexis's wife, and their daughter, Maude, sometimes perform a novel act. Nathalie, Stéphan's wife, is a foot juggler, and all are expert horsewomen. Maude has presented the St. Petersburg Courier act handling no fewer than seventeen horses.

In addition to all the artistry seen in the various displays of skill, the physical trappings of the performance are extraordinarily tasteful, stylish, and elegant. Nary a sequin or spangle is to be seen on any costumes, which depend instead on fabric, drape, and detailing for their effect. Even the color palette is restrained, oftentimes echoing the colors of the horses.

No wonder Binder and Caron were so in awe of what they saw under the Gruss big top. There was nothing like it in the world of circus before 1974, and, one is tempted to say, it is still without peer despite recent equestrian-based productions like Althoff's Zauberwald in Germany, Theatre Cheval and Cavalia (both out of Canada), the UK's Equestrian Theatre, and France's Zingaro, all of which feature a wide variety of horsemanship in their productions.

Of the more recent equestrian extravaganzas, Zingaro produces the strongest evocation of the circus's equestrian heritage. Both of its productions were to visit America and the communal, almost monastic existence of the troupe reminded noted circus historian Hovey Burgess of nothing less than his imagined view of the early equestrian circuses of Astley and Fanconi.

In America, the Big Apple Circus has managed to honor its original inspiration thanks to the equestrian base provided for many seasons by Binder's wife, Katja Schumann. Cirque du Soleil, founded in 1984, seven years after the Big Apple Circus, expanded the horizons of the contemporary circus by abandoning the circus's historic use of animal performers and making its human ensemble the centerpiece of its productions, with astonishingly brilliant acts of a size and complexity that were vanishing everywhere else. It further opened the new circus movement to hitherto unexplored possibilities with its determination to bring all the theatrical arts to bear on the creation of its performances. Under the guidance of its first director, Franco Dragone, and its artistic director Guy Caron, often in collaboration with Gilles Ste-Croix, Cirque du Soleil also brought the contemporary circus something else that was new: an intellectual component, with its heavily atmospheric, often surrealistic, imagistic performances.

The company's two greatest achievements to date have been its touring production, *Quidam*, and its resident, spectacular water-circus, *O*, both of which are thrilling examples of its sorties into the subterranean world of the subconscious and surreal. The world of *Quidam* is the darker of the two, and its characters are more detached from one another than they have been in any of the company's previous work. And yet, while the trappings of the physical production provided by Michel Crete and the costumes of Dominique Lemieux are quite striking, nothing provokes the imagination quite as thrillingly as the company acts that have been created specifically for each of these extraordinary journeys.

Looking back to the company's origins in the streets, for instance, *Quidam* raises the schoolyard game of jumping rope to the level of spectacle by continually compounding the difficulty, adding more and more ropes and an ever-increasing number of jumpers. Few circus companies in the world can present acts that are as big, complex, and beautifully put together as those seen in *Quidam*. The most thrilling of these is based on an ancient form of Italian acrobatics known as *banquine*, in which no fewer than fifteen acrobats demonstrate the flexibility of the human body in a gorgeously choreographed display that is literally breathtaking, not only for the amazing physical prowess of the performers (one tower rises to four high, the top mounter being propelled aloft without the aid of trampoline or teeterboard) but also for the beauty with which it is all accomplished. Here is a display worthy of any stage in any theatre in the world. It is equal parts brilliant dance and stunning acrobatics, enhanced by the lighting, the costumes, and perhaps most importantly the musical score. It should also be noted that in *Quidam*, the level and amount of dance incorporated into the performance have risen appreciably. Much of it is classically based and performed by exquisite dancers.

Because of the ambiguity of the imagery found in the productions of Cirque du Soleil, they have often been called obscure and impenetrable. In contrast there is certainly nothing ambiguous about the messages or the level of audience involvement engendered by another novel approach to circus witnessed in the performances of the African–American UniverSoul Circus.

There can be no more powerful example of what has been called "participatory celebration" than the electric excitement created by this audience, whipped up to a near frenzy by the ringmaster, Casual Cal Dupree. The audience cheers; they sing; they dance in the aisles; they shout, whistle, clap their hands, and stamp their feet. They are indisputably an essential and intrinsic part of the experience.

Dupree, part cheerleader, part revivalist, and part entertainer, is the show's main attraction. He guides the audience through the evening like a preacher shepherding his flock to salvation. He uses each of the acts as a parable to expound upon such issues as being a good father, being an obedient and respectful son or daughter, self-discipline, charity, cultural awareness, striving for excellence, and spiritual uplift in riffs that approach the operatic.

When the audience reacts with its cheers, Dupree exhorts them to further bursts of enthusiasm: "It's all right," he assures his wildly stimulated audience. "Have a good time." Do they ever!

But that is what the UniverSoul Circus is all about: prying its audience loose from its uptight inhibitions, its negative attitudes, and its failure to appreciate the beauty and wonder of its own accomplishments—thereby proving that there can be more to a circus than tricks.

In a very different venue, the three-ring arena, Ringling Bros. and Barnum & Bailey Circus has managed to walk a very delicate line, balancing the traditional with the contemporary. But that is not to say its creative people are uninterested in the one-ring format and other elements of the contemporary circus, as both its current Hometown Edition (or Gold Unit) and *Barnum's Kaleidoscope*, its first excursion into that genre, lavishly illustrate.

But the Ringling organization has also acquired a contemporary look and feel in its three-ring circuses. These represent an ongoing effort to make the arena circus more theatrical. Rather than following the lead of Cirque du Soleil into abstract symbolism, Ringling's creative staff has embraced a style of showmanship that has opted for an in-your-face, all-stops-out style of showmanship rivaling that of Broadway. Ringling Bros. and Barnum & Bailey's 133rd edition of The Greatest Show on Earth was so loaded with eye candy, so crammed full of high-energy excitement, that the circus, more than ever, became a nonstop feast of sensory stimulation.

A year later, the 134th edition took another step toward becoming its own form of musical theatre thanks to the addition of a female vocalist and an original score that was as melodic and jazzy as any Broadway show, its production numbers fully replacing the pageants that used to be called "spec." There is a subtle but important difference between the two forms, spec and production. The former relies on pageantry, floats, and a lavish array of gorgeously costumed characters. Production numbers, on the other hand, integrate all the theatrical elements and eliminate both the pageantry and the floats in favor of music, dance, scenic, and special effects. The pattern of movement is no longer confined to the inevitable counter-clockwise march around the hippodrome. There is activity everywhere all the time, including the air as well as the track, often going in several directions at once, usually in counterpoint to the attractions that are simultaneously working in the rings.

While all of the contemporary circuses avidly acknowledge the effectiveness of combining circus with the theatrical arts, some have attempted to embrace the dramatic arts, incorporating narration into their productions. Circus Flora has managed to do this through several noteworthy productions, none more effectively than in its farewell to Flora, the elephant that gave the circus its name.

The show's narration of events, Circus Flora's unique feature, not only gave each act a context and a conclusion but always seemed more than welcome, given the charm of the story and the deftness of the tone and manner in which it was told by Cecil MacKinnon as YoYo the clown, mistress of ceremonies and revealer of the circus's inner mysteries. The acts were so nicely woven into the plot that it all moved along with a logic that seemed close to being inevitable.

If one were looking for a textbook example of how the circus and the dramatic arts can be successfully married, the search need go no further than the Midnight Circus and its production *All the World's a Stage*, in which no less a personage than old Will Shakespeare himself presided over the marriage.

All the World's a Stage was a brilliant conception that imagined what would happen if the Bard of Avon were suddenly to find himself surrounded by a circus. That such a meeting seemed perfectly logical was only the first of several *coups de theatre* that this amazingly deft production was able to pull off. Shakespeare appeared in the midst of a magician's classic transformation act, the one in which the magician stands on top of a trunk and a curtain is raised around him. When it is dropped, he has been transformed into a beautiful showgirl or a tiger. In this instance, it was Shakespeare who appeared in place of the magician, uninvited, unexpected, and decidedly unamused.

Thus began the real transformation, turning Shakespeare from a skeptic who looked at the circus about him rather suspiciously and asked, "Where are the words?" to a believer more than ready to take part in a charivari that ends the show on a level of triumph and celebration that could only be achieved when the audience has been made to identify with the characters to such a degree that they can participate fully in their victory.

So here is a theatrical circus that has all the best elements of drama: conflict, character development, and an exciting denouement, as well as the clowns, acrobats, and aerialists of the circus.

Another significant characteristic of the contemporary circus is its dependence on clowning to knit its productions into a unified whole, as we have seen with the Big Apple's Grandma, Ringlings Bello and David Larible, and Floras YoYo. Circus Oz, from Australia, takes that concept to its ultimate conclusion by turning everyone into a clown. Like many other new circuses, Circus Oz is certainly a show with an attitude, but happily that attitude is one of wild irreverence. Almost every act in its offerings has a satiric edge.

While everyone in the show has a specialty, all of them, including the three members of the band and even the rigger, take part in various ensemble pieces. That kind of interaction and their versatility have turned Circus Oz into an example of that much desired but seldom seen paragon, a true ensemble, found first in the Gruss family circus.

* * *

elements

While the individual circuses of the contemporary circus movement share many of the characteristics already enumerated—the single ring, an equestrian foundation, a commitment to the theatrical and dramatic arts, the use of music, highlighting the pre-eminence of women, and the integration of the related performing arts like dance and acting as a means of enhancing the work of its performing artists and thereby achieving a greater degree of audience involvement—each is a unique combination of these elements, as personal as the work of the men and women who have collaborated to raise the circus to a level of artistic achievement equivalent to that of any of the performing arts, and whose work is as provocative and as stimulating as any of their fellow artists.

Note

1. Hovey, Burgess. (Winter 1998). "Zingaro Gives a New Meaning to the Term 'Horse Opera.'" *Spectacle*: 31.

Questions

1. How has circus changed over the years?
2. What are the key characteristics of contemporary circus?
3. What are some of the primary companies today and the differences between them?
4. How does contemporary circus exemplify Kellner's idea of "seductive spectacles"?

View

Web

Ringling Brothers (www.ringling.com)
Universoul Circus (www.universoulcircus.com)
Cirque du Soliel (www.cirquedusoleil.com)

Film/Video

Laugh, Clown, Laugh (1928)
The Big Circus (1959)
Circus (2010)
Water for Elephants (2011)
Madagascar 3: Europe's Most Wanted (2012)

Read

Babinski, Tony. *Cirque du Soleil: 20 Years Under the Sun.* New York: Harry N. Abrams, 2004. Print.

Fletcher, Stephen J. and Sharon Lee Smith. *Life in a Three-Ring-Circus: Posters and Interviews.* Indianapolis, Ind.: Indiana Historical Society, 2001. Print.

Kohne, Eckart and Cornelia Ewigleben, eds. *Gladiators and Caesars: The Power of Spectacle in Ancient Rome.* Berkeley: University of California Press, 2000. Print.

Sloan, Mark and F. W. Glasier. *Wild, Weird, and Wonderful: The American Circus 1901–1927, as seen by F. W. Glasier, photographer.* New York: Quantuck Lane Press, 2003. Print.

The Mouse and the Musical

Scholars and critics often refer to musical theatre as a uniquely American performance genre—and one that often straddles the line between highbrow (elitist) art and middle- or lowbrow (popular) entertainment mentioned in the introduction to this edition. Most historians point to the hugely popular mid-nineteenth century musical spectacle *The Black Crook* (which ironically was a British import) as the predecessor to what became the standardized form and structure of the American musical. Thanks to this highly successful extravaganza, producers of popular entertainment began integrating chorus girls performing extensive and often risqué dance numbers, ornate costuming, and complex production and staging techniques that rival the spectacle on Broadway stages today.

Spectacle continues to drive both the artistic development and financial success of musical theatre and commercial Broadway theatre as a whole. Producers continually vie for the attention of audiences accustomed to the technical wizardry and effects available on the web, on TV, and in film. It is not surprising then that one of the entertainment industry's most successful organizations, whose work spans all aspects of popular entertainment, would want to apply its expertise to the Broadway musical. In 1994, The Walt Disney Company launched its theatrical division when they adapted the wildly successful animated film *Beauty and the Beast* to the stage. Disney built on the familiarity of the characters from the film, yet expanded the content in order to enhance the live experience and encourage the audience to see a musical as a mode of engagement complementary to their film-viewing experience. Disney solidified its presence on Broadway by following *Beauty and the Beast* with an adaptation of *The Lion King*, which won six Tony awards including Best Musical and Best Direction of a Musical.

In these productions, Disney took advantage of the beginnings of convergence, and developed innovative ways to engage audiences with their materials across media. In particular, *The Lion King* afforded an opportunity to cross cultural performance boundaries by involving an international team of designers and performers with their own cultural perspectives, exploring the cross-cultural questions of who we are and why we are here. However, as John Bell's essay in this section points out, many scholars and artists chafed at the corporatization of Broadway, and saw Disney as both the leading culprit and the leading benefactor of New York City's 42nd Street Development Project. Bell's article, written as *The Lion King* hit Broadway, poses many questions about the effect of industry and convergence on the American Theatre then, and helps contextualize some of the spectacular developments since The Mouse first made a musical for the Broadway stage.

Ideas

Musical
Mediated performance
Consumer performance
Theatre as a reflection and creator of communities
Cultural entrepreneur

Disney's Times Square

The New American Community Theatre

By John Bell

W hat is the place and the function of live performance (theatre, as it were) in late 20th-century United States culture? The specific instance I'm looking at in this article is the 42nd Street Development Project now underway at Manhattan's Time Square area, and in particular the Walt Disney Company's renovation and coming operation of the New Amsterdam Theatre. How much and what kind of change in the nature of Broadway theatre does the Disney redevelopment represent?

Near the beginning of this century, in 1913, Vladimir Mayakovsky asked, "Can contemporary theatre survive the competition of cinema?" (1980:181). Of course, live theatre has survived, existing today not only in the context of film, but of other technology-based performance media: television and computers. But as the century has developed, it has become clear that the relationship between live theatre and mediated performance is not so much that of competition as it is of synergy, especially for live theatre, which has become an element of the overall network of consumer activities defining the performance of American capitalist society in the last decades of this century. These activities want to create a community of consumers through the participatory performances of buying information, entertainment, and objects (to "Get Stuff," as recent Marlboro and Pepsi promotional campaigns so clearly put it). The Walt Disney Company is perhaps the most sophisticated, integrated, and well-established of these networks.

The two-billion-dollar 42nd Street Development Project, according to its administrators, is:

> the largest development effort the City and State [of New York] have ever undertaken [...] a far-reaching attempt to turn 42nd Street

John Bell, "Disney's Times Square: The New American Community Theatre," *The Drama Review*, vol. 42, no. 1, pp. 26–33. Copyright © 1998 by MIT Press. Reprinted with permission.

between Broadway and Eighth Avenue into an inviting commercial/ cultural throughfare *[sic]* for private business and the public, (42nd Street 1987:Appendix).

This public project to promote private capital seeks to counter the area's 60-year "decline" into the sensual entertainments of arcade games, burlesque, and other types of erotic performance. One nonprofit playhouse, the New Victory Theatre (already in operation as a children's theatre) anchors the project as Culture, but as *New York Times* columnist Frank Rich pointed out, it was the Walt Disney Company's "embrace" of the New Amsterdam Theatre that "helped create a gold-rush atmosphere in the entire Times Square neighborhood" (Rich 1995:A27). In addition to the renovation of nine historic Times Square theatres, the project includes "four new office buildings, a new hotel, a merchandise trade mart, and the reconstruction of the Times Square Subway Complex" (42nd Street 1987:np). The Walt Disney Company's stake in this real estate is not only the New Amsterdam, but, equally important, the new hotel, as well as a nearby store for Disney "stuff."

It's not that a discussion of the banality of Disney culture or its calculated and depressing definitions of family, entertainment, and community is needed here, since those subjects have been well covered by recent additions to the burgeoning realm of "Disney studies." What seems important here is how Disney's development of the New Amsterdam Theatre will put that historic Times Square playhouse and its theatre productions squarely into the middle of the Disney corporate network of consumer performance. In that network live theatre will serve, like theme-park performance, as a place where Disney consumers can participate in (consume) a Disney event with other Disney customers, helping to establish in person a temporary Disney consumer community. This is a different type of community and a different type of theatre than the community attracted to and the theatre produced by the New Amsterdam in its heyday in the 1920s, when the Ziegfeld Follies played inside the theatre and Eddie Cantor appeared on its "Midnight Roof" (Ewen 1961:63).

Theatre and Community

I take it as an axiom that all theatre is both a reflection and an active creator of communities. Greek tragedy was a community performance of Athens, the Rose Playhouse served the community of Elizabethan London, Shaliko dances are part of Hopi communities in the Southwest, raves serve (or served) their own floating subcultural community, and the Bread and Puppet Theater's *Domestic Resurrection Circus,* with which I have been involved for over 20 years, serves and helps create a community attracted to post-1960s eco-political puppet ritual.

My research into 1920s New York performance has made me realize that my idea—my ideal—of Broadway as America's classic theatre of the 20th century is connected to its heyday in the '20s, when the Times Square area was the glamorous home for the work of Eugene O'Neill, Duke Ellington, Mae West, Flo Ziegfeld, and George Sissle and Eubie Blake. In my idea(l), Broadway performances of that time (whether box-office play, art theatre, vaudeville, revue, burlesque, or speakeasy entertainment) served and helped define the metropolitan community of New York, a "mongrel Manhattan," as Ann Douglas calls it, which was in the process of creating a United States version of urban modernism (1995:5). In theatres and bars on Broadway and Times Square, New Yorkers found all forms of live performance somehow vital, somehow a necessity, to such a degree that, in 1928, an unsurpassed record of 264 shows opened in one Broadway season (Atkinson 1974:179).

But the "decline" of 42nd Street followed this high point rather quickly, beginning in the '30s. Compounded by the economic pressures of the Depression, live theatre on Broadway and especially the "serious" theatre of such groups as the Theatre Guild had to compete with film and radio, and the audience for live theatre could not support as many theatres as it earlier had. Broadway became less of a "local" New York community cultural center, for two reasons: first, new suburban towns were creating different types of communities on the fringes of the city, and second, the technological media of radio and film were effectively reaching nationwide audiences, superseding the ritual of live performance in theatres like the New Amsterdam. Hollywood rivaled New York as America's symbolic cultural center, pulling talent and money from the East Coast to the West, from live theatre to film work.

Leaving New York

One of those drawn to the west was Walt Disney, an entrepreneur whose under-standing of the possibilities of new performance technologies was matched by his ability to gauge what American audiences wanted to see. In 1927, according to an oft-repeated story, Disney came from Hollywood to New York to renegotiate his contract with Charles Mintz. Mintz was the nationwide distributor of the "Oswald the Rabbit" cartoons Disney had been making in California and wanted to pay Disney less money for them. When Mintz told him he was planning to hire away Disney's animators and continue the Oswald cartoons himself (Mintz held the copyright), Disney walked away from the project, and on the train back to Hollywood—leaving the city of theatre and returning to the city of film; he decided to replace the rabbit with a mouse (Schickel 1968:108–09).

Disney's business trip to New York—and his inspirational train ride back to Hollywood—point out the increased importance of Hollywood over New York and the obvious economic advantages of mass-distributed entertainment over the more localized means of live theatre. A perceptive cultural entrepreneur like Disney was not interested in live theatre on Broadway; he was preoccupied with the possibili-ties of cartoon animation and probably thought of Broadway theatre the way others in the film industry did: as a source of talent to lure westward.

Disney probably did not care, at this moment, what happened to live theatre in the film and radio age, but Lee Simonson did. Simonson, a designer and one of the founders of the Theatre Guild, saw that organization take the Greenwich Village "art" theatre of Eugene O'Neill and others—which had grown out of America's "Little Theatre" movement—to Broadway, in a process that made the commercial Broadway stage a place for serious modern intellectuals. But by the early '30s, in the midst of the Depression and what Simonson himself referred to as the "competition of the movies" (1932:398), he wondered (like Mayakovsky) about the future of live theatre in the modern age.

When he offered his prognostications about modern performance in *The Stage Is Set* (1932), Simonson tried to present them in a realistic economic framework, offering a plan for decentralized community theatre centers across the country as an alternative to the old touring networks that had fed Broadway (381). Simonson's vision wasn't exactly the regional theatre system that developed after World War II. Instead, he focused on the automobile-centered suburbs rather than urban sites like 42nd Street; he imagined suburban community center buildings as multi-use per-formance spaces capable of presenting everything from poultry shows and tennis matches to *The Cherry Orchard* and the Metropolitan Opera. Simonson looked to the existing Westchester Community Center as a model. It was:

> a building constructed at a cost of nearly one million dollars, paid for by a bond issue, […] supporting two theatres, one seating five thousand and the other four hundred and fifty. The building stands on the Bronx River Parkway, one of the finest examples of landscape road-building in the East, which connects the northern end of New York City with the Hudson Valley at Peekskill. And several hundred thousand commuters, without scurrying back on the last midnight local, are able to ride in comfort to hear the Metropolitan Opera Company, […] recitals by Paderewski, Percy Grainger, and Paul Robeson. (1932:417)

Simonson's vision of "how a theatre can be made a center and can also begin to pay its way by being related to a program of recreation for an entire community" (419) is a modernist (even socialist) idea of planned community and planned culture—the kind of thinking that led to Roosevelt's New Deal, the Federal Theatre Project, and eventually the urban renewal projects of the 1960s, and the Times Square Development Project itself. Simonson's plan, which combines car culture and pastoral visions with serious theatre, attempts a nationwide scope:

> These playhouses should exist in gardens of which an open-air arena might easily be made a part, where local gardeners could compete for annual prizes, where lovers could meet and children could play. Every such community center would tap a population on a radius of sixty miles that could reach it by automobile and so serve a territory of approximately eleven thousand square miles. (420)

Simonson's 1932 vision of vital community-center theatres linked by parkways didn't come to pass as he had imagined. Across the United States live performance in the automobile age became more often linked to film-going, tourism, shopping, or (especially in California) to the performance of the car itself than to roadside versions of *The Cherry Orchard*. And television, like radio, offered suburbanites a chance to be entertained without even leaving their homes. In 1954, Walt Disney entered into the new medium of television. But Richard Schickel points out that despite this epochal innovation in Disney corporate history, Disney's central focus at that moment was his new concept for a total-environment theme park, Disneyland, which would be completed the following year (1968:303). With Disneyland, Walt Disney turned to, and in fact redefined, live performance in America, making this and later theme parks all-encompassing theatres in which every Disneyland (or Walt Disney World) employee is a member of the cast.

The live performance (the theatre) of the theme park exists as only one aspect of the Disney cultural network. Which is to say that quite early on in the '50s Disney used television, film, merchandise, and theme-park performance to support one another in a system of constant reinforcement urging the Disney audience to watch, visit, and buy Disney products. Live performance at the theme park then and now reinforces already-existing images from film, television, and other media, encouraging consumer spending on Disney products or the products of allied corporations.[2] The theme-park actor, whether a ride operator, a "walkaround" character in a masked costume, a performer in *Broadway at the Top* at Disney World's Disney Resort, or a live re-enactor of *Indiana Jones* (at Disney-MGM studios), repeats as closely as possible images already existing within the Disney image network crisscrossing the United States and the world.[3]

Returning to New York

According to a factoid I read somewhere in 1996, the three top tourist destinations in the United States are Disney World, New York City, and Minnesota's Mall of America.

The Disney version of Times Square redevelopment seems to want to define its Broadway theatre as a popular-performance form fitting cleanly into its existing corporate image network. After Disney redevelopment, the typical Broadway tourist experience might not be much different than it has been in the past two decades (which is to say, one travels into New York, stays in a hotel, shops, and sees a Broadway show), but in the Disney version one would stay in the Disney hotel, shop in the Disney store (perhaps eat in a Disney restaurant?), and see the Disney musical in the New Amsterdam Theatre.

The community served and in part created by live Disney performances, such as the long-running *Beauty and the Beast* at the Palace Theatre or *The Lion King* production at the New Amsterdam, is one segment of a worldwide cultural community identifying itself with Disney productions. In this community, attendance at live events assumes the status of tourist pilgrimage: an obligatory trip (by plane or car) to Disneyland, Disney World, Mall of America, or to Disney's Times Square.

And the Disney pilgrimage is like other pilgrimages, in that it is a fulfillment of something already established, something already understood—the enactment of a long-imagined action suggested and reinforced by the constant presence of images in one's daily life (a photograph of the Kaaba at Mecca, a plastic model of the Black Madonna, a videotape of *Mickey Mouse: Golden-Edition* cartoons). In terms of Disney's theatre, the live performance *of Beauty and the Beast* or *The Lion King* depends for its success on its connection to the pre-existing Disney film on which it is based, as well as to other products: television spin-off shows, fast-food Happy Meals, books, videos, and clothing.

How does the Disney concept of popular theatre as theme-park pilgrimage define American community, and what does that vision mean for American theatre? Most importantly, the community defined by Disney theatre, the community to be defined by the New Amsterdam theatre, lacks the kind of local origin and local definition that characterized New York theatre of the 1920s and that Lee Simonson wanted to promote in his parkway theatres of the suburbs. What is obviously missing is the possibility of the small community which "local" theatre could create, or the possibility of the "local" theatre which the small community could create, even on the large scale of 1920s Broadway theatre. The theatre of a "local" community can articulate a variety of sentiments and ideas from that community. The theatre of a corporate image network like Disney's can express only the sentiments and ideas of that body and its owners.

Notes

1. Significant writings on Disney include Bryman (1995), Eisenstein (1988), Schickel (1968), Fjellman (1992), Smoodin (1994), and The Project on Disney (1995).

2. General Electric, Met Life, and United Technologies, for example, at Disney's Epcot Center.

3. By this I mean the saturation of images for the purposes of film promotion, as in Disney films such as *101 Dalmatians* or *The Hunchback of Notre Dame,* whose marketing strategy involves a massive assault through as many advertising media as possible. But the Disney image network also depends on the possibilities of media control, for example, Disney's ownership of the Capital Cities/ABC television conglomerate.

References

Atkinson, Brooks. (1974). *Broadway*. New York: Limelight.

Bryman, Alan. (1995). *Disney and His Worlds*. New York: Routledge.

Douglas, Ann. (1995). *Terrible Honesty: Mongrel Manhattan in the 1920s*. New York: Noonday Press.

Eisenstein, Sergei. (1988). *Eisenstein on Disney*. Edited by Jay Leyda. London: Methuen.

Ewen, David. (1961). *The Story of America's Musical Theater*. New York: Chilton.

Fjellman, Stephen M. (1992). *Vinyl Leaves: Walt Disney World and America*. Boulder: Westview Press.

42nd Street Development Project Non-Profit Theatre Advisory Committee. (1987). *Final Report*.

Mayakovsky, Vladimir. (1980). [1913] "Theatre, Cinema and Futurism." In *The Ardis Anthology of Russian Futurism*, edited by Ellendea Proffer and Carl Proffer, (pp. 181–82). Ann Arbor: Ardis.

The Project on Disney. (1995). *Inside the Mouse: Work and Play at Disney World*. Durham: Duke University Press.

Rich, Frank. (1995). "Goodbye to All That." *The New York Times*, 30 December: A27.

Schickel, Richard. (1968). The Disney Version: *The Life, Times, Art and Commerce of Walt Disney*. New York: Simon and Schuster.

Simonson, Lee. (1932). *The Stage Is Set*. New York: Theatre Arts Books.

Eric Smoodin, ed. (1994). *Disney Discourse*. New York: Routledge.

John Bell teaches theatre history at New York University and Rhode Island School of Design and is a Contributing Editor to *TDR*. He is a founding member of Great Small Works theatre collective and has worked with Bread and Puppet Theater since 1973.

Questions

1. What do you think it means to be a *cultural entrepreneur*?
2. How is Disney's theatre "a reflection and creator of communities"?
3. What assumptions does the author make about how Disney's presence would affect popular theatre? Now that Disney is firmly entrenched in Times Square, how would you describe its effect?
4. How is Disney's integration into commercial Broadway theatre an example of what Henry Jenkins refers to as cultural convergence?
5. Bell poses the question "How does the Disney concept of popular theatre as theme-park pilgrimage define American community, and what does that vision mean for American theatre?" How do you respond to this question today?

View

Web

Disney on Broadway (www.disneyonbroadway.com)

The Broadway League (www.livebroadway.com)

The Internet Broadway Database (www.ibdb.com)

The American Theatre Wing Tony Awards (tonyawards.com)

Film

The Broadway Melody (1929)

Broadway: The American Musical (2004)

Smash (2012)

Read

Cerniglia, Ken and Aubrey Lynch II. "Embodying Animal, Racial, Theatrical, and Commercial Power in *The Lion King*." *Dance Research Journal* 43.1 (2011) Supplement: 3–9. Print.

"Disney Takes Over Times Square." *New York Amsterdam News.* 11 November 2010. 18.

Do Rozario, Rebecca-Anne. "Reanimating the Animated: Disney's Theatrical Productions." *TDR/The Drama Review* 48.1 (2004): 164–177. Print.

Nelson, Steve. "Broadway and the Beast: Disney Comes to Times Square." *TDR* 39.2 (1995) 71–85. Print.

Wollman, Elizabeth L. "The Economic Development of the 'New' Times Square and Its Impact on the Broadway Musical." *American Music* 20.4 (2002): 445–465. Print.

Film and the Hollywood Blockbuster

Coming on the heels of the popular entertainers traveling the world performing for live audiences, the invention of motion pictures offered cheaper and simpler ways of providing entertainment to the masses. With movies' superior ability to capture spectacle, motion pictures drew audiences away from attending live performances. Throughout the 1900s to 1920s, the film industry expanded exponentially. While films were initially shown in venues designed for live performance, permanent movie theatres soon became the norm. Films grew longer, using more shots and telling more complex stories. Filmmakers explored new techniques for conveying narrative information. French cinema led the way in innovation—making comedies, historical films, thrillers, and melodramas. Italian filmmakers included large, sweeping vistas of landscape and rousing historical spectacle. In the US, the first film companies were located in New York and New Jersey. Because filmmakers worked outdoors, poor weather hindered production for several months out of the year. Film production moved to California's warmer climate in 1910 and Los Angeles became the country's major production center—what we know today as Hollywood.

Technical innovations continued to improve film production. Color was an obvious way to differentiate movies from the fledgling media of television. When the wonders of Technicolor were combined with wide-screen processes, audiences experienced spectacle beyond their imaginations. Filmmakers first introduced 3-D in the 1950s, but it lasted only two years. Larger than life and more colorful films shown on wider screens led to large-scale, popular, and profitable blockbusters. King's essay focuses attention on the spectacular qualities of Hollywood's blockbuster films and the role of narrative structure. King argues that despite an increasing emphasis on spectacle, blockbuster films continue to tell "carefully organized, more or less linear cause/effect stories, organized around central characters" (181),

Ideas

Spectacle
Blockbuster
Small scale attraction/large scale attraction
Film technologies (3-D, wide screen, Technicolor)

Spectacle, Narrative, and the Spectacular Hollywood Blockbuster

By Geoff King

Spectacle, spectacular imagery; sheer scale, lavishness and (hopefully) quality of big-screen audio-visual sensation: however the blockbuster is defined, qualities such as these have often been close to the center of its appeal, from the early Italian historical epics of the 1910s to today's digital special-effects extravaganzas. Overt, large-scale spectacle is not a major feature of all films that enjoy blockbuster-scale success at the box office. But it is often a major ingredient at the high-budget end of the spectrum and in production and/or distribution-led definitions of the blockbuster. The spectacular variety of blockbuster, on which this chapter focuses, is usually meant to constitute an "event," something that stands out from the cinematic routine. It is sold this way even if the formation of the "event" itself becomes routinized, as is the case in contemporary Hollywood, where the heavily preplanned and presold prospective blockbuster is a central feature around which each year's slate of production revolves, rather than something that departs from the norm. A substantial part of the appeal of many blockbusters lies precisely in the scale of spectacular audio-visual experience that is offered, in contrast to the smaller-scale resources of rival films or media. The definition of the blockbuster in terms of spectacle (as with other attributes such as length and budget) tends to be relative rather than absolute.

Two aspects of the spectacular movie blockbuster are considered in this chapter. The first part looks more closely at the production of spectacular qualities, primarily in terms of visual strategies. Two alternative modes of spectacle are outlined, in relation to shifting contexts of production and consumption: one based on the visual scope of the big-screen experience offered by the cinematic blockbuster, the other related to the impact of visual strategies drawn in recent decades from small-screen media such as advertising and music video. The second part of the chapter focuses on the issue of narrative. If spectacle is so central to a particular kind of blockbuster experience, what is the role of narrative structure? Many have been quick to announce the death, or at least the fading, of narrative in the spectacular context of recent Hollywood blockbuster production, a judgment that, as I and others have argued, is precipitate. To what extent, though, does the spectacular blockbuster adhere to the conventions of "classical" narrative structure? Has it utilized other types of narrative organization? If so, to what extent, and what challenge might this pose more generally to our understanding of the classical Hollywood style?

Spectacle: From Large-Screen Vista to (Large and Small-Screen) Montage-Impact

An epic scale of spectacular representation unavailable in rival media products is one of the promises that has long been made by the would-be blockbuster. From the early 1910s, Italian epics such as *The Fall of Troy (La caduta di Troia*, 1910) and *Quo Vadis?* (1913) attracted crowds by offering a scale of events and production values that dwarfed and stood out from more routine cinematic fare (Bowser 1990). The American film industry's response included D. W. Griffith's *Judith of Bethulia* (1913), *The Birth of a Nation* (1915), and *Intolerance* (1916) and the tradition of biblical-historical epic in the studio era most commonly associated with the films of Cecil B. DeMille. Ingredients these early blockbusters have in common include expense, length, a focus on "weighty," "important," or epic-mythical subject matter, and—of more central relevance here—a largeness in the *staging* of the spectacular on-screen events. Great vistas are offered, along with more intimate moments, often involving the reconstruction of epic events on a grand scale: the Civil War battlefield in *The Birth of a Nation*, massive teeming edifices of Babylon in *Intolerance*, the exodus from Egypt in *The Ten Commandments* (1956); the proverbial "cast of thousands," and large outlays on the building of massive sets and/or travel to exotic locations.

An emphasis on spectacular epic production of this kind gained particular prominence in Hollywood in the 1950s and 1960s, decades in which the industry struggled to regain equilibrium in the face of the combined threats of the divorcement of exhibition from production and distribution, the decline in cinemagoing that resulted from broader social changes such as migration to the suburbs, and the rival attractions of television and other leisure pursuits. As a more or less habitual pattern of visiting the cinema declined, the spectacular blockbuster was envisaged as potential savior of Hollywood. Its quality as extra-larger-than-life special event was seen as a way to attract back to the cinema viewers whose more routine attendance could not be guaranteed. Hence, the advent of widescreen formats, among others, institutionalized in the form of 20th Century-Fox's CinemaScope process. Visually, the emphasis was put, again, on sheer scale of imagery: the width of the screen and the vast panoramas it could encompass.

The particular forms of spectacular blockbuster adopted in the 1950s and 1960s ran into difficulties, especially in the later decade, and especially the Roman-historical epic (in the shape of *Cleopatra*, 1963) and the epic musical after what proved to be the deceptive triumph of *The Sound of Music* (1965). The foregrounding of the large-scale, big-screen vista has remained an important ingredient in more recent blockbusters, however, including the successful revisiting of the Roman epic in *Gladiator* (2000). Blockbusters continue to base much of their appeal on the promise of providing a variety of spectacle that befits the nature of the specifically *cinematic* context of exhibition. From *Star Wars* (1977) to *Titanic* (1997), *Pearl Harbor* (2001) and the heavily pretrailed *Lord of the Rings* trilogy (2001, 2002, 2003), epic or fantastic events are designed to play strongly to the audio-visual qualities of the theatrical experience. There appears to be a paradox, however, in the economic basis of contemporary Hollywood's blockbuster production. The large vistas of spectacular attraction are designed to work at their best on the big screen. But the bulk of revenues are currently earned through viewings on the *small* screen, via videotape/disc or broadcast television of one variety or another.

The big-screen vista remains important in Hollywood today. But it has been supplemented, in the creation of overt visual spectacle, by the use of techniques more suited to the creation of spectacular impact within the confines of the small-screen image. At the risk of over-simplification, two varieties of spectacle might be suggested. One has its roots in the creation of impact on the big screen. The other draws on techniques associated in part with small-screen spectacle. In the former case, as in much of the tradition of spectacular blockbuster production, the emphasis is put on the presentation before the viewer of large vistas, at the level of what appears to be the *pro-filmic* reality. For the purpose of this argument, I include here elements of special effects that are not strictly pro-filmic, but that are designed to create that impression (matte paintings or models, for example, or digitally composited images, meant to blend more or less seamlessly with more substantially "real" sets, locations and action). Images such as extreme long shots of the construction of Goshen, the exodus from Egypt, or the parting of the Red Sea in *The Ten Commandments*, or of the ship in *Titanic*, are offered as forms of large-scale spectacle the viewer is invited to sit back and admire on the big screen in a relatively leisurely fashion. This is a form I have described elsewhere as offering a "contemplative" brand of spectacle (King 2000). Time is permitted for a certain amount of scrutiny of the image: admiration of texture or detail produced by lavish expenditure on sets, locations, props and extras, or of the latest illusions available with the use of state-of-the-art special effects. The viewer might as a result be taken more effectively "into" the diegetic world on screen—if the overall effect is a "convincing" representation and helps in the process of "suspending disbelief." Alternatively, or at the same time, the viewer might admire the spectacle *as* impressive construct, testament to the illusionary powers of high-cost, resource-heavy spectacular cinema (for more discussion of this in relation to special effects, see LaValley 1985; Landon 1992; Barker and Brooks 1998; Darley 2000; King 2000). The latter effect, based on the selling of the spectacular capabilities of the medium itself, has always been a significant component of the attraction of large-scale blockbuster production.

What happens, though, when spectacle of this variety is reduced to the spatial limits of the small screen? Widescreen spectacle is particularly vulnerable, either being shown in pan/scan versions, in which only parts of the image are visible and original compositions are subjected to reframing, or "letterbox" screenings that maintain more of the integrity of the frame but reduce still further the scale of the image. The large-scale spectacular qualities of blockbusters such as *The Ten Commandments* and *Titanic* are not entirely destroyed in this process but they are substantially reduced in impact. Other forms of spectacle, however, suffer relatively less in the move from big screen to small—specifically, those based on techniques such as rapid editing or rapid and/or unstable movement of the camera. Constant change of image-content is needed to maintain heightened levels of visual stimulus on the small screen (Ellis 1989), a strategy Hollywood appears to have learned from formats such as advertising and music video.[1] Hyperbolically rapid editing and camera movement have become important sources of heightened spectacular impact in contemporary Hollywood, either replacing or (probably more often) being used in conjunction with images of grander visual scale. This is especially the case in action-oriented blockbuster production, with its basic currency of explosive destruction. The impact of the contemporary action film is often constructed through patterns of rapid montage-effect editing combined with "unstable" camera movement designed to create an impression of subjective immersion in the action, an "impact aesthetic" often increased by the practice of propelling debris and other objects out toward the viewer (for detailed analysis of examples, see King 2000).

Particularly notable, given its generic allegiance to the large-vista Roman-biblical tradition, is the use of such techniques as the dominant aesthetic in the action-fighting scenes of *Gladiator* (for more detail, see King 2002a).

A typical strategy today is to combine moments of broader, more expansive spectacle with those of tightly framed explosive-montage-impact effects. The central action sequence in *Pearl Harbor*, for example, offers larger shots, the spectacle of a large number of American ships in various stages of destruction during and after the initial Japanese attack, and closer and more rapidly cut detail—making claims to a more "subjective" location—including the obligatory outward-moving fireball/debris effects and a bomb's-eye-view perspective. What this offers in the realm of heightened spectacle is, in fact, in keeping with a central aspect of the classical Hollywood *decoupage* more generally: a combination of relatively "objective," distanced and closer, quasi-subjective perspectives. The difference, however, is that the more subjective-seeming position is constructed as a variety of spectacular impact (as opposed, for instance, to a less frenzied, more quotidian point-of-view shot).

The appeal of the more "contemplative" end of the spectacular spectrum might be understood in the context of a long tradition of larger-than-life spectacular representation. This includes pre-cinematic forms such as the magic lantern show and the diorama as well as earlier forms of spectacle, both secular and religious in origin. The pleasures offered might include a sense of being taken beyond the scale of everyday life to something suggesting a grandeur, an awe, or a sense of the sublime, even if a format such as blockbuster cinema might offer a rather debased and commercialized version of such an experience. Richard Dyer's attempt to analyze some of the characteristics of the pleasurable/entertaining dimension of the more spectacular varieties of Hollywood cinema (specifically, in his case studies, the musical) offers a useful vocabulary in which to understand some of these pleasures. Of most direct relevance are the qualities of "abundance" and "intensity" identified by Dyer (1992) that can be contrasted with the scarcity and banality that characterizes much of the typical reality of everyday life. The pleasure of experiencing greater-than-life intensity also applies to the high-impact variety of spectacle, a form that offers an intense engagement for the viewer. This is a quality actively discussed as a source of enjoyment by some enthusiasts of the action genre (Barker and Brooks 1998) and also offered by other media targeted at a similar audience, such as action-adventure videogames (King 2002b). The prominence of this format in contemporary Hollywood can be explained by more than just its suitability for translation to the small screen, which may or may not be a consciously exploited causal factor. A more indirect route can also be suggested, given the tendency of

Hollywood to embrace styles used in other popular media consumed by its key target audience of younger viewers, including music video, and the employment of directors (such as Michael Bay, director of *Armageddon* [1998] and *Pearl Harbor*) with backgrounds in music video and/or advertising, two of the key training grounds for recent generations of filmmakers.

Whatever the precise causal factors behind—and audience appeals of—the two, a combination of large-scale and more impact-centered spectacle makes sense in the contemporary industrial context. Video and television screenings are the principal sources of revenue, in the longer term. But their potential remains dependent to a large extent—especially at the prestigious, high-budget blockbuster end of the market—on success in the theatrical realm. It is success at the box office, in most cases, that determines the likely scale of revenues to be earned in subsequent forms such as video sales/rentals and sales to pay- and free-to-air television broadcast. Spectacular dimensions that play especially well on the big screen remain important. They help to create the "event movie" impact, in terms of wider media coverage as well as promotion and box office returns, that translates into subsequent success on the small screen for a franchise or a one-off blockbuster.

Narrative Still Matters

What, though, of narrative in the spectacular blockbuster? It is common parlance in both journalistic criticism and some academic writing to assume or to assert that the emphasis on visual spectacle is at the expense of narrative. "Impressive effects, shame the same effort wasn't put into the plot," is a standard response. The plot of the typical Hollywood spectacular blockbuster may not be terribly challenging or complex; a basic mistake that is often made, however, is to confuse this—a perfectly valid qualitative judgment, but one that could be applied to many other Hollywood films—with the idea that narrative is in some way *absent* or *displaced* by spectacle. It is surprising how often this slippage seems to occur, as if prominent narrative dimensions somehow become invisible once the focus turns to the production of spectacular impact. Different aspects of this argument can be related to the two different versions of spectacle considered above, each of which has been cited as an impediment to narrative. In what follows, I begin by sketching briefly some of these claims and suggesting why they are often mistaken. Having established that narrative remains important, and usually quite central, to the contemporary blockbuster, this section concludes by examining some of the specific qualities of the kind of narrative structure found in the context of spectacular production. My principal focus here will be on the recent spectacular Hollywood blockbuster, rather than earlier examples, as it is here that arguments about the decline of narrative have been concentrated.

Contemporary blockbusters of the large-scale spectacular variety are often lumped together with spin-off forms such as movie-based theme-park rides or videogames. The fact that films are sometimes converted into such formats is used by some commentators as a basis on which to imply that the films themselves exhibit the far less narrative-based qualities of rides or games (see, for example, Bukatman 1998). Narrative is said to be subordinated to the provision of a spectacular "thrill-ride." The logic of this kind of argument is flawed, however, other than as a species of rhetoric, a way to "bash" Hollywood rather than to engage in serious analysis. Even if constructed with one eye on their potential for conversion to ride or videogame, it does not follow in principal that the films should be lacking in narrative dimensions, so different are the requirements of cinema from those of ride or game. Another major strain in these arguments focuses on the prominence of special-effects sequences in the spectacular blockbuster. Narrative dynamics are said to be "bracketed" in many cases by major effects sequences (Pierson 1999), powerful illusions/spectacles that threaten to "overwhelm traditional concerns with character and story" (Darley 2000: 103). The style of visual spectacle and impact that draws on techniques used in advertising and music video, including rapid and emphatic montage-editing, has also been identified as a threat to narrative, most notably in Justin Wyatt's much-cited book on "high concept" in Hollywood (Wyatt 1994).

The fact remains, however, that spectacular Hollywood blockbusters, of both varieties, continue to invest strongly in narrative dynamics, and at more than one level. They tell carefully organized, more or less linear cause/effect stories organized around central characters. They also manifest what a structuralist analysis would term "underlying" narrative structural patterns, on which I have written at length elsewhere (King 2000). Take, for example, *Terminator 2: Judgment Day* (1991), a quintessential example of the recent Hollywood spectacular blockbuster production, and a blockbuster in all contemporary senses of the term (expensive, large-scale, spectacular, and a substantial box-office hit). *Terminator 2* is one of the films regularly cited by commentators such as Pierson and Darley. As such, it is a useful example to revisit in a little more detail, with attention to exactly how it is structured in terms of the relationship between spectacle and narrative.

Terminator 2 is, clearly, a film *driven by* the dimension of spectacle more than that of narrative, which is one reason why it is a good test case. It is safe to assume, I think, that the reason for making the film was to capitalize on the success of *The Terminator* (1984), a modestly budgeted film, in the typical contemporary Hollywood manner of producing a "bigger," "better," more spectacular and special-effects-oriented sequel. The distinctive spectacular attraction of *Terminator 2*, the morphing transformation scenes involving the new-generation shape-shifting T-1000 terminator, was also driven by specific developments in special effects technologies—principally the adaptation and extension of 3-D computer generation techniques used to create the water pseudopod in director James Cameron's earlier film *The Abyss* (1989). The principle *raison d'être* of *Terminator 2* is the production of special-effects-based spectacle, along with the more conventional action-movie recipe of chase, combat and destruction. *The Terminator* left plenty of undeveloped *narrative* potential—an ending in which the central character Sarah Connor (Linda Hamilton) drives off ready to bear a son who will lead the human resistance in a post-apocalyptic future—but it seems reasonable to conclude that fulfilling this potential was not the major factor in the decision to fashion a sequel. Even if some of the narrative dimensions of the film might be interpreted as responses to socio-cultural issues or anxieties, it is difficult to make any very direct argument to support the claim that these are an identifiable *causal factor* in the appearance of the film.

If *Terminator 2* owes its existence primarily to its potential to create a particular form of spectacular blockbuster attraction, a product of the particular Hollywood regime in place at the time (and very much with us today), it does not follow that, as a result, it is lacking in narrative dynamics, or even that narrative is in a particularly secondary position in the actual structure of the film. The distinction between these two propositions is important, but one that tends to be overlooked in many accounts. *Terminator 2* has strong and carefully orchestrated narrative dimensions. Like most other spectacular blockbusters, it offers a combination of spectacular and narrative appeals, a quality clearly marked from the outset. In its opening moments, *Terminator 2* supplies both large-scale spectacle (images of apocalypse and post-apocalyptic warfare between human and machine) and narrative exposition (a voice-over from Sarah Connor that establishes the narrative context). Outbursts of spectacle and special effects are narratively situated; they serve narrative purposes. The opening vision of apocalypse—repeated later, when located in Sarah's dreams—hangs over the film as its basic, narratively located fulcrum of suspense (will it really occur, or be averted?). Celebrated sequences such as the transformation in which the figure of the T-1000 emerges seamlessly from a checkerboard floor, or when it passes through the metal bars in a hospital hallway, gain their *full* impact also through their location at narratively heightened moments of tension: the ability of the T-1000 to perform such maneuvers directly places the sympathetic characters in danger.

Such sequences arc designed to show off the effects. If they are experienced *as* effects, something less than total engrossment in the ongoing events of the diegetic universe must be entailed: the viewer "sits back," as it were, distanced to some extent from the on-screen world, aware of the nature of the image as construct. To interpret this as a spectacular/special-effects *interruption* or bracketing of narrative, however, is to assume a rather one-dimensional model of the experience of film viewing—as if, for example, the *normal* experience of spectator ship was anything close to *total* and undivided engrossment or "suspension of disbelief." The example of special-effects-led spectacle might be used, more helpfully, to illustrate the complex and multidimensional modalities in which any particular film, type of film, or individual sequence is likely to be consumed.[2] If high-definition computer-generated special effects can be experienced simultaneously as "highly realistic and convincing" and as "amazing *illusions* of the highly realistic and convincing," the same kind of oscillations might be available more widely—between that which draws the viewer acceptingly "into" the fictional world on screen and that which marks its more distanced status as pleasurable illusion (the pleasure resulting partly from awareness of its status *as* illusion).

If the major spectacular sequences of *Terminator 2* are themselves narratively situated, the film also exhibits many other features usually associated with the "classical Hollywood" style of narration (as defined by Bordwell 1985). It has a primarily linear, forward-moving structure, across the different narrative threads, based on cause-and-effect relationships between one event and another. It is organized around the qualities and experiences of a distinctive small group of characters who undergo significant development. This would not need to be stated, so obvious does it seem, were it not for some of the sweeping claims made about such films. It does not take any great feats of academic ingenuity, either, to suggest a number of not very deeply "underlying" narrative dynamics of a structural variety, often entailing the establishment and imaginary reconciliation of thematic oppositions. Obvious examples include the theme of "humanity vs. technology" and issues of gender roles and parenting. Plenty has been written about these (for example, Telotte 1995; Tasker 1993), but such dimensions often seem to be lost from sight during discussion of spectacle or special effects. A full and adequate understanding of spectacular blockbusters such as *Terminator 2* requires simultaneous attention to the various dimensions that make up the experience offered to the viewer. The same can be said of films that use the montage-based form of spectacular impact, whether in the form of hyperkinetically edited action sequences or the surface-style oriented music-video aesthetic examined by Wyatt. They still exhibit most if not all of the qualities usually associated, loosely, with "classical Hollywood" narrative and are structured around various thematic oppositions (for more on this in detail, see King 2000 and 2002a).

The continued importance of narrative structure in Hollywood blockbuster-style production has been acknowledged by some recent commentators, in an attempt to redress the balance against assumptions that narrative has been undermined (especially Buckland 1998; Cowie 1998; Thompson 1999). But does narrative have any distinctive characteristics in this context, when combined with an emphasis on the production of spectacular impact? Does it depart in any way from the "classical" version? Spectacular blockbusters of recent decades have sometimes been associated with the more episodic structure of B-movie serials produced in Hollywood in the 1930s and 1940s, a structure in which less emphasis is placed on overarching narrative dynamics. Some of the landmark spectacular blockbusters of the 1970s and 1980s are designed very much with the serial template in mind, obvious examples being *Star Wars* (1977) and *Raiders of the Lost Ark* (1981). As Warren Buckland suggests, the latter can be broken down into a series of six distinct episodes, but these are tied together quite strongly through their position in the development of a feature-length narrative that reaches resolution in the final episode; "The point to make here is that this pattern transcends individual episodes, and is dependent for its very existence on the presence of a feature-length story" (1998: 172). The dynamic is very different from that which results from the shorter serial format, in which a substantial gap occurs between one episode and another.

One quality often associated with recent spectacular blockbuster production is pace. For Thomas Schatz, the distinguishing characteristic of a film such as *Star Wars* is not an absence of narrative drive but a hell-bent and careening form of narrative that emphasizes "plot over character" (1993: 23). This account seems to contradict the claim that the production of spectacular or impact aesthetics has an interruptive or bracketing effect in relation to narrative. The accusation is of lack of narrative depth, rather than of narrative itself (and, whatever the distinctive characteristics of the film, it is hardly the case that character is other than a central component in the armature that drives *Star Wars* or other titles in the franchise). The generation of spectacular impact within what might be described as an incessant, forward-driving narrative-spectacle context is characteristic of many recent Hollywood blockbusters and less-than-blockbuster-scale action films. Exactly *how* major sequences of spectacle or special effects occur within this kind of framework is variable, however, on more than one ground. Large-scale computer-generated effects remain expensive, which is one reason why they are unlikely to overwhelm narrative at present, even if filmmakers were prepared to dispose of the narrative dimension in any substantial manner (which itself seems highly unlikely). *Terminator 2* is a prominent example in this respect, the trademark transformational effects being absent from large stretches of the film.

The rapid succession with which moments of spectacular impact come in some films—a strong example is *Armageddon*—might be seen as a point of distinction from earlier spectacular blockbusters, which tend to be more "stately" in their mode of presentation, moving (in some cases, lumbering) more slowly between larger scale spectacular set-pieces and sequences of greater intimacy. In this sense, it might be said that narrative momentum is "bracketed" a good deal less in the contemporary Hollywood spectacular blockbuster than in some other examples. An alternative might be suggested, in these two different forms of spectacular, between degrees of narrative momentum (forward-moving drive) and narrative depth (complications, ramifications, nuances, etc.), but these are only relative. The trouble with any sweeping judgments, either way, is that narrative/spectacle dynamics vary within as well as between different industrial-historical contexts. Some contemporary spectacular blockbusters are clearly designed to hark back to the "grander" earlier style, prominent examples including *Titanic, Gladiator*, and *Pearl Harbor*. The duration and pacing of these films, in particular, is very different from that of the *Star Wars/Raiders of the Lost Ark/Armageddon* variety. Lengthy scenes of slow-paced, character-based narrative development account for large segments of the running time. For viewers attracted by the promise of spectacle, it might be these sequences that are experienced as the interruptive dimension. The same might be said of *The Ten Commandments*, in which extra-large-scale spectacle is witnessed only on occasion and accounts for a small fraction of the running time (compared, say, to the large-scale scenes of conflict in *The Birth of a Nation*, which are held for more extensive periods). The typical rhythm of the film during its set-pieces is to move quite swiftly from the enormous vista to a more conventionally studio-bound scale of more localized detail at which the principals interact.

Differences can also be identified between films in the same blockbuster franchise. *Jurassic Park 3* (2001), for example, has a structure rather different from that of either of its two predecessors. Less time is spent dwelling on the broader ramifications of the creation of the dinosaurs (a substantial component of the first film, especially) and there is no new twist of a corporate-conspiratorial nature (as there is in the second in the series). There are no human enemies this time. The film, as a result, is some thirty minutes shorter than the first two instalments. Emphasis is put on a forward-driving rescue-survive-escape scenario that delivers a tight succession of spectacular engagements with dinosaurs. This might seem to confirm the suggestion by Timothy Corrigan (1991) that the prevalence of sequels has been a major factor in what he describes as the attenuation of narrative in Hollywood since the mid-1970s in favor of the spectacle provided by the display of cinematic technology. In the sequel, the series film, and the remake, Corrigan argues, "figures of technological or stylistic extravagance ... detach themselves from the path of character psychology and plot incident" (1991: 170). The main *point* of the blockbuster sequel, in this case as in *Terminator* 2, might be to provide the opportunity to display the latest advances in special-effects capabilities (as well as simply providing "more of the same," as a "thrill ride"). But plenty of narrative structure is still in evidence, even in the relatively stripped-down second-sequel format used by *Jurassic Park 3*. The experience of the special-effects-led spectacle is closely linked to character (including differences in the attitudes and reactions of different characters to the dinosaurs); it also drives the basic "jeopardy" narrative. The narrative structure of events embodies a typical Hollywood moral economy: the fact, for example, that the cavalier young assistant to the dinosaur expert will redeem himself and appear to die in the process (rescuing a young boy from the clutches of a pterodactyl) after being castigated for stealing a pair of eggs from the nest of a velociraptor. Judgments such as that of Corrigan tend to flatten the picture, overstating certain tendencies to the detriment of close understanding of precisely how such films are structured. Broad historical-industrial factors are clearly important in shaping the spectacle/narrative dynamics of blockbusters, but accounts in these terms usually need to be supplemented by more local and specific analysis. Differences of genre, for example—which might include the favoring of different genres on different occasions—seem to play as important a part as shifts from one era to another in accounting for some of the specific qualities found in examples such as *Gladiator* and *Star Wars* or *Jurassic Park 3*.

If some contemporary Hollywood blockbusters are relatively episodic, they are far from alone, historically speaking. As Elizabeth Cowie suggests, episodic structure—in which narrative events are sometimes displaced by set-pieces and not always given clear causal explanation—is found in plenty of products from the "classical" period (for examples see Cowie 1998: 185). This is the case from the levels of "prestige" and spectacular blockbuster production to the B-movie tradition on which one trend in more recent blockbuster filmmaking has drawn. Hollywood production in the studio era, in general, was often not as "classical" as is sometimes implied (most notably in David Bordwell's influential account). Once reasonably coherent narrative became established as a primary basis of organization (by the 1910s) it was constantly subject to combination with all sorts of other appeals, ranging from the presence of larger-than-role star performers to the vicissitudes of melodramatic coincidence and the pleasures of large-scale spectacular attraction (see, for example, Altman 1992; Maltby 1995). This may sometimes be foregrounded to an extra degree in the spectacular blockbuster, but the differences, generally, are relative and of degree rather than absolute. Narrative has never since played less than a substantial role, either, in combination with other dimensions, whether in the most hell-bent or the most heavy-handed and lumbering varieties of spectacular blockbuster production. The experience of spectacle in the blockbuster is usually organized and given resonance by narrative dimensions, in an assortment of different combinations and styles, each of which merits careful analysis in its own right: a weighing up of the balance between narrative and spectacle, their interactions, the specific qualities of each, and the industrial and historical contexts in which a particular format is encouraged.

Notes

1. These devices also have cinematic precedents, of course, most notably the montage style adopted by Sergei Eisenstein.
2. For more on the subject of varying "modalities of response," in reference to special effects sequences and to Hollywood films more generally, see Barker with Austin (2000: 55, 79, 81).

References

Altman, Rick. (1992). Dickens, Griffith, and Film Theory Today, in Jane Gaines (ed.), *Classical Hollywood Narrative: The Paradigm Wars.* (pp. 9–47). Durham, NC: Duke University Press.

Barker, Martin, with Austin, Thomas. (2000). *From Antz to Titanic: Reinventing Film Analysis.* London: Pluto Press.

Barker, Martin, & Brooks, Kate. (1998). *Knowing Audiences: Judge Dredd, Its Friends, Fans and Foes.* Luton: University of Luton Press.

Bordwell, David. (1985). The Classical Hollywood Style, 1917–60, in Bordwell, David, Staiger, Janet, & Thompson, Kristin, *The Classical Hollywood Cinema: Film Style and Mode of Production to 1960.* (pp. 1–84). London: Routledge & Kegan Paul.

Bowser, Eileen. (1990). *The Transformation of Cinema 1907–1915.* Berkeley: University of California Press.

Buckland, Warren. (1998). A Close Encounter With Raiders of the Lost Ark: Notes on Narrative Aspects of the New Hollywood Blockbuster, in Steve Neale & Murray Smith (eds), *Contemporary Hollywood Cinema.* (pp. 166–77). London: Routledge.

Bukatman, Scott. (1998). Zooming Out: The End of Offscreen Space, in Jon Lewis (ed.), *The New American Cinema.* (pp. 248–72). Durham, NC: Duke University Press.

Corrigan, Timothy. (1991). *Cinema Without Walls: Movies and Culture After Vietnam.* London: Routledge.

Cowie, Elizabeth. (1998). Storytelling: Classical Hollywood Cinema and Classical Narrative, in Steve Neale & Murray Smith (eds), *Contemporary Hollywood Cinema.* (pp. 178–90). London: Routledge.

Darley, Andrew. (2000). *Digital Visual Culture: Surface Play and Spectacle in New Media Genres.* London: Routledge.

Dyer, Richard. (1992). *Only Entertainment.* London: British Film Institute.

Ellis, John. (1989). *Visible Fictions: Cinema, Television, Video.* (Rev. edn). London: Routledge.

King, Geoff. (2000). *Spectacular Narratives: Hollywood in the Age of the Blockbuster.* London and New York: I. B. Tauris.

King, Geoff. (2002a). *New Hollywood Cinema: An Introduction.* London: I. B. Tauris.

King, Geoff. (2002b). Die Hard/Try Harder: Narrative, Spectacle and Beyond, From Hollywood to Videogame, in Geoff King & Tanya Krzywinska (eds), *ScreenPlay: Cinema/Videogames/Interfaces.* London: Wallflower Press.

Landon, Brooks. (1992). *The Aesthetics of Ambivalence.* Westport, CT: Greenwood Press.

LaValley, Albert J. (1985). Tradition or Trickery?: The Role of Special Effects in the Science Fiction Film, in George E. Slusser & Eric S. Rabkin (eds), *Shadows of the Magic Lamp: Fantasy and Science Fiction Film.* (pp. 141–58). Carbondale: Southern Illinois University Press.

Maltby, Richard. (1995). *Hollywood Cinema: An Introduction.* Oxford: Blackwell.

Pierson, Michele. (1999). CGI Effects in Hollywood Science-Fiction Cinema 1989–95: The Wonder Years. *Screen*, 40, 2: 158–76.

Schatz, Thomas .(1993). The New Hollywood, in Jim Collins, Hilary Radner & Ava Preacher Collins (eds), *Film Theory Goes to the Movies*. (pp. 8–36). New York and London: Routledge. [Reprinted in this volume].

Tasker, Yvonne. (1993). *Spectacular Bodies: Gender, Genre and the Action Cinema*. London: Routledge.

Telotte, J. P. (1995). *Replications: A Robotic History of the Science Fiction Film*. Urbana: University of Illinois Press.

Thompson, Kristin. (1999). *Storytelling in the New Hollywood*. Cambridge, MA: Harvard University Press.

Wyatt, Justin. (1994). *High Concept: Movies and Marketing in Hollywood*. Austin: University of Texas Press.

Questions

1. What was the first movie you ever saw? What do you remember?
2. Think about how you watch large-scale action films. Are you drawn into the fictional world completely? Or do you enter the fictional world while at the same time admire the technique that is creating spectacular effects?
3. Some people complain that blockbusters today are "theme-park movies". What do you think? Are movies today over designed?
4. Compare and contrast the large scale attractions with smaller scale attractions. What are the main differences and similarities?

View

Film
Trip to the Moon (1902)
The Fall of Troy (1910)
The Birth of a Nation (1915)
Hugo (2011)

Read

Davis, Blair. "Made-from-TV Movies: Turning 1950s Television into Film." *Historical Journal of Film, Radio and Television* 29.2 (2009): 197–218. Print.

Lavik, E. "New Narrative Depths?: Spectacle and Narrative in Blockbuster Cinema Revisited." *Nordicom Review* 30.2 (2009): 141-157. Print.

Schirato, et al. The Film/Television as Spectacle" in Tony Schirato, Angi Buettner, Thierry Jutel, and Geoff Stal, *Understanding Media Studies*, 136-155. Oxford University Press, 2010. Print.

Thompson, Kristin and David Bordwell, eds. *Film History: An Introduction.* 3rd ed. New York: McGraw-Hill, 2010. Print.

Exercises

1. Contemporary circus companies use spectacle in different ways and for different purposes. Find a company on the web and try to figure out how they use spectacle.

2. What musicals are familiar to you? What is the role of spectacle in those musicals?

3. Spectacle in film is achieved mainly through special effects. Consider a current Hollywood blockbuster. How do you think the special effects help to achieve spectacle? How do the special effects engage the audience?

4. Deconstruct your own convergence. Keep a log of the popular entertainment performances you watch and the various media platforms you use to access those performances. Note moments of convergence (i.e., where the same content is accessed from different platforms).

Part 3

When Culture Becomes

Entertainment

Part Three builds on the theoretical foundation constructed in Parts One and Two by shifting the focus of performance, adaptation, and the marketplace to representations of culture and identity. What constitutes culture and how culture is studied has changed dramatically over the last century, as anthropologists, sociologists, and performance theorists all examine it from the perspective of their own fields while technology and globalization have begun to blur the geographical and philosophical boundaries between cultures. Cultural and media convergence has given us more access to other cultures, but has also led to tensions as some attempt to protect their identities and beliefs from cultural poaching. Issues of authenticity and definitions of culture become increasingly problematic in a post-convergence world.

Part Three acknowledges the challenge of creating a specific and inclusive definition of culture when studying it not just as performance, but as popular entertainment. John Bodley's characterization of the three basic components of a culture—what people think, what they do, and what they produce—provides a base for critical examination that works across cultural boundaries constructed by race, ethnicity, geography, philosophy, or aesthetic.

Acknowledging the challenge of creating a specific and inclusive definition of culture, Part Three instead offers several examples of culture as popular entertainment to give a broad sense of types of cultural performances. The first half of Part Three focuses on cultural tourism as popular entertainment by examining living history museums, historical re-enactments, and tourist performances. These cultural performances can also as be read as adaptations of culture for entertainment purposes, as Hutcheon's expansive definition of adaption "includes almost any act of alteration performed upon specific cultural works of the past and dovetails with a general process of cultural recreation." (99)

However, cultural performance as popular entertainment extends well beyond tourism, which tends to maintain the distinction between producers, performers, and audiences. Many cultural performances blur the boundaries between these three roles, and engage audiences as producers and performers in cultural activity. The essays that serve as examples of cultural entertainment beyond tourism intersect not only with Schechner's approach to performance and Hutcheon's analysis of adaptation from Part One, but also explore issues of ritual, identity, and authenticity, and offer an opportunity to both engage and complicate the analysis of cultural performance as popular entertainment.

Cultural Tourism
Culture as Entertainment
    Cultural Ritual, Popular Entertainment
    Performing Identity
    Cultural Authenticity

Cultural Tourism

Cultural tourism, or cultural heritage tourism, is leisure time spent experiencing places and events that attempt to provide an authentic representation of people and their stories. Cultural tourism includes popular entertainment forms such as living history museums, historical re-enactments, and tourist performances. These can be narratives of a community or culture in the present, but most often cultural tourism relies on representations of the past. Yet who defines this idea of authenticity—the producers of the tourist site or event, the performers charged with interpreting the history and stories, or the audiences experiencing them through their unique perspectives shaped by their own histories and experiences? Producers of these forms of popular entertainment must constantly attend to cultural shifts in values and beliefs, discoveries of new documentation or alternative histories, and the convergence of cultures in order to maintain relevance—and popularity.

Schechner's essay, "Tourist Performances: Leisure Globalization," puts into practice the model he provides in Part One, and offers specific examples of the unique dynamic between producers, performers, and audiences of cultural tourism. While Schechner's analysis critiques cultural tourism primarily from the audience's perspective, Modlin, Alderman, and Gentry turn their analysis to the role of the performer in "Tour Guides as Creators of Empathy: The Role of Affective Inequality in Marginalizing the Enslaved at Plantation House Museums." In this essay, the authors acknowledge that the idea of a single, unified representation of authenticity in tourist performances is highly problematic, and instead focus on the tour guide's role in helping the audience negotiate contested representations of a culture.

Ideas

Tourism and virtual tourism
Living history museums
Interpreters vs. actors

Historical re-enactments
Affective inequality
Heritage tourism
Historical empathy
Oppositional interpretive community
Counter-narrative

Tourist Performances

Leisure Globalization

By Richard Schechner

Tourism is no simple matter. To satisfy an enormous and still rapidly growing market of intercultural, international, intracultural, and intranational tourists, performances of all kinds have been found, redesigned, or invented. There are many kinds of tourism—culture, sports, sex, wildlife, historical, etc.—where at the destination the tourist witnesses or, increasingly, takes part in a performance of one kind or another. While on safari, for example, tourists become hunters-with-cameras, living in a refurbished and toileted "wild." Sports tourists at the Olympics or the Superbowl more than watch athletes. They party, sightsee, vicariously take part in the competition while identifying with their heroes and their city or nation. These tourisms, for we must use the plural to describe them, can transport people to distant places or back in time by means of restorations and re-enactments.

It is common wisdom to disparage tourism and tourist performances as shallow and tawdry, a pastime for the rich and an exploitation of "native" or "local" peoples, their beliefs, and skills. Tourists yearn for the "authentic" and the "real," even as most of them know they are being fed the ersatz and the invented. Although all this is too often true, it is not always the case, nor is it the whole story. In Bali very similar performances may be part of a temple ceremony in one instance and presented in unconsecrated space for tourists at another time. The quality suffers, but not as much as those who condemn tourism say. *Ketchak*—the "monkey chant dance" which re-enacts an episode from the *Ramayana*—is performed by the Balinese both in their own ceremonies and as a big tourist attraction. Ironically, ketchak began in the 1920s as a tourist performance.

There are performances not made for tourists which attract them in droves all the same. Many religious observances are open to visitors—sometimes in the hopes of proselytizing, or to earn money, or just to be hospitable. When tourists enter churches, temples, synagogues, shrines, or mosques, are they enjoying (and paying for) an entertainment or experiencing the sacred? Need one strictly separate these orders of experience? And insofar as the tourists are present at the "real thing," what adjustments are made in the performances to accommodate the outsiders? The answer cannot be given briefly or definitively because the changes may be subtle and slowly transformative.

There is virtual and media tourism—film and television are so enormously popular partly because they give people a chance to experience "the other" without leaving home. Brazilians watching reruns of *Seinfeld* or Americans watching a *National Geographic Special* (or any number of programs on the Discovery Channel) are virtual tourists. Surfing the web yields similar opportunities for experiencing the far away. Does virtual tourism create a pressure for the places depicted to attempt to live up to their media images?

When tourism involves actual travel, this can take many forms. Pilgrimages, popular the world over, and undertaken by poor and rich alike combine religious devotion and tourism. Hindus are continually in circulation around India, visiting literally thousands of *tirths* (pilgrimage spots)—temples, caves, mountains, rivers. Multitudes journey to performances such as the Raslila at Mathura or the Ramlila at Ramnagar. At Raslila *Krishna*, and at Ramlila, *Rama*, are manifest. People come from far and near to *hadarshan*—a vision or view—of the gods who the devoted believe are incarnate in the guise of young boys. In 1978 at Ramnagar, I met a man who had been carrying his mother around India in a basket for two years so that she could visit as many pilgrimage sites as possible. Millions of Muslims make the Hajj to Mecca at least once in their lives. Places sacred to Christianity abound, attracting tourists to the Holy Land and to miracle shrines in Europe and the Western Hemisphere. People make these journeys not only to fulfill a religious obligation but also to see the world, sharing in the camaraderie that "going away" enlivens—a liminal time-space well known to poet Geoffrey Chaucer as recounted in his *Canterbury Tales*.

> Geoffrey Chaucer (1342–1400): English poet, best known for *The Canterbury Tales,* written between 1386 and 1400. In this poem, persons old and young, women and men on a pilgrimage to Canterbury, England, tell stories to pass the time.

Tourism within nations is at least as big a business as travel among nations. Protecting local peoples, practices, wildlife, or landscapes can turn into selling them, or imitations of them, to tourists. In India, city-dwelling Rajasthanis flock to a specially built "authentic" village to view craftspeople at work and to enjoy music, dance, and supper. The tourists sit on the floor of a large thatch-roofed house eating traditional foods dished onto banana leaves by young women dressed in "traditional" garb. As Jaipur's Rex Tours puts it, "Take a peek into the lives of rural folk, their abodes, social set up, religious beliefs, and innovative cuisine." The night I was there most of the tourists were visibly middle class. My hunch was right that at least some of the visitors were returning to a sanitized version of their own past. "This is very authentic," a man told me. "It is just like the village my parents came from." So why didn't he simply make a trip back to his parents' village? Tourism simplifies, idealizes, and packages. When the show is over, you can wash your hands of the whole thing. The actual village may have been far away or held some disturbing reminders—or even relations to whom he would be obligated. Or maybe his own village had changed so much that the tourist village was a better representation of his past. But most probably, seeing his own experience reified gave him a sense of mastery over his past. He could literally purchase his past. Tourism does that—allows the tourist to purchase the other, the past, the exotic, the sexy, the exciting … whatever is up for grabs. And if "purchase" means to buy with money, it also means to get a hold on, to grasp firmly, to be in charge.

In Kenya, Mayer's Farm—a homestead owned by white settlers—attracted tourists who wanted to experience "authentic" colonial life including members of the Mayer family and Maasai employees all playing their colonial roles. So for the "eternal past" of the tourist experience, the vanished world was back in place, if only in the realm of the performative make-believe. Mayer's Farm no longer exists—but the Maasai continue to be exploited by hordes of camera-toting tourists who treat them as little more than part of the area's wildlife (see Maimai box). What about the economics of this kind of tourism? Much tourism feeds on the needy and, like globalization generally, depends on a sharp imbalance of economic opportunity. The tourist is free-floating, a consumer with a lot of cash (relatively speaking) who could in theory go anywhere.

The international tour agency has access to local operators who, in turn, organize the "workers," the Maasai or whoever are the destination objects. As in globalized industries, the money is unevenly distributed: the agency and local operators take the lion's share. The Maasai—and their case is not unusual—get less than 10 percent of the tourists' dollars. They are in effect working in a sweatshop.

Visiting the "eternal past" is not just an overseas thing. The Rajasthanis seeking a replica of their own village are matched in the USA by a host of historical re-enactments, theme parks, and restored villages. "Living *museums*" such as

Kakuta Ole Maimai
Commercial photographers in the Maasai region

The Maasai people are among the indigenous people hunted by photographers who found free access into a land filled with exoticism, wildlife, and tribal people, where the law to protect indigenous people remains scarce. Some western photographers are stepping over boundaries; they are not being sensitive to our culture and way of life. They are invading and exploiting our people and culture for profit purposes.

Here are some questions to ask yourself, when looking at a portrait book with Maasai images: Who is this person in the picture? What is her name? How does she feel being in a portrait book? Does she know that her picture is being sold in the Western world? Did she receive anything in return? Has the photographer obtained a letter of consent from this person or from the community? Now look at a portrait book, or magazine, with images of Western people. Repeat the same questions stated above.

It appears that a wild animal is given a better recognition than a Maasai person. When you visit a zoo […] the keeper will present that animal to you by its name. Why can't a photographer name a Maasai if s/he can name a wild animal? A Maasai is not less of a human being. Recently, we came across images of a circumcision event, a sacred rite of passage that is not intended for the public. This discovery was shocking, sad, and disappointing to us, as this is a personal and sacred rite of passage that should have not been photographed, published, and sold to the public.

The photographers must stop invading the privacy of the Maasai people, community, and culture. There are other ways to take images of the people without humiliating, invading, and exploiting the culture. Photographers can make profits without disrespecting the culture. On the other hand, the reader/viewer can learn about Maasai culture without supporting a disrespectful photographer. The reader has the power to change this behavior of a misbehaving photographer. […] Do not buy books with nude images of indigenous people. […] Encourage your bookseller to buy books that are culturally sensitive to indigenous cultures. […] Write to the photographer and encourage her/him to give something back to the community in which s/he photographed. […]

It is important to make clear that we are not opposed to ordinary and respectful photographers. A tourist, for example, is free to take family pictures, as s/he wishes, so long as s/he has obtained a consent from the individual. Also, we are not opposed to learners who wish to understand the Maasai culture. In fact, we are glad to learn that people from all corners of the world are willing to learn about our culture. What we are opposed to is commercial photography obtained without consent. […] We respect other cultures and their way of life. As such, we expect the outside world to respect us in return. What might be accepted in your culture might not be accepted in our culture. Cultural boundaries must be obeyed. Our culture must be represented in a respectful manner.

(2005). *http://maasai-infolme.org/index.html.*

Plimoth Plantation in Massachusetts and Colonial Williamsburg in Virginia pride themselves on the historical verisimilitude of their environments. Because no houses survive from the seventeenth-century pilgrim settlement, Plimoth is not a restoration but a "re-creation." And the location of the present-day plantation is about a mile from the original site. The "interpreters"—the word "actor" is shunned because of the association with theatrical inauthenticity—are dressed in period costumes and coached in the language and manners of the New England pilgrims or the Virginia planters. Interpreters not only improvise dialogue with tourists, but enact specific persons and scenes. At Plimoth, interpreters study "personation biographs" written out in colonial English script describing the settler to be enacted along with a full body portrait. The interpreter is expected to develop an in-depth characterization and maintain it at all times while on site during the hours that the public is admitted. Needless to say, there are slips and even larger difficulties. Similar to living museums are many "historical re-enactments" researched, costumed, and staged by amateur adepts. For example, American Civil War buffs re-enact with meticulous detail hundreds of different events from the bloody battle of Gettysburg in 1863 to the surrender of Confederate General Robert E. Lee at Appomattox Courthouse, Virginia, ending the war in 1865 (see Wisconsin Historical Society box). Re-enactments are simulations, reconstructions, popular entertainments, living histories, and commercial ventures all rolled up into one package. There are hundreds if not thousands of other kinds of re-enactments ranging from fanciful medieval fairs to famous courtroom trials.

Plimoth Plantation had a "problem" with how to represent the Wampanoag Native Americans who in colonial times occupied the land near the Pilgrim settlement. Most tourists come for the pilgrims, and just as in the colonial past, the natives are pretty well pushed out of the picture. Their "summer settlement" consists of a few tepees. One peculiar detail: A brochure informs visitors that the Wampanoags are "staffed by Native Americans." Why tell us this? Those who interpret the pilgrims are not advertised as descendants of white Britishers (which most probably most of them aren't). There is both an intercultural apology and a bragging about authenticity encoded in detail about the "natives." The brochure goes on to invite tourists to "meet the Native American people who have lived for centuries along the New England coast." But are these interpreters from coastal tribes? And what difference would that make when there is no engagement with the circumstances of native "removal"—the wars, the European diseases, and the general decimation of both cultures and peoples that took place? Tourist pleasure trumps historical

---

Wisconsin Historical Society
Fifteenth Annual Civil War Weekend

In what has become the biggest and best Civil War reenactment in Wisconsin, Confederate and Union armies set up camp on the sprawling, wooded grounds of Wade House State Park. Visitors meet and mingle with the troops as well as civilian sutlers—civilian merchants who follow troop movements and sell Civil War-era merchandise. The event's emphasis for 2005 is civilians and medicine helping to save lives. Each afternoon at 2 o'clock the opposing armies clash in a full-scale historic battle reenactment featuring cavalry, infantry and artillery duels.

Ticket Info: Adults $10; children (5–12) $5; family (two adults and two or more dependent children 5–17) $27. Horse-drawn transportation on the site included in ticket cost.

(2005). (http://www.wisconsinhistory.org/wadehouse/events.asp?id=203).

---

accuracy even in a museum site that exults in its accuracy. Something similar haunts Colonial Williamsburg.

When Colonial Williamsburg began in 1926, and for many years thereafter, it was a white-only living museum recreating the life of the eighteenth century. African–Americans were present, of course, but behind the scenes, mostly as menial laborers. No African–Americans were allowed onto the premises as visitors during the period of segregation. But from the 1960s onward, things changed. Yet it was one thing to admit African–Americans as tourists, another to integrate their history into a site that depended on slave labor for its very existence. African–American interpreters performed certain aspects of enslavement—working the fields, plantation servants. Then in the 1990s, it was decided to enact a slave auction. Some of the African–American actors, though recognizing the need for the depiction, felt demeaned and humiliated. But they persevered because they believed that only by performing the auction could people really understand the abomination of African slavery in America.

Tour Guides as Creators of Empathy

The Role of Affective Inequality in Marginalizing the Enslaved at Plantation House Museums

By E. Arnold Modlin Jr; Derek H. Alderman; Glenn W. Gentry

Abstract

Criticized for ignoring or misrepresenting slavery, some docents at plantation house museums have responded by including more references to slavery, but rarely move beyond mere factual references of the enslaved. This contrasts with the emotionally evocative accounts tourists hear about the planter-class family. We refer to this disparity as affective inequality. At plantation house museums, affective inequality is created and reproduced through specific spatial and narrative practices by tour guides. By retracing docent-led tours at Destrehan Plantation, Louisiana, this article engages, conceptually and empirically, with the concept of affective inequality—how it contributes to the marginalization of the history of the enslaved community, and how it becomes reproduced within the practices of tour guides at plantation house museums in the Southern US.

Keywords

Affect; Destrehan Plantation; docent; historic house; inequality; memory; museum; plantation.

E. Arnold Modlin, Derek Alderman, and Glenn Gentry, "Tour Guides as Creators of Empathy: The role of affective inequality in marginalizing the enslaved at Plantation House Museums," *Tourist Studies*, vol. 11, no. 3, pp. 3–19. Copyright © 2011 by Sage Publications. Reprinted with permission.

Introduction

Historic house museums play an important role in the heritage tourism experience (West, 1999). While visiting these museums, tourists hear about events and people of the past, and are actively encouraged to place themselves there historically—to identify with and form emotional bonds with individuals from the past. While many history museums appear to consider the past in objective ways, a tour through any historical site is a selective, political process which makes certain people, places, and perspectives appear legitimate while rendering others invisible (Buzinde, 2007; Eichstedt and Small, 2002). Tour guides or docents are extraordinarily important to the politics of retelling the past in selective and emotionally evocative ways.

Traditional studies tend to view tour guides in monolithic and categorical terms, emphasizing the extent to which they serve as mere 'mediators' of the tourist experience. More recent studies focus on the agency and cultural politics of tour guides, how they participate in the social construction of destinations, and actively shape the meanings that tourists read and interpret from historic sites (Dahles, 2002; MacDonald, 2006). In developing this theme further, we focus on how guides operate as 'creators' of historical empathy. The concept of historical empathy recognizes that a full understanding of the past requires people to adopt, cognitively, a perspective different from their own and to establish an emotional connection with historical actors from different eras and walks of life. In the words of Barton and Levstik (2004: 207–8), historical empathy 'invites us to care with and about people in the past, to be concerned with what happened to them and how they experienced their lives'.

Plantation house museums in the Southern US are places where the political and emotional stakes of tour guiding are particularly high, especially in terms of the depiction of the history of slavery. A growing number of scholars have addressed the controversies that surround the portrayal of the enslaved at historic sites and museums (Alderman, 2010; Butler, 2001; Buzinde, 2007; Buzinde and Santos, 2008, 2009; Handler and Gable, 1997; Hanna, 2008; Modlin, 2008). Tourism plantations across the South often ignore or marginalize the story of slavery while valorizing the accomplishments and possessions of the planter class, thus carrying out a 'symbolic annihilation' of the history and identity of enslaved Africans and African–Americans (Eichstedt and Small, 2002: 105). While this annihilation is carried out through many channels, tour guides play an especially influential role. Traditionally, tours at most plantation house museums present vivid, detailed accounts of the lives of members of planter families while reducing enslaved people—whose presence made the master/planter's lifestyle possible—to stock characters who receive less attention than the furniture and china owned by the master. These representational inequalities, 'not only annihilate the histories of marginalized groups from the official heritage narrative but also foster feelings of disinheritance and exasperate historical and contemporary issues of racism' (Buzinde and Santos, 2008: 484).

The disinheritance of Africans and African–Americans from Southern plantation history has not gone unchallenged, however. Not all tourists acquiesce to this traditionally dominant reading of the plantation. Some tourists fall into what Buzinde and Santos (2009) call an 'oppositional interpretive community' that views the plantation much more in terms of racial politics. Some African–Americans actively seek to reclaim their plantation heritage (Redford, 1988), producing counter-narratives that bring the slave struggle front and center within the re-telling of the Old South (Hoelscher, 2003). Some site managers and docents have responded by incorporating slavery into their representations of the past (Butler et al., 2008; Litvin and Brewer, 2008). Academicians have contributed their research to document and challenge the marginalization of the enslaved at historic sites (for example, Loewen, 2000). It is out of this intellectual and political context that we write this paper.

Previous analyses of the representation of slavery in plantation tourism tended to document the number of times that the enslaved are mentioned (or not) on docent-led tours and marketing materials (Alderman and Modlin, 2008; Butler, 2001; Eichstedt and Small, 2002; Modlin, 2008). Our many onsite observations of plantation house museum tours over 5 years convince us that increasing the number of references to slave life on tours is an important *first* step in developing a more socially responsible discourse at plantation sites. However, we have also observed that even some of the most conscientious docents fail to move the dialogue beyond making factual descriptions of enslavement or simply referencing the aggregate number of slaves owned by a particular planter/master, thus perpetuating an 'inventory discourse' that continues to view the enslaved as mere property rather than human beings. These factual mentions of slavery certainly represent an improvement over traditional representations of plantation life, but do not necessarily help tourists empathize or identify with the enslaved community.

The lack of historical empathy created for the enslaved lies in contrast to the way in which many guides work to make the lives of the planter family come alive for tourists, offering dramatic accounts of the family's losses, pains, power, and wealth.

At some sites, docents might ask tourists to imagine briefly some aspect of slavery, but such emotive adventures are often little more than short detours from what remains a 'white-centric' representation of the plantation (Eichstedt and Small, 2002: 4). The uneven way in which tourists are encouraged to invest emotionally in the planter versus the enslaved is what we call *affective inequality*. As creators of historical empathy, tour guides play a major role in not only reaffirming but also potentially challenging this affective inequality. Indeed, we have found instances of some guides creating highly emotional moments for tourists to learn about enslavement (Alderman and Campbell, 2008). Bringing about broader change requires understanding, more fully, the role that empathetic engagement between guide and tourists plays in shaping representations of slavery at plantation house museums.

In this paper, we define tours of plantation house museums as emotive journeys and focus on the empathy-producing capacity of tour guides. Our purpose is to engage the concept of affective inequality, how it contributes to the marginalization of the history of the enslaved, and how it becomes reproduced within the practices of docents at Southern plantation house museums. In exploring the representational practices of tour guides, it is important to pay attention not only to how they tell emotionally evocative stories about certain people from the past, but also how they arrange or configure these historical narratives within the historical spaces of the plantation. The practice of retelling the past happens in and through places and landscapes, and space represents an important medium for storytelling rather than simply a backdrop for history (Azaryahu and Foote, 2008). As we illustrate through a retracing of docent-led tours at Destrehan Plantation in Louisiana, guides create affective spatial–historical storylines by anchoring certain narrative themes in particular spaces and through the sequential ordering of spaces and stories within the tour. First, we present a background discussion of the political agency of tour guides and the role of emotion and affect at historical museum sites.

Creating Empathy, Creating Inequality: The Politics of Tour Guiding

Much research has been written on the function and role of tour guides. Some of this research addresses tour guide practices in terms of competence, quality assurance, training, and the optimization of service and product delivery (Black and Weiler, 2005; Curtin, 2010; Huang and Wang, 2007; Mason and Christie, 2003). While these aspects are important, our interest in this paper is on the larger social and cultural dimensions of the docent–tourist relationship and how bodily and verbal performances of guides work to 'sacralize' or transform an unassuming site of history into a socially important historical sight (Fine and Speer, 1985).

Ap and Wong (2001: 551) describe tour guides as the 'essential interface' between tourists and destinations. Dahles (2002: 783) agrees, saying 'tour guiding constitutes a strategic factor in the representation of a destination area'. Tourists certainly can form their own independent impressions of destinations (Banyai, 2010), but guides exert great influence on tourist interpretation and experience of place (Baum et al., 2007). Tour guides act as 'gatekeepers of the destination, not only to provide interesting information and an enjoyable experience but also a physical and cultural familiarity with destinations. They can recommend to tourists what to see, control what is supposed to be seen, and what the destination does not want them to see' (Nelson, 2003: 114). To categorize the role of guides in tourism, Cohen (1985) establishes a tour-guide typology of pathfinders and mentors. The pathfinder guide 'provides privileged access to an otherwise non-public territory' and the mentor guide is more active in the 'mediation' and 'cultural brokerage' of the tourism experience (Cohen, 1985: 10).

Ap and Wong (2001: 557) find this split between pathfinding and mentoring lacking. To them, tour guiding is 'more complex than the usually accepted and straightforward roles of being "information giver", "environmental interpreter", or "cultural broker", as described by the literature'. The pathfinder–mentor dichotomy is also questionable in light of the post-modern tourist experience, in which tour guides are expected 'to bring something extra, something that the visitors cannot get through any other media' (McGrath, 2003: 16). With this typological rethinking, research is expanding to look at additional roles fulfilled by tour guides. Cohen et al. (2002) explore the tour guide as an ethical and moral leader, or *Madrich,* in religious pilgrimages. Reed (2002) emphasizes the importance of storytelling as an essential skill for tour guides, for they are able to present the 'personality' of both place and subject through the use of narratives. Salazar (2005: 642) focuses on guides as agents of 'glocalization' and 'the way they (re)present and actively (re)construct local culture for a diversified global audience'.

Dahles (2002) argues that the traditional conceptualization of tour guides as cultural mediators does not capture the extent to which they function as political actors. By examining government control of place images presented by tour guides in Indonesia, where 'decisions regarding the "true" story or the "most appropriate" interpretation are subject to relations of power and dependence', she highlights how guides work to maintain cultural images supported by an authoritarian state and hence assist in the nationalistic scripting of place and history (Dahles, 2002: 797). While Dahles' work is important in pushing us to realize the larger politics of tour guiding, it emphasizes only the standardization and governmental control of guides as they engage in historical representation, and therefore fails to fully acknowledge their agency. In fact, training and certification do not ensure consistency, especially when the tour narrative falls outside of the certification process as it often does at plantation house museums. As Hanna et al. (2004) indicate, docents improvise as they recite a previously established tourist narrative, drawing from their own background and experiences. In these instances, guides function as 'creative storytellers' who sometimes question and challenge popular discourses about people, places, and the past (Salazar, 2006: 833). As Salazar (2006: 848) observes, tour guide narratives 'are not closed or rigid systems, but rather open systems that are always put at risk by what happens in actual encounters [with tourists]'.

MacDonald (2006) does not support abandoning the 'mediator' metaphor, but recognizes how the encoding of meaning through tour guiding is a negotiated and contested process. According to her, tour guides do exercise agency, 'positioning' themselves in relation to the official narrative, the organization or industry for which they work, and the wider social and political context of tourism. This agency includes both how they deal with the 'social dynamics of the tour group' and also the 'materiality of the [tourism] site', controlling the 'place and space of the tour itself' and actively managing the meanings that tourists read and interpret from sites (MacDonald, 2006: 119–24). Hanna et al. (2004: 476) argue that tour guides are crucial in constructing historical narratives and directing 'the tourists' collective gaze at particular buildings and memorials'. We would add that guides are also important in directing the collective gaze of tourists toward particular people from the past, thus shaping who—and not just what—is commemorated. Docents are active participants in a 'reputational politics' in which the meaning and legacy of historical figures—rather than being fixed historical facts—are open to social control (Alderman, 2002).

Bruner (2005) contends that tour guides are influential stakeholders in struggles to define and 'enact' the historical and cultural meaning of people and places, even to the point that they may subvert the assertions of professional historians and compete with other stakeholders over historical narration. Handler and Gable (1997) consider the struggles of guides to incorporate the history of African–Americans into tours of colonial Williamsburg. They saw a tension between African–American docents and white docents, who, unlike their black counterparts, tend to avoid talking about the topic of miscegenation and the sexual exploitation of slaves by masters. This reluctance to discuss occurred even though there is no dispute among historians that such sexual relations happened among planter and slave and the public appeared to yearn to hear about these relations, according to Handler and Gable.

Remembering the past can be a highly politicized and racialized process (Hoelscher, 2003; Regis, 2001) in which docents are active participants. Through the representational and performative activities of guides, museums, and other heritage tourism sites work to remind the public that certain pasts should be remembered and by extension, that certain pasts should be forgotten. Underlying the tensions between docents in Williamsburg was a conflict over facts, with white guides arguing that there is not enough archival documentation to discuss sensitive topics, such as miscegenation (Handler and Gable, 1997). This echoes what we heard at many plantations when docents tell us that they would be willing to include more information about slavery, if they only knew more about the lives of the enslaved. However, we also observed during field research that a lack of documentation does not keep guides on tour from engaging in historical conjecture about details of the planter-class family.

It is misguided to think of museums as simply sites designed to disseminate information and tour guiding as merely a recitation of facts. Katriel (1993: 70) characterizes heritage museums as 'arenas for ideological assertion'. As performers of these ideologies, tour guides make claims to narrative and cultural authority over the past and its interpretation. Museums assert certain ways of thinking and knowing the past and reinforce particular community identities through ordering knowledge in ways that naturalize particular worldviews. Focusing merely on the presentation of knowledge by the museum misses how it naturalizes these worldviews (Anderson and Smith, 2001). While docents certainly bring legitimacy to certain interpretations of history by choosing to narrate certain things and not others, they also exercise agency through the manner and style in which they talk about, perform, and represent the past. As Iles (2008) suggests, tourists, particularly those who visit places with highly charged memories of suffering, want more than to sightsee. They desire 'to identify and empathize' and it is the job of tour guides to 'capture their clients' emotional engagement with the area' in addition to providing them with 'comprehensive accounts of the history' (Iles, 2008: 151).

Remembering the past at historic museums is often an emotive, even affective, process because museums are spaces of emotion as well as information (Tyson, 2008). Docents shape people's moods and feelings about the past, directing tourists in deciding what and who from the past should receive emotional investment, which directly shapes how tourists think about and value certain historical events, people, and places. Issues of emotion are most obvious when museums and their guides engage with controversial subjects.

What concerns us are not only emotions at the historic site, but also the actions called for, and resulting from, the emotional journey through the site. Associated with emotion, we follow the understanding of 'affect' proposed by geographer Nigel Thrift (2004: 60), who maintains that affect is more than emotion, without being separated from emotion, that is, 'emotion in motion both literally and figuratively'. Affect could be considered as emotion packaged with action—actuated, and potential. We do not attempt to cleave emotion apart from its resulting action, as such a division can unnecessarily distance a call for an emotive reaction and the expression of that reaction, and thus potentially open up a space for an oversimplification of the emotion-laden responses a person might have (Thrift, 2004). For example, a sad story told by a docent might immediately elicit tears, but changing the listener's mood for the day is also an affective response, as is changing—or possibly changing—the way the audience feels about the person of whom the tale is expressed.

In thinking about the power of stories told on tours to elicit feelings and affect, it is worth considering how the agency of tour guides lies in their ability to create historical empathy among tourists. While historical empathy is a concept identified with the pedagogical literature, the application to tourism appears appropriate given the stated educational mission of museums and other historic sites. A lively debate exists among history educators about the exact definition and nature of historical empathy (Brooks, 2009). The term is defined, on one hand, in terms of people developing an historical understanding by taking on the perspectives of people from the past through a close non-emotional, non-sympathetic engagement with historical evidence (for example, Foster, 1999). The emphasis here is on empathy merely as a cognitive act. On the other hand, other scholars argue for a conception of historical empathy that also includes an affective component, not mutually exclusive from the cognitive reconstruction of historical perspectives and experiences (Barton and Levstik, 2004; Endacott, 2010).

The development of historical empathy by docents can be done unevenly and potentially unfairly, hence our use of the word 'affective inequality'. Our interest in unevenly developed historical empathy focuses on the representational environment that tour guides create and how this environment, beyond what it may say about the past on a factual level, favors the affective portrayal of certain individuals and communities from the past over others. Guides at Southern plantation house museums tend to celebrate the planter lifestyle in emotionally evocative ways that aggrandize the reputation of the master over other people and themes. The presence of such affective inequality has the dangerous potential to reaffirm the marginality of the enslaved—reducing them to a lifeless historical fact of the plantation if they are mentioned at all. To challenge this affective inequality in the representation of the enslaved requires understanding how such inequality is constructed and normalized within and through the geography of specific plantation sites. Space constitutes and shapes the meaning and politics of public memory (Dwyer and Alderman, 2008). There is growing recognition of the emotional intersections between people and places, both within and outside the study of tourism (Davidson et al., 2005). The rest of this article presents a case study that advances our understanding of how tour guides use the stories and spaces of the plantation to emotionally engage the tourist in socially uneven ways.

A Tour Through Destrehan: Ordering Space to Compel Historic Empathy

Destrehan Plantation is a former indigo and sugar plantation 25 miles west of New Orleans, Louisiana, in St. Charles Parish along the Mississippi River Road (Highway 48), a scenic route with several prominent 18th and 19th century antebellum plantations that host visitors. Listed on the National Register of Historic Places, Destrehan Plantation was established in 1787 and once covered 6000 acres. Private ownership of Destrehan ended in 1910 when it was bought by a series of industrial owners. In 1971, the River Road Historical Society, a not-for-profit organization, received the main plantation house as a donation (Cizek et al., 2008). At the time of writing this article, Destrehan was accessible to tourists daily for US$15 per adult visitor.

Based on our fieldwork at more than 100 plantations across the South, Destrehan arguably presents more information about slavery than other plantation house museums (Modlin, 2008). Indeed, site managers recently collaborated with the New Orleans African American Museum and Tulane University to commemorate the 1811 River Road Slave Revolt. Although Destrehan's docents mention the enslaved more than guides at many museums we have toured, the primary focus remains the planter-class family who owned the site, the affective dimensions of their lives, and their connection to local, regional, and national history. Enslaved persons, while certainly a subject on the tour, tend to be dealt with through a mere recounting of facts.

For two years starting in 2008, we toured Destrehan Plantation on 12 different occasions, accompanying tour groups that averaged six to ten people, although one group did number as many as 30 tourists. The tour groups we accompanied were overwhelmingly comprised of white tourists with women only slightly outnumbering men. Most tourists arrived with others, usually family members. Each tour was approximately 50 minutes long and our observations are a selective summary of tours led by seven different docents—approximately half of the 15 guides who worked there over the study period. Docents did not appear to utilize a standard script, but they do receive ongoing training and some supplement tours with their own independent research. Guides presented tour narratives in their own words while maintaining a continuity of key points and themes across all tours, which suggest that there is an interpretive and performative fluidity in tours that could be used to portray the enslaved in more emotionally evocative terms. Yet, we did not find significant evidence of this at Destrehan.

On each tour, we conducted a non-intrusive form of participant observation in which we allowed our emotive gaze to be directed by the docent. Similar to Eichstedt and Small (2002), we did not ask questions about the enslaved, but sought to experience the tour as it would normally be presented. In terms of understanding how guides at Destrehan reproduce affective inequality and identification with the planter over the enslaved, it is important to understand that docents engage in evocative story telling. But stories alone do not necessarily create historical empathy among tourists. Tour guides ground their stories in the emotive meaning of certain rooms and certain artifacts found in those rooms. This material culture reminds visitors of the veracity of the docent's claims, thus becoming a tool in the politics of historical interpretation (Alderman and Campbell, 2008).

The rooms within which Destrehan's docents tell their stories are more than simply background settings. Rooms, furnishings, and artifacts, by virtue of how they are represented, become characters in the story and serve important ideological functions on the tour. Within some of these interpretive spaces tourists hear why the site and its past planter-class resident(s) are still important. In other spaces, visitors, particularly white, middle-class tourists, receive cues that they have things in common with the planter and his family. Some spaces within the plantation house, such as bedrooms, become especially poignant as docents provide tales of loneliness, uncertainty, and joy felt over courting or childbirth, and experiences of loss through the death of loved ones, particularly spouses and children. These stops on the tour arguably compel tourists to empathize with the planter-class family by drawing upon their own feelings, fears, and experiences.

In understanding more fully the affective practices of docents at Destrehan, it is important to recognize that tour stop locations and spatial order shape the interpretive and empathetic arc of docent narratives. A spatial narrative develops in which each storied room and artifact builds upon previous ones, building up to a crescendo of empathy for the planter family and then refocusing the attention of tourists back to larger themes beyond the house before ending the tour. In light of the importance of these spatial narratives, we feel it is important to reconstruct the historical and spatial chronology of the tour itself.

Destrehan Plantation's docent-led tours start with a seven-minute video on the history of the plantation and the people who lived there. This video focuses on the planter-class family who lived in the 'Big House'. After the video, a docent leads the tour group to the house and through it in a series of 18 interpretative stops.

The first three stops on the tour of Destrehan Plantation are exterior stops, which we categorize as 'public' because of the visibility or accessibility of these places to antebellum visitors of the plantation. At the first stop, guides feature the live oaks at the site, including one named after Azby, the grandson of Jean Noel Destrehan, the featured owner/master of the plantation. The second stop, by the rear corner of the main house, is in front of two single-story, two-room slave cabins, relocated to the site from another plantation. The tour does not include the cabin interiors, although docents encourage tourists to return and examine the cabins after the tour. We view the slave cabins as a sorely missed opportunity for docents to help tourists to empathize and connect with the lives of the enslaved.

A room in one cabin is an interpretive room reflecting what the interior of a slave cabin might have looked like. The other room in the same cabin displays an artist's rendition of the 1811 River Road Slave Revolt. While in front of the cabins, guides discuss Destrehan's plantation store, where slaves purchased their clothing and other items, 'at little or no profit to Mr. Destrehan, because of his generosity'. At the third stop, the opposite rear corner of the house, docents point out the wash-house and the re-created kitchen. Docents inform tourists that antebellum kitchens were located away from the main house because of extreme heat, smells, and the frequency of kitchen fires, which risked burning down the house. Although slave labor operated the kitchen, the risk of cooking is largely represented in relation to the planter family.

Next are the first of three rooms at Destrehan, which we define as 'verifying' spaces. These spaces build symbolic capital for docents by verifying the importance of stories shared about the property and the planter-class family through the presentation of unique, even extraordinary, artifacts. In the fourth stop, called the Jefferson

Room, tourists see copies of treaties, portraits, and maps on the walls, which together with the tour guides' dialogue, connect Jean Noel Destrehan to Louisianan, US, and international history. The focal point of the room is the 1804 Jefferson Document with its signatures of President Jefferson and then-Secretary of State James Madison. The Jefferson document occupies a special, protective case. The document announced the appointment of Destrehan and three other prominent Louisianan men to handle matters related to the transition of Louisiana into the US.

The next three stops are in 'semi-private' spaces—where certain people were allowed access under particular circumstances. For antebellum visitors, a degree of intimacy with the family was implied by access into these spaces. Occasional connections between the family and larger historical themes are made in these spaces, but they actually serve as places to shift emotive attention toward planter-class individuals who lived in the house and to help tourists identify with these figures. Docents discuss architecture and possessions, particularly the furniture, making the material culture of the house the focus of these spaces. The fifth stop, the warming kitchen, located on the bottom floor of the upriver garçonnière, was used for preparing food that did not need to be cooked. Docents contrast it with the main kitchen in the back yard.

Stop six is the pantry inside the main house. Here tourists see a mannequin representing an enslaved Creole named Marguarite. Each tour guide explains that Creole meant 'born in the New World from parents who were born in Europe or Africa'. Two of the docents who led our tours suggest that Marguarite's husband was sold, thus separating the couple. A few guides say that some of her children lived through the Civil War and received their freedom. After this brief connection to larger themes of Creolization and slavery, docents shift quickly to talking about a plate warmer and a tea safe in the room, thus missing another opportunity for tourists to learn more about the enslaved and invest emotionally. The plate warmer was used to warm up plates with food from the exterior kitchen before being served in the dining room. This item is often compared with a microwave. Dried blocks of tea—a luxury in the colonial and antebellum periods—are used to discuss how the packaging of tea has changed compared with what is found in tourists' kitchens. Docents use items like these to encourage tourists to make connections or comparisons with the planter-class family who owned these items. Through this discussion, tourists are told that the planter class is similar to them—at least in some ways. Sadly, the story of Marguarite never really moves her representation beyond that of a mannequin. She has a place in the plantation, but not in the same animated and humanized ways as the Destrehan family.

The seventh stop, the storage room, is not made by all tour guides. Docents who stop here explain the architectural features of the room, which kept goods cool. Three of the guides who directed our tours reflected upon slavery in Southern Louisiana, stressing factors that made it unique compared with other parts of the US, particularly during the early 19th century. Having this moment to reflect on slavery is important, but is more of an intellectual reflection on the institution of slavery rather than an emotive reflection on slave life at Destrehan.

Stops eight and nine—the dining room and the formal entry—are public spaces because docents interpret these spaces as where formal guests were welcomed. In the dining room, tour guides tell tourists that the main meal of the day for the planter-class family started about 2 pm and often lasted for two hours. Visitors handling business at Destrehan were invited to eat at the table. Multiple tablecloths were used, which indicated the wealth of the owner and how many courses were being served. The final course, dessert, was eaten on the uncovered table to indicate the meal's conclusion. Children were fed separately in the pantry. Women and teen-age girls could not leave the table until the entire meal ended, though men could get up between courses. At the ninth stop, tourists learn about the renovation of the house in the 1830s, which enclosed the back porch, added two lavish interior stair-cases, and inadvertently disrupted the flow of air through the main (second) floor of the house. In both of these spaces, tourists received explicit direction to imagine themselves as antebellum visitors to Destrehan. Most docents use second-person reference, saying such things as, 'if you visited, this would be the door you would come in', while pointing to the door at the ninth stop. The irony of this empathy-producing exercise is that African–American visitors would not have entered the house at this location in the 1800s and docents never ask tour groups to imagine their place in the house if they had been enslaved.

The second verifying space, the tenth stop, is an upstairs room with unfinished walls so tourists see what the house looks like under the plaster. Docents note indentions from the thumbs of enslaved workers who put mud filling between the posts in the walls—called bousillage-entre-poteaux. A clear plastic-covered open-ing in the ceiling reveals carpentry details in the attic. There is an acknowledgment of enslaved labor, but not the kind of engaged discussion that would help tourists identify with that labor in affective ways. Rather, this room is used to reaffirm to tourists that those who historically lived in Louisiana were uniquely American—applying American ingenuity in a uniquely Louisianan way, the emphasis being on the architect rather than the laborer. Thus, it reinforces the remarks of the docents about the uniqueness of the Creole Destrehans, as well as the uniqueness of the expression of institutions, including slavery, at Destrehan Plantation. Off this room is a cabinet room, interpreted as a temporary office for the Freedman's Bureau, of which little is usually said. This represents a lost opportunity to connect visitors, in an affective way, to what freedom would have meant to the enslaved.

The women's parlor, the eleventh stop, is a semi-private space. Docents used semi-private rooms nearest the bedrooms to mention details about the family, using these spaces to transition toward private areas of the house. In this parlor, tourists see Eliza Destrehan's portrait on the wall. She outlived three husbands. Some guides note that in the portrait, Eliza wears three wedding bands to reflect her love for each of her deceased husbands. In this room, tourists are also shown a 'courting' candlestick holder with an unlit candle. Tour guides inform the group that the father decided whom the daughter married. When men called to visit the daughter, the father lit the candle and adjusted the height of the candle in the holder to indicate how long a suitor could stay. The suitor was expected to leave once the candle reached the top of the candleholder's metal wire. Docents explain that the more candle above the wire when the candle was lit, the more favored the suitor was to the young woman's father.

The room of the twelfth stop is the first room on the tour that we categorize as private space. Viewing the bedroom as a private, intimate, often gendered, space emerged among the middle class, out of Victorian sensibilities (Gan, 2009). In these spaces, guests hear tales of childbirth, sickness, loneliness, and death as well as allusions to conjugal activity. In private spaces, docents encourage intimacy with the planter-class family. Docents rarely say anything about the enslaved in these spaces even though it is likely that slaves were in and out of these rooms serving the planter family. Stop twelve is the bedroom of Lydia Rost, daughter of Louise and Pierre Rost and granddaughter of Jean Noel Destrehan. A portrait of 14-year-old Lydia is on the wall above the fireplace while her bed with a canopy and a mosquito net is in one corner. After discussing the bed, docents inform tourists that Lydia died three years after the painting was completed, which usually evokes an emotional response from visitors. In 1853, Lydia and thousands of others died in the worst yellow fever outbreak to hit the area. Docents tell tourists that after Lydia's death, the father would not allow the priest to return to attend to her younger brother, Henri's spiritual needs. Evidently, the parents worried that seeing the priest would scare Henri as he was ill with yellow fever too. Henri died two weeks after his sister. After allowing some somber moments', docents turn their attention to a 1200-pound marble tub in a second cabinet off of Lydia's room, illustrating how artifacts are used to relieve as well as build up emotional drama on the tour.

Stop thirteen is interpreted as the planter's wife's bedroom. This room together with Lydia's bedroom served as the area for young children to sleep near their mother. According to docents, the planter (who slept in the room that is the fifteenth stop) made appointments to visit his wife's room for conjugal purposes. Guides mention that the bed in the wife's room was constructed by a local, free African–American furniture maker. However, docent narratives quickly turn to involved explanations of how making the bed was done first thing in the morning because women were viewed as lazy if they returned to the bed later in the day, unless they were very sick.

The fourteenth stop is the men's parlor, a semi-private space. This room is also a site where docents mention black workmanship but in a rather limited, factual way. Guides point to a desk built by a slave at Destrehan. Yet, most of the docent's empathy-producing narrative revolves around the social function of parlors. After formal dinners, men and women moved to their respective parlors—spaces divided by pocket doors that, once retracted, turn the two rooms into one. Once opened, this larger room is, at least theoretically, open to both men and women, though the only example given of this occurring are the aforementioned visits by prospective sons-in-law who visited the daughter in the women's parlor, while under the watchful eyes of the father sitting in the men's parlor. What visitor cannot relate to the struggles of courting and prying eyes of parents? Thus the parlor narrative becomes an empathy-producing moment on the tour.

Stop fifteen is in the planter's bedroom, a private space. In this room, docents share the story of Azby Destrehan. His father, Nicholas, was afraid Azby would contract yellow fever in Louisiana and die so he sent Azby to school out of state, forbidding him from returning to Louisiana until he was 21 years old. Ironically, Azby died from smallpox in Europe while his wife was pregnant with their only child, a daughter. The interpretative value of this room and other private spaces cannot be underplayed in terms of creating a powerfully evocative image of the planter and his family. The degree to which docents cover so many intimate details about the living spaces of the master/planter class stands in stark contrast to the lack of attention that life in slave cabins received earlier in the tour.

The final three stops are public spaces, visible to antebellum visitors. These stops, all on the upper porch, are outside the planter's bedroom (sixteen), downriver garçonnière (seventeen) and overlooking the backyard (eighteen). Docents use these exterior areas, in their spatial narrative, to move the visitor away from the detailed, compelling personal histories of the planter family and discuss the larger context of Destrehan, acknowledging the many buildings no longer present on the plantation, the importance of the Mississippi River as an antebellum transportation route, and reminding visitors of the demonstrations going on that day behind the main house. A rotating set of free demonstrations, including hearth cooking, African medicinal plants, and bousillage-entre-poteaux, are held six days a week. These demonstrations could help tourists identify with enslaved life and labor, but participation in them is up to the visitors after the tour and not docent-initiated. In effect, these demonstrations—like the slave cabins—are not part of the spatial narratives created by guides, which works to reproduce an affective inequality at Destrehan while also tending to segregate the discussion of slavery from the main house.

Conclusion

Many plantation house museums fail to acknowledge that historically, the Southern plantation was an economic enterprise with the control and exploitation of slave labor at its heart. Nevertheless, a growing number of plantation house museums, including Destrehan Plantation, recognize their responsibility to discuss slavery. Our discussions with docents at Destrehan indicate that some have done research about slavery beyond their initial training and they genuinely wish to give accurate, factual information on their tours. In doing so, these guides take an important step toward coming to terms with and publicly remembering the enslaved.

However, tours through plantation house museums are more than mere factual adventures; these journeys are emotional, indeed, affective. The process of remembering means coming to terms with more than facts. Inequality can exist on tours even at sites that are committed to more fully addressing the historical facts of slavery. This inequality is not just about whether docents talk about the planter-class more than the enslaved, but also the unevenness in how tourists are encouraged to connect with these historical groups emotionally. The stakes of this inequality are high. Tourists are encouraged by docents to empathize with the planter-class family who lived in the 'Big House', which communicates clear ideas about whose lives really mattered at plantations. Planter-class family members made up only a small part of the population that lived on the plantation. While their lives might have been difficult, the focus placed on the extreme moments of their lives further marginalizes the everyday lived moments of enslaved individuals. In the end, the constant, poignant struggles of the enslaved are lost. Forgotten is the tremendous daily burden of living under a violent system, weighted down with thoughts that subjection to this coercive system was an inheritance parents passed to their children. Stories such as Louise and Pierre Rost's loss of their children to yellow fever are presented absent of stories of the same loss that some enslaved parents at the same plantation might have experienced—and we can be assured that many enslaved children were among the thousands of Louisianans who died from yellow fever in the 19th century. Forgotten too are the thousands of 'social deaths' of slavery (Patterson, 1982). The exercise of power by slaveholders over enslaved individuals, such as selling someone and forcing them to live elsewhere, effectively killed—socially—the enslaved. Just the possibility of such a separation made each potentially joyful birth of an enslaved baby an ambivalent moment for the parents. Despite the very real dangers ever-present for any newborn, this potentiality had no equal among planter-class families.

Moving beyond a focus on mere fact when we consider slavery opens up new possibilities for these museums. In concluding their article, Buzinde and Santos (2009: 456) mention that researchers of plantation house museums should consider how these sites can potentially present 'healing and holistic messages'. This requires representing the plantation house as more than just a site of ownership, which tends to be white-centric. The plantation was also a lived space from which the enslaved drew identity and life even if they did not own it. Such a perspective necessitates a fuller, more empathetic presentation of the stories and spaces associated with the slave community. The importance of space cannot be overlooked since the narrative meanings attached to places and the order in which they are toured shape the tourist experience and the ability to create affective connections with people from the past.

As we consider how to combat the affective inequality taking place at Southern plantation house museums, future work might focus on historic sites with tour guides that have been successful in helping tourists identify and empathize with the enslaved. Studying the representational strategies and spatial–historical narratives that these guides employ could be instructive for site managers and docents at other plantations. A noteworthy example of such a guide is Kitty Wilson-Evans, a former slave interpreter and storyteller at Historic Brattonsville in McConnells, South Carolina. She retired in 2010 after 16 years of service, much of it as a volunteer. Wilson-Evans was widely acknowledged for her powerful portrayals of the struggles and contributions of the enslaved through her re-enactment of an 18th century slave named Kessie, to the point of bringing some visitors to tears (Bates, 2005). Creating such highly charged emotions is not simply about creating better entertainment for tourists, but taking them to an affective place where the struggles of the enslaved can be more fully realized and understood. As Ira Berlin (2004) argues, remembering slavery in emotive ways is necessary to achieving social justice not only for African–Americans in the past, but also in the present.

The performative activities at Brattonsville also prompt us to consider another aspect of the affective impact of plantation tours—the issue of gender. Finding women docents leading plantation tours is rather common, although finding an African–American female docent such as Wilson-Evans is unusual, which undoubtedly contributes to the emotive gravity she is able to bring to the story of the enslaved. As Taft (2010) finds, the representation of race and gender at plantation museums can take on complex forms that give voice to certain men while marginalizing women in addition to African–Americans. We have no doubt that gender is an important variable in shaping how docents present information about the plantation and the tactics they use to create affective empathy. Of the seven docents who guided our tours of Destrehan, all were white, and all were female except one. We saw clear evidence of a gendering of certain rooms of the plantation in terms of what stories and artifacts docents used to help visitors identify with the planter family. The identity of tourists is perhaps also a key factor in shaping the historic portrayals communicated to them by guides. As Eichstedt and Small (2002: 20) observe in their major study of Southern plantation house museums, docents generally assumed that white female visitors would be 'interested in decorative arts produced by white women', while white male visitors would be 'interested in the maps and firearms' used by the planter/master. The gendered and racialized assumptions, which perhaps reflect the proclivities of the guide as much as they do the visitor, represent a significant barrier to telling a more emotionally compelling story of the enslaved. In reality, some white tourists have shown interest 'in the slave experience as compared to hearing about other, more established plantation narratives' (Butler et al., 2008: 296). Nevertheless, future work on the affective dimensions of Southern plantation house museum tours needs to take on the task of measuring visitor responses and emotive bonds, thus providing more specific empirical evidence about the degree and nature of historical empathy created by docents.

Note

We wish to thank the two anonymous reviewers of this paper for their helpful comments and suggestions, and the employees of Destrehan Plantation for allowing us access to the site for participant observation. This paper was supported, in part, by the Center for Sustainable Tourism and the Department of Geography at East Carolina University and the Department of Geography and Anthropology at Louisiana State University. The paper was produced in affiliation with the multi-university and inter-disciplinary Race, Ethnicity, and Social Equity in Tourism (RESET) Initiative (www. tourismreset. org).

References

Alderman, D. H. (2010). 'Surrogation and the Politics of Remembering Slavery in Savannah, Georgia', *Journal of Historical Geography* 36(1): 90–101.

Alderman, D. H. (2002). 'Street Names as Memorial Arenas: The Reputational Politics of Commemorating Martin Luther King, Jr. in a Georgia County', *Historical Geography* 30: 99–120.

Alderman, D. H., and Campbell, R. (2008). 'Symbolic Excavation and the Artifact Politics of Remembering Slavery in the American South: Observations from Walterboro, South Carolina', *Southeastern Geographer* 48(3): 338–55.

Alderman, D. H., and Modlin Jr., E. A. (2008). '(In) visibility of the Enslaved within Online Plantation Tourism Marketing: A Textual Analysis of North Carolina Websites', *Journal of Travel and Tourism Marketing* 25(3/4): 265–81.

Anderson, K., and Smith, S. (2001). 'Editorial: Emotional Geographies', *Transactions of the Institute of British Geographers* 26(1): 7–10.

Ap, J., and Wong, K. F. (2001). 'Case Study on Tour Guiding: Professionalism, Issues and Problems', *Tourism Management* 22: 551–63.

Azaryahu, M., and Foote, K. E. (2008). 'Historical Space as Narrative Medium: On the Configuration of Spatial Narratives of Time at Historical Sites', *GeoJournal* 73(3): 179–94.

Banyai, M. (2010). 'Dracula's Image in Tourism: Western Bloggers versus Tour Guides', *European Journal of Tourism Research* 3(1): 5–22.

Barton, K. C., and Levstik, L. S. (2004). *Teaching History for the Common Good*. Mahwah: Lawrence Erlbaum.

Bates, K. G. (2005). *Toll, Rewards of Playing a Slave at Brattonsville*. (Available at www.npr. org/templates/transcript/transcript.php?storyId=4992408.) Accessed 15 June 2010.

Baum, T., Heams, N., and Devine, F. (2007). 'Place, People, and Interpretation: Issues of Migrant Labor and Tourism Imagery in Ireland', *Tourism Recreation Research* 32(3): 39–48.

Berlin, I. (2004). 'American Slavery in History and Memory and the Search for Social Justice', *Journal of American History.* 90(4): 12 51–68.

Black, R., and Weiler, B. (2005). 'Quality Assurance and Regulatory Mechanism in the Tour Guiding Industry: A Systematic Review', *Journal of Tourism Studies* 16(1): 24–37.

Brooks, S. (2009). 'Historical Empathy in the Social Studies Classroom: A Review of the Literature', *Journal of Social Studies Research* 33(2): 213–34.

Bruner, E. M. (2005). *Culture on Tour: Ethnographies of Travel.* Chicago: University of Chicago.

Butler, D. L. (2001). 'Whitewashing Plantations: The Commodification of a Slave-free Antebellum South', *International Journal of Hospitality and Tourism Administration* 2(3/4): 163–75.

Butler, D. L., Carter, P. L., and Dwyer, O. J. (2008). 'Imagining Plantations: Slavery, Dominant Narratives, and the Foreign Born', *Southeastern Geographer* 48(3): 288–302.

Buzinde, C. N. (2007). 'Representational Politics of Plantation Heritage Tourism: The Contemporary Plantation as a Social Imaginary', (pp. 229–52) in McCarthy, C., Filmer, A. A., Giardina, M. D., and Malagreca, M. (eds). *Globalizing Cultural Studies: Ethnographic Interventions in Theory, Method and Policy.* New York: Peter Lang.

Buzinde, C. N., and Santos, C. A. (2008). 'Representations of Slavery, *Annals of Tourism Research* 35(2): 469–88.

Buzinde, C. N., and Santos, C. A. (2009). 'Interpreting Slavery Tourism Representations', *Annals of Tourism Research* 36(3): 439–58.

Cizek, E. D., Lawrence, J. H., and Sexton, R. (2008). *Destrehan: The Man, the House, the Legacy.* Destrehan: River Road Historical Society.

Cohen, E. (1985). 'The Tourist Guide: The Origins, Structures and Dynamics of a Role', *Annals of Tourism Research* 12(1): 5–29.

Cohen, E., Ifergan, M., and Cohen, E. (2002) 'A New Paradigm in Guiding: The Madrich as a Role Model', *Annals of Tourism Research* 29(4): 919–32.

Curtin, S. (2010). 'Managing the Wildlife Tourism Experience: The Importance of Tour Leaders', *International Journal of Tourism Research* 12(3): 219–36.

Dahles, H. (2002). 'The Politics of Tour Guiding: Image Management in Indonesia', *Annals of Tourism Research* 29(3): 783–800.

Davidson, J., Smith, M., and Bondi, L. (eds). (2005). *Emotional Geographies.* Burlington: Ashgate.

Dwyer, O. J., and Alderman, D. H. (2008). *Civil Rights Memorials and the Geography of Memory.* Athens: University of Georgia.

Eichstedt, J., and Small, S. (2002). *Representations of Slavery: Race and Ideology in Southern Plantation Museums.* Washington: Smithsonian.

Endacott, J. L. (2010). 'Reconsidering Affective Engagement in Historical Empathy', *Theory and Research in Social Education* 38(1): 6–47.

Fine, E. C., and Speer, J. H. (1985). 'Tour Guide Performances as Sight Sacralization', *Annals of Tourism Research* 12(1): 73–95.

Foster, S. (1999). 'Using Historical Empathy to Excite Students about the Study of History: Can you Empathize with Neville Chamberlain?' *The Social Studies* 90(1): 18–24.

Gan, W. (2009). 'Solitude and Community: Virginia Woolf, Spatial Privacy, and *A Room of One's Own*' *Literature and History* 18(1): 68–80.

Handler, R., and Gable, E. (1997). The New History in an Old Museum: Creating the Past at Colonial Williamsburg. Durham: Duke University.

Hanna, S. (2008). 'A Slavery Museum? Race, Memory, and Landscape in Fredericksburg, Virginia', *Southeastern Geographer* 48(3): 316–37.

Hanna, S., Del Casino Jr., V., Selden, C., and Hite, B. (2004). 'Representation as Work in "America's Most Historic City"', *Social and Cultural Geography* 5(3): 459–81.

Hoelscher, S. (2003). 'Making Place, Making Race: Performances of Whiteness in the Jim Crow South', *Annals of the Association of American Geographers* 93(3): 657–86.

Huang, R., and Wang, W. (2007). 'An Investigation of the Intercultural Competence of Tour Guides in Great Britain', *Acta Turistica* 19(2): 126–49.

Iles, J. (2008). 'Encounters in the Fields: Tourism to the Battlefields of the Western Front', *Journal of Tourism and Cultural Change* 6(2): 138–54.

Katriel, T. (1993). 'Our Future is Where Our Past Is; Studying Heritage Museums as Ideological Performative Arenas', *Communication Monographs* 60(1): 69–75.

Litvin, S. W., and Brewer, J. D. (2008). 'Charleston, South Carolina Tourism and the Presentation of Urban Slavery in an Historic Southern City', *International Journal of Hospitality and Tourism Administration* 9(1): 71–84.

Loewen, J. (2000). *Lies Across America: What Our Historic Sites Get Wrong*. New York: Touchstone.

MacDonald, S. (2006). 'Mediating Heritage: Tour Guides at the Former Nazi Party Rally Grounds, Nuremberg', *Tourist Studies* 6(2): 119–38.

McGrath, G. (2003). Myth, Magic, Meaning and Memory—Mentor Tour Guides as Central to Developing Integrated Heritage Tourism at Archaeological Sites in Cusco, Peru. *Proceedings of 12th International Tourism and Leisure Symposium, Barcelona*: 1–26.

Mason, P., and Christie, M. (2003). 'Tour Guides as Critically Reflective Practitioners: A Proposed Training Model', *Tourism Recreation Research* 28(1): 23–33.

Modlin Jr., E. A. (2008). Tales Told on the Tour: Mythic Representation of Slavery on Docent-Led Tours at North Carolina Plantation Museums', *Southeastern Geographer* 48(3): 265–87.

Nelson, V. (2003). 'Representation and Images of Ecotourism in Grenada', Unpublished Master's thesis, Greenville: East Carolina University.

Patterson, O. (1982). *Slavery and Social Death*. Cambridge: Harvard University.

Reed, A. (2002). 'City of Details: Interpreting the Personality of London', *Journal of Royal Anthropological Institute* 8(1): 127–41.

Regis, H. A. (2001). 'Blackness and the Politics of Memory in the New Orleans Second Line', *American Ethnologist* 28(4): 152–11.

Redford, D. S. (1988). *Somerset Homecoming. Recovering a Lost Heritage*. New York: Doubleday.

Salazar, N. (2005). 'Tourism and Glocalization: "Local" Tour Guiding', *Annals of Tourism Research* 32(3): 628–46.

Salazar, N. (2006). 'Touristifying Tanzania: Local Guides, Global Discourse', *Annals of Tourism Research* 33(3): 833–52.

Taft, K. E. (2010). 'Silent Voices: Searching for Women and African Americans at Historic Stagville and Somerset Place Historic Sites', Unpublished Master's thesis. Raleigh: North Carolina State University.

Thrift, N. (2004). 'Intensities of Feeling: Towards a Spatial Politics of Affect', *Geografiska Annaler. Series B, Human Geography* 86(1): 57–78.

Tyson, A. (2008). 'Crafting Emotional Comfort: Interpreting the Painful Past at Living History *Museums in the New Economy*', Museum and Society 6(3): 246–62.

West, P. (1999). Domesticating History: The Political Origins of America's House Museums. Washington: Smithsonian.

E. Arnold Modlin Jr. is a geography doctoral candidate at Louisiana State University. His dissertation research explores the roles tourists play in remembering slavery at plantation house museums. His previous published research considered the role of tour guides and museum management in creating and maintaining myths about the US Southern plantation past. *Address:* Department of Geography and Anthropology, Louisiana State University, 227 Howe-Russell Geoscience Complex, Baton Rouge, LA 70803, USA. [email: emodli2@lsu.edu]

Derek H. Alderman is Professor of Geography and a Research Fellow in the Center for Sustainable Tourism at East Carolina University. His research interests include the politics of public memory and heritage tourism in the American South, particularly the commemoration of the civil rights movement and the slave experience. He is the co-author (with

Owen Dwyer) of *Civil Rights Memorials and the Geography of Memory* (University of Georgia Press, 2008). *Address:* Department of Geography and Research Fellow, Center for Sustainable Tourism, 221-A Brewster, East Carolina University, Greenville, NC 27858, USA.
[email: aldermand@ecu.edu]

Glenn W. Gentry is Lecturer in Geography at State University of New York at Cortland. His research interests include the representation of dissonant heritages and memories through the bodily performances of people, having examined the role of sense of place and movement in ghost walk tourism in Savannah, Georgia, and the use of tattoos as memorials among survivors of Hurricane Katrina in New Orleans, Louisiana. *Address:* Department of Geography, State University of New York at Cortland, Old Main, Room 138, Cortland, NY 13045, USA.
[email: gwgentry@gmail.com]

Questions

1. What are the tensions between authenticity and entertainment in tourist performances?
2. What is the role of the tourist as an audience for cultural performances? Are there multiple roles?
3. Why is the distinction between "interpreter" and "actor" important? How does the tour guide/docent/interpreter participate in a process of historical adaptation?
4. Have you ever had an "intercultural moment," when you have miscommunicated or been misunderstood because of a difference in cultures? What did you do in that situation? What should be done in such circumstances?
5. Why is historical empathy important? How is it defined?

View

YouTube

"Civil War Re-enactment, Wade House, Wisconsin" (2008)
 "Colonial Williamsburg interpreter brings history to life" (2008)
"Mondo Black: Colonial Williamsburg" (2010)

Web

Colonial Williamsburg (colonialwilliamsburg.com)
Plimouth Plantation (www.plimouth.org)
Living history Farms (http://www.lhf.org/)
"The Black Watch of Canada Living History Association" (home.myfairpoint.net/paullev/)
"Actors, Interpreters Bring US Colonial Past Alive" (www.npr.org)

Film/Video

"Medieval Mayhem," *Dinner Impossible* (S03E03, 2008)

Read

Baker, James W. *Plimoth Plantation: Fifty Years of Living History*. Plymouth: Plimoth Plantation, 1997. Print.

Bridal, Tessa. *Exploring Museum Theatre*. Walnut Creek, CA: Altamira Press, 2004. Print.

Crosby, Olivia. "You're a What? Historic Interpreter." *Bureau of Labor Statistics*. 2003. PDF file.

Lamb, Jonathan. "Historical Re-Enactment, Extremity, and Passion." *The Eighteenth Century: Theory and Interpretation*. 49.3 (2008): 239–250. Print.

Manteuffel, Rachel. "Colonial in: The Complicated History of Colonial Williamsburg." *Washington Post*. 9 June 2011. Web. 14 June 2012.

Pavis, Patrice. "Introduction." *The Intercultural Performance Reader: London and New York: Routledge*, 1996. 1–21. Print.

Shatwell, Justin. "Two Mornings in April." *Yankee* 76.2 (2012): 72–81. Print.

Stupp, Jason. "Slavery and the Theatre of History: Ritual Performance on the Auction Block." *Theatre Journal* 63.1 (March 2011): 61–84. Print.

Culture as Entertainment

While the two previous essays focused on cultural entertainment designed to reinforce ideas of history and heritage, the essays that follow offer three varied perspectives on cultural performances defined by specific cultural identities. The idea of a stable identity—that the notion of "self" could be empirically defined—dissolved in the late twentieth century as theories of postmodernism began to take hold. Where cultural tourism is in many ways designed around master narratives that seek to offer universal truths, cultural performances of identity in the post-modern era acknowledge that identity is a process rather than a product, and that the self can be examined through performances that engage in ritual, that are bounded by a specific time and place dedicated to that exploratory performance—or a combination of the two. The following three essays offer varying and unique perspectives on the dynamic of culture and identity performance as entertainment.

Cultural Ritual as Popular Entertainment

In the first essay, "Day of the Dead in the U.S. Media: The Celebration Goes Mainstream," Marchi offers an example of how cultural ritual can become popular entertainment beyond the community the ritual was designed to serve. Here, ideas of adaptation move beyond text-based sources to those grounded in specific cultural phenomena, yet the process of adaptation is also engaged in the movement of rituals from one culture to another.

Ideas

Imagined communities
Agency
Multiculturalism
Demographic shift

Day of the Dead in the U.S. Media

The Celebration Goes Mainstream

By Regina Marchi

Ten years ago, says an elderly native of San Diego, "I saw just one article, one tiny little mention in the paper saying. 'Come see Day of the Dead.' Now you see feature articles in the newspapers, which ten, fifteen, or twenty years ago, you never saw. Nothing ever done to honor the Latino culture anywhere here in San Diego County, which is staggering, if you think about it, because we have lots of Latinos here and we're kissing the border."[1]

If the growth of Day of the Dead celebrations and their coverage in mainstream media is news to natives of California, where there has long been a large Mexican presence, it is even bigger news in areas of the United States that, until recently, have had few, if any, Latino residents. Newspaper articles about Day of the Dead were barely on the media radar in the 1970s, but the holiday today is routinely featured in the front pages of the metro, region, culture, arts, and calendar sections of mainstream newspapers across the country, usually accompanied by colorful photos.[2] As the following examples illustrate, the growing popularity of the celebration is itself a topic of headlines:

> Homage to the dead in Día de los Muertos draws thousands to Seattle Center—Maria Gonzalez, *Seattle Times*, November 2, 2003, Local News, B1.
>
> For a growing number of Atlantans: Navigating life requires honoring the dead—Yolanda Rodriguez, *Atlanta Journal-Constitution*, November 6, 2002. 1E.

> Celebration carries a legacy; Day of Dead marks launch of new pro-
> grams—*Grand Rapids Press,* [Michigan], November 2, 2005, City &
> Region, B4.
> Day of the Dead celebration is alive and well in Cleveland—Jesse Tinsley.
> *Cleveland Plain Dealer.* October 21, 2006, Metro, 3.
> Día de los Muertos is bustin' out all over the place—Eduardo Cuan, *San
> Diego Union Tribune*, October 28, 2004, Entertainment, 21.

Media coverage has not only popularized the celebration among the general
U.S. public, but has helped facilitate an imagined community of Latinos. In seeing
themselves and their communities depicted positively in the mainstream media,
commonly in the front pages of newspapers and magazines, many Latinos feel a
sense of cultural pride. Although Day of the Dead articles are not the only positive
stories written about Latinos, they represent a sizeable number of stories published
each fall. As we shall see, media coverage of Day of the Dead has helped teach about
this celebration, dispelling misunderstandings and legitimizing it in the eyes of potential funders, the general public, and Latinos themselves. This has contributed to
the growth of the celebration, to the point where it is fast becoming a new American
holiday, embraced by Latinos and non-Latinos alike. In fact, the mainstreaming of
Day of the Dead itself is a topic of news:

> "From San Francisco to Austin to New Orleans. 'The Day of the Dead' is
> becoming more and more widespread. It's not just something for Latinos
> anymore."—Anne-Marie O'Connor, Day of the Dead crosses borders, *Los
> Angles Times*, October 31, 1998, Metro, 1.
> "Day of the Dead has become an event whose meaning crosses ethnic and
> social boundaries … The first day of November marks a transborder hap-
> pening whose regional popularity rivals that of St. Patrick's Day."—John
> Carlos Villani. There's lot of life in Day of the Dead. *Arizona Republic*,
> October 29, 2000, A&E, 1.
> "The holiday was once a rare sight in New England, but will probably
> become routine for many here."—Raphael Lewis, Locals fete ancestors
> with Day of the Dead, *Boston Globe*, November 5, 2000, Metro, B5.

Widespread Media Attention

Media coverage of Day of the Dead comes in a variety of forms. There have been Día de los Muertos episodes on prime-time television shows such as PBS's *American Family* (2002 season) and the popular HBO series, *Six Feet Under* (2002 season) and *Carnivale* (2003 season). A recent John Sayles movie, *Silver City* (2004), included a Day of the Dead scene, and the Tim Burton Film *Corpse Bride* (2005) was filled with Day of the Dead imagery. Widely read travel publications such as the American Automobile Association's *Horizons* and *Westways* magazines and the *Elderhostel Annual Program* promote Day of the Dead excursions in New Mexico, Texas, and California, while lifestyle magazines such as *Better Homes and Gardens, Ladies' Home Journal, Parent, Travel and Leisure,* and *Holiday Celebrations* have featured articles on the holiday. The celebration is the subject of more than 28.6 million nonprofit, personal and commercial Internet Web sites geared toward an English-speaking audience. These Web sites serve "regulars" already familiar with the celebration (who simply want to download schedules or directions for events) as well as neophytes searching for information.[3] National news organizations such as the Associated Press, National Public Radio. *U.S. News and World Report*, the *New York Times*, and the *Washington Post*, as well as local TV stations and documentary filmmakers now provide regular coverage of the holiday.

During the "Muertos" season, which in the United States extends from late September through mid-November, a given newspaper may publish multiple Day of Dead articles and listings, ranging from coverage of children's school activities, to instructions for holiday recipes and crafts, to discussions of avant-garde altar exhibits, community celebrations, political manifestations, or religious syncretism. Unlike family Day of the Dead rituals in Latin America, where cameras would be intrusive, U.S. activities are meant to be publicly showcased. Journalists and members of the general public are allowed and encouraged to photograph the proceedings, which has been an important way of sharing the celebration with wide audiences. The news coverage these celebrations attract is a ritualized opportunity for Latinos to communicate information about themselves to the larger U.S. public.

This media space is significant, given that Latinos have been underrepresented in U.S. media for most of the twentieth century.[4] Historically, news coverage has reinforced negative stereotypes by depicting Mexicans and other Latinos as lazier, less intelligent, less moral, and more prone to crime than Anglos (Carveth and Alverio 1997; Friedman 1991; C. Rodriguez 1997; Wilson and Gutierrez 1985). Although such stereotypes are not as blatant today as in the past, Latinos in the news are still frequently portrayed as lacking agency—presented as objects rather than authoritative subjects of news (Gerbner 1993; Vargas 2000). Moreover even newspapers attempting to offer positive images of Latinos publish disproportionately high numbers of stories focused on token athletes or entertainers, rather than on the pursuits of everyday people (Kraeplin and Subervi-Velez 2003, 119–121).

The same pattern of under-representation and negative representation exists in magazine and television advertising (Combating the network 'Brownout' 1999; C. Taylor and Bang 1997; Wilson, Gutiérrez and Chao 2003) and Hollywood films (Fregoso 1993; Noriega and Lopez 1996; Ramirez Berg 2002), where Latinos have long been stereotyped in tropes such as the *bandido*, the gang banger, the over-sexualized Latin lover, the dangerous temptress, or the dim-witted buffoon. Studies done from the 1960s through the beginning of the 2000s conclude that mainstream U.S. newspaper coverage has reinforced many of the negative stereotypes found in generations of Hollywood films, portraying Latinos primarily within "problem" and "social disadvantage" frames, as people who live in crime-infested neighborhoods, lack basic educational and job skills and are probably not legitimate U.S. citizens (Carveth and Alverio 1997; Fishman and Casiano 1969; Quiroga 1997; Wilson and Gutiérrez 1985). The National Council of La Raza, the largest national Hispanic civil rights advocacy organization in the United States, argues that such media imagery helps legitimize prejudice and undermines public support for policy interventions aimed at addressing discrimination (C. Rodriguez 1997, 18).

Day of the Dead coverage diverges from such portrayals by presenting Latino culture as a vibrant and positive, rather than deviant, part of U.S. society. Moving beyond sports and entertainment tokenism, the news sources interviewed for Day of the Dead articles represent a range of "everyday" Latino voices, including educators, librarians, students, artists, poets, folk dancers, staff of community-based organizations, political activists, home-makers, immigrants, and shopkeepers. As the most widely covered Latino festivity in the United States, Day of the Dead season brings more media attention than usual to Latino cultural and political messages.

From their onset, Chicano Day of the Dead celebrations were formulated as performances of identity whose creators anticipated public viewing. Both Latinos and non-Latinos attending early Day of the Dead events experienced a mixture of surprise, admiration, and awe at the rituals they observed, but Latinos in particular experienced feelings of cultural validation and pride. Media coverage publicized Day of the Dead to millions among the general public who were not personally connected to the Chicano Movement, Latino community centers, the art world, or multicultural education initiatives. For Latinos, this coverage facilitated the development of an imagined community, or "a community of sentiment"—a group that begins to imagine and feel things together, coming to see themselves as people with historical, religious, and social commonalities (Appadurai 1996).

Media coverage of Day of the Dead portrays Latinos as having valuable contributions to offer mainstream society, both in terms of artistic and ritual practices, and in terms of alternative metaphysical views. In a country where the commercial celebration of Halloween begins to occupy people's minds (or at least space in stores, restaurants, schools and magazine covers) from late August through October 31, news coverage of Day of the Dead has introduced people to an alternative autumn ritual. In fact, articles often portray Day of the Dead as a more meaningful way to engage with the spirit world, as in the following clips:

> "Halloween gets most of the hype, but of this weekend's two spooky holidays, Día de los Muertos has the most heart and soul."
> "For most people who grow up in the United States, Halloween is little more than an excuse to wear tacky costumers, gorge on the plastic waxiness of candy corn, maybe get a few pleasant thrills at the local haunted house. But for many Mexicans and Mexican–Americans, the days at the end of October and the beginning of November are both more solemn and more festive—involving the entire family rather than only the children."
> "For many Americans, the colors of death squeeze into a narrow spectrum. Funeral attire is black, while the pallor of the dead is described as ashen or ghostly. Red, green, blue, fiery orange, deep lavender, the vibrancy of the rainbow—this is not death's palette. That might change for those who take in a new exhibit at Harvard's Peabody Museum on Días de los Muertos (Days of the Dead), a Latin American festival that celebrates the links between the living and the deceased."
>
> "In Latin America, death is seen as an inevitable, natural part of life. This healthy attitude toward our potentially disturbing fate finds expression in annual Día de los Muertos (Day of the Dead) celebration."
> "This is about an attitude change and looking at life a little differently. Life is short and death is long. Let's enjoy it while we're here."[5]

Unlike Day of the Dead celebrants in Latin America, where the holiday's ritual activities are part of the quotidian fabric of community life, most people in the United States, whether Latino or non-Latino, rely on some form of mass media to get information about Day of the Dead activities.[6] In the weeks preceding November

1 and 2, newspapers announce Day of the Dead events, explaining the "who, what, when, where, and why" of the celebration. Promotional posters are hung in windows of commercial establishments, social service agencies, and schools, while banners and billboards are placed in malls, parks, and university campuses. Early each fall, community centers, art galleries and museums mail thousands of post-cards to their constituents, announcing the dates of their Day of the Dead exhibits, workshops and related events. Entertainment magazines and the calendar or arts sections of newspapers include Day of the Dead listings, while galleries, museums, universities, folk art stores, and community centers include schedules of their Day of the Dead activities in their Web pages and newsletters. The following examples, showing the type of events typically listed in newspapers, were taken from the *San Diego Reader* during the weeks of October 24, 2002 (in which there were six Day of the Dead events advertised) and October 31, 2002 (in which there were eight Day of the Dead events advertised).

> *"Art for the Dead*: This celebration is at the Chicano Park Gazebo on Friday November 1. Expect to find altar building, spoken word, music and a marketplace to celebrate Days of the Dead. A special offering will be built to commemorate the second cycle of mourning for the twin tow-ers victims. Free."
>
> "Día de los Muertos is being celebrated all over town this week. Bazaar del Mundo has activities planned from Saturday October 26, through Sunday, November 2, with traditional decorations, activities and artists' demonstrations. Hours 10:00 am to 9:00 pm ... Admission is free."
>
> *"Bring Mementos, Photographs and Objects* that remind you of deceased loved ones. San Diego State University. The event begins with a slide-illustrated lecture ... and ends with a community altar-making ceremony. "The altar will be on view in Love Library through Friday November 22. Free."
>
> "The Day of the Dead Festivities at Casa Familiar Civic and Recreational Center take place on Friday, November 1. There's altar-making all day, with the observance getting underway at 6:00 pm and a *velación* [com-munal vigil for the dead] ... from 8:00 pm to midnight. Free."
>
> "Noche de Muertos, head to Voz Alta Cultural Center to celebrate life and death with a poetry reading honoring those who have passed away. ... The event starts at 8:00 pm on Friday November 1. Free."

During this same period in San Diego, there were also announcements in the *San Diego Union Tribune,* the *North County Times, La Prensa San Diego,* and smaller newspapers in San Diego County. Similar listings appeared the same month in newspapers across the United States, such as the *Boston Globe,* the *New York Times,* and the *Village Voice.*

These listings illustrate how, from a primarily internal or family-oriented religious observance in Latin America, Day of the Dead is transformed in the United States into an external, advertised cultural happening, organized primarily by nonprofit organizations that use the mass media to attract participants. Mary Ann Thiem, chief organizer of the annual Day of the Dead Festival in Oceanside California, explains, "We advertise it in the *North County Times,* the *San Diego Reader,* and the *Union Tribune. We* have a newsletter that goes out to all our Mainstreet members. Telemundo promoted it. ... This year we may be working with Uniradio. We're planning to do more advertising on Spanish-speaking stations. It gets written up in *Oceanside Magazine.* Last year the *North County Times* did a huge spread on it. There were something like thirty-three different articles on Day of the Dead, in a huge spread. Not just writing about ours, but other events happening in the county."[7]

Estela Rubalcava Klink notes that while most participants in San Diego's Sherman Heights Day of the Dead events are local residents, the mass media also attract people from throughout greater San Diego County: "It's really grown and we have press releases in local magazines and newspapers. ... We get people from San Ysidro, North County, Oceanside ... Los Angeles. There are bus tours that come, organized by another organization. There are tourists, a mixture of Caucasians, African–Americans, and Latinos, and professors and students from universities. Last year we were written about in *Smithsonian Magazine* and we were announced in *Night and Day* and the *San Diego Reader.*"[8]

Similarly, the owner of the Folktree Gallery in Pasadena, which holds annual Day of the Dead altar exhibits, sells Day of the Dead merchandise, and organizes Día de los Muertos travel tours to Mexico, also notes that media coverage has helped promote Day of the Dead: "There's usually at least one article in one of the local papers about us; The *Star News* and the *Pasadena Weekly.* Once I was on the cover of the *L.A. Reader.* One year we got a blurb in an opera handbook ... Oh, and we were in the *New York Times* once. We were also in *Travel and Leisure* magazine and AAA's *Westways.*"[9]

In contrast, early California Day of the Dead events were publicized through hand-typed flyers and word of mouth. According to René Yañez, "We were too busy just trying to organize the exhibits. We weren't thinking about publicity."[10] A review of cultural news coverage in the *San Francisco Chronicle* and the *Los Angles Times* during the 1970s yielded no full-length articles about Day of the Dead events in either paper.[11] However, word of mouth spread quickly, particularly in arts circles, and growing numbers of people attended the Chicano-organized events each year. Neighborhood exhibits attracted the interest of major museums that in turn attracted media attention from newspaper and television stations. Chicana artist and educator Yolanda Garfias Woo, affectionately known in San Francisco circles as "La Madrina" (the godmother) of Day of the Dead for her pioneering work conducting Day of the Dead workshops in California schools, recalls her surprise when all three major television networks covered the opening of an ofrenda exhibit she was invited to create at San Francisco's prestigious De Young Fine Arts Museum in 1975:

> It was the first time a major museum was interested in Día de los Muertos, something so ethnically outlandish … Channels 4, 5, and 7 were all there with camera crews, filming and asking all kinds of questions that no one on the museum staff could answer. They were doing community interest stories. But Channel 7 had an ABC program called *Perspectives* that was an hour long, and they returned and we filmed one hour about the exhibit and the whole history of Día de los Muertos. It was great because since Galería was doing a Muertos exhibit at the same time, we got invited to a lot of TV programs to do a combined effort about the exhibits and about what this was. This was a real turning point for the community, as well as for me, in terms of being public.[12]

Other prominent museums began to hold Day of the Dead exhibits by Chicano artists, and as the celebration gained popularity (and legitimacy) in the mid-1980s, full-length articles and photos appeared in newspapers with increasing frequency. As these events became better organized, planners sent press packets to media outlets, held press conferences, and conducted interviews with journalists to educate them about the tradition.

Reasons for Increased News Coverage

The 1980s and 1990s brought an exponential growth in Day of the Dead activities across California, growing from only five organizations holding celebrations in the 1970s, to double that number in the 1980s, and triple the number in the 1990s. By 1990, the Mission District's Day of the Dead celebration was featured on page A1 of the *San Francisco Examiner*, with a large photo of the procession.[13] By the early 2000s, coverage in each of California's two largest newspapers, the *San Francisco Chronicle* and the *Los Angles Times*, had grown to an average of seven articles annually, almost always accompanied by large photos and detailed listings. The rise in Day of the Dead events during these years corresponds with a growth in financial support for multicultural programming in schools and community-based agencies funded by public and private sources. During an era of energized civil rights advocacy, the Bilingual Education Act (also known as Title VII) was enacted in 1968 and reauthorized several times from the 1970s through the 1990s, to provide federal funding for bilingual and multicultural curricula. Providing learning opportunities in art, poetry, history, social studies, and the Spanish language, Day of the Dead became one of the most popular educational activities in California and the Southwest, later appealing in multicultural teaching curricula used by teachers across the country.

Rising interest in multiculturalism was cited by journalists as an important reason for increased news coverage of Day of the Dead:[14]

> "The middle-class white liberal affection for multiculturalism is one reason, as many newsrooms are run by editors who came of age journalistically and politically between the 60s and 80s. It's genuine … however, because their view in many ways reflects the view of their readership, particularly in large urban centers."
> "The editors of a lot of newspapers realize the importance of diversity and that celebrating diverse cultures will attract readers to their paper."
> "I think it's the growing interest in multiculturalism. This is an interesting cultural event that many readers don't know about but might want to see. We also write about the African–American Juneteenth celebration and other ethnic celebrations."[15]

Another factor in the growth of Day of the Dead news coverage is the higher number of Latino reporters working at newspapers since the latter twentieth century. Given increased national attention to racial diversity as a result of civil rights work, affirmative action policies at universities nationwide resulted in higher numbers of Latinos graduating from college and attending journalism schools. Editors at news organizations responded to affirmative action requirements by hiring more people of color—previously rare in the historically White and male profession of journalism. Twelve Latino journalists I surveyed indicated that their ethnic background played a role in their choice to write about Day of the Dead: all except one reported that he/she had initiated stories on the topic, pitching the subject in editorial meetings or (in the cases of editors and columnists), simply deciding to cover the subject. The following are a few of their comments:

> "I can't and shouldn't cover every Latino event, but I do take care to make sure that I'm not short-changing Latino events and prominent individuals."
>
> "I brought the idea up, as I do all my stories, to my editor, who is also Latin, and she said Ok. I cover an area that is predominantly Latino, near the San Diego–Tijuana border, and so many of my stories, at least the feature-type stories, are about Latinos."
>
> "I brought the topic up to my editor at the time. There is a fear among some Latino journalists of ghettoizing themselves if they pitch too many articles on Latino culture and life, preventing them from climbing the newsroom ranks … I resist this idea because a) if we don't do it, who will? And more importantly, b) Latinos in the U.S. happen to be the most interesting national story around, if you ask me."
>
> "I was working the night shift and had the choice of covering two evening events. I picked Day of the Dead because it was something I was familiar with."[16]

Non-Latino journalists also initiated Day of the Dead stories, such as a reporter at the *San Diego Union Tribune*, who said, "I brought up the subject because I cover everything that happens in the city of Oceanside. Although I am not Latina, I am bilingual, did postgraduate work at the University of Mexico, and have been an officer in the San Diego chapter of the California Chicano News Media Association. My editor, also not Latino, was immediately interested."[17] A veteran Latino reporter for more than thirty-five years, working at the *Houston Chronicle*, affirmed that while he initiated writing Day of the Dead stories at his paper, he observed both Latino and non-Latino journalists bringing up stories: "I've initiated any stories I've done on Day of the Dead, but I see my colleagues (both Latinos and not) in other parts of my newspaper doing so as well, like feature writers and arts writers."[18]

Both Latino and non-Latino journalists felt that the record numbers of Latin American immigrants settling in the United States over the past two decades has made the Latino population more attractive as a market for media and other commercial enterprises. Journalists expressed the following thought on the relationship between the growing Latino population and increased news coverage of Day of the Dead:

> "I think the media in general is beginning to wake up to the powerful Latino market … The Latino population is really growing and you will be dead in the water in those growing markets if you don't begin doing more to cover Latino issues."
>
> "[Increased coverage of Day of the Dead] is probably about trying to appeal to Latino readers and advertisers … More and more cities throughout the country are growing in their Latino population [and this] means that media outlets need to hurry and find ways to appeal to those readers."
>
> "With the Latino population on the rise, more and more people are taking an interest in Day of the Dead as an alternative to the traditional American Halloween. Newspapers reflect this trend."
>
> "More Latinos are moving to California, graduating from college, and entering newsrooms. More are running community organizations that alert editors of their community celebrations. It's a natural demographic shift … It's also a copycat phenomenon. As more papers watch other papers give it play, they fall in line."[19]

News Coverage as a Resource for Financial and Institutional Support

In addition to educating the public about the tradition, media coverage has provided another tangible benefit for U.S. Day of the Dead celebrations attracting foundation funding and commercial sponsors. This has made it possible to expand activities to new sites and larger audiences. Almost all of the gallery curators and community center staff I interviewed showed me binders, or in some cases compact discs, of collected press coverage of their organization's Day of the Dead events. These displays included newspaper and magazine articles and/or transcripts of radio and TV coverage received over the years. Such media coverage is routinely used as supporting material for grant applications and press packets, indicating the importance of news coverage for the continued public visibility and financial support of Day of the Dead activities. Whereas some event organizers asserted that, regardless of funding, their constituents would continue to engage in Day of the Dead celebrations even if it meant paying expenses, out of pocket, others expressed concern that without continued outside funding the exhibits, workshops, and other activities offered free to the public could not continue. Most spoke of the financial strain that funding cuts to the California Arts Council, the National Foundation for the Arts, and other funding sources had placed on their organization's arts and cultural programming.

Recognizing the power of the media to educate the general public about Latino culture, event organizers have welcomed press coverage of the celebration, both as a way to promote the tradition and to prevent misunderstandings of it. Given the general unfamiliarity of mainstream U.S. audiences in the 1970s with non-Western cultural practices and belief systems, a celebration of "the dead," replete with "offerings," smoldering incense, and other unusual rites, was initially misinterpreted by some as the handiwork of Satan worshippers. For example, in reaction to the 1976 Day of the Dead exhibit at La Galería de la Raza in San Francisco the word "necrophiliacs" was found scrawled on the front windows of the gallery.[20] People who did not understand the tradition accused the Galería staff of being members of a death cult. René Yañez, who organized the first Day of the Dead exhibit at La Galería, notes. "The Irish captain of the Mission Police Station refused to give me a permit to hold the Day of the Dead procession. He called me a 'devil' … [and] said, 'Over my dead body!' People thought we were a death cult. They made references to Charles Manson."[21]

Along with non-Latinos disturbed by what they perceived to be sacrilegious communing with the dead, were Latinos who were unfamiliar or uncomfortable with the indigenous aspects of the holiday. When she first began teaching school-children about Day of the Dead, Yolanda Garfias Woo was criticized by both Anglo coworkers and a Mexican American school superintendent:

> I taught in an area that was predominantly Black. It was a very difficult area. There were a lot of deaths, a lot of murders, suicides, violence. And because I realized that the students had no outlet, I began doing Muertos in the classroom and found that it was extremely successful in opening things up and being able to talk about death. I was criticized by the staff for teaching "witchcraft," even though the teacher next door to me one

year during Halloween was standing in her doorway, wearing a long black gown with a pointed witch's hat, and she said to me. "You know you can't do that in your classroom because it's witchcraft."

Later, when Garfias Woo conducted a teachers' workshop about Day of the Dead, she learned from the teachers that the school superintendent, who was Mexican–American, had adamantly resisted the teachers' request for the workshop: "He had told the teachers that it was barbaric and that only the poorest areas of Mexico, only the uneducated people did it and that it wasn't part of mainstream Mexican culture and had no place in the school curriculum. The teachers fought and fought to get him to approve the workshop."[22]

Whereas some onlookers criticized the festivities as being too "pagan" or too "barbaric," others accused organizers of celebrating a "Catholic" tradition in publicly funded schools. Patricia Rodriguez, gallery curator of the MCCLA in San Francisco, recounts: "I was teaching at the University of New Mexico—doing an altar and talking about the tradition—and the local newspaper wrote me up as being pagan. Others said it was too Catholic, too religious, and that religion didn't belong in the university."[23] Given such misunderstandings and resistance, even among sectors of the Mexican–American community, Chicano artists had to work hard to clarify that the celebration bore no relation to zombies, witchcraft, or the devil, and that their renditions of Day of the Dead were important not only in terms of achieving a positive representation of cultural identity, but also in terms of acquiring institutional support. Event organizers regularly clarified the meaning of the celebration when meeting with school groups and other audiences, and published explanations of the tradition in exhibit brochures and museum catalogs. News media elucidate the ritual's intention for wide audiences.

Explaining the meaning of the holiday—something that would be unnecessary in Latin America—has been a consistent theme in U.S. media coverage. From the 1980s to the present, articles, television news, and radio segments have observed that the custom is a joyous rather than morbid time, which celebrates life and loved ones, rather than death. Cognizant of the gruesome images that the words "Day of the Dead" might conjure in the minds of people unfamiliar with the tradition, journalists often acknowledge the "strangeness" of the name and preemptively dismiss morbid associations, as in the following front-page examples:

"Despite its somber-sounding name, el Día de los Muertos, the Day of the Dead, is a day of music, food, and decoration in the Latino community."

"Although it *sounds* macabre, celebrating the Day of the Dead is actually about life, affirming the belief that death is the final arc of life's circle, bringing it to its inevitable close. And it is about love, about honoring the people you once knew so intimately that death could not fully take them from you."

"This is not a grim, morbid affair. With touches of humor and a festive air, it is a form of honoring the dead and acknowledging death as a part of life."

"Día de los Muertos is not a worship of death, but a recognition that life and death are one in the same, part of the same cycle."[24]

News coverage has helped contextualize U.S. festivities as non-denominational celebrations with roots in the spiritual beliefs of Indigenous Latin American cultures.[25] As more people gain knowledge of the tradition, misunderstandings are less common, although they still exist.

Publicity and Validation for Latino Communities

For politically and economically marginalized populations who do not generally occupy powerful positions as newsmakers, mainstream media coverage provides public validation of their existence to the larger world (Cook and Hartnett 2001; Gitlin 1980; Ryan 1991). For decades, the association of Latinos with crime, drugs, and poverty in the media rendered Latino neighborhoods devoid of the cultural cachet necessary for inclusion in the arts and culture sections of citywide newspapers. However, as Day of the Dead exhibits brought the barrio to the academy, representing the first time, in many cases, that works of Chicano artists were exhibited in prestigious museums, they also brought the academy to the barrio.[26]" Exhibits at neighborhood-based Latino art galleries drew art lovers to communities that had long been ignored by the cultural cognoscenti. Coverage of Day of the Dead exhibits in major newspapers encouraged middle-class suburbanites and wealthy city dwellers to venture into Latino neighborhoods for gallery exhibits. Muertos art, or fresh pan de muerto. Today busloads of schoolchildren and tourists visit San Francisco's Mission District, East Los Angeles, San Diego's Sherman Heights, and Latino communities elsewhere during Day of the Dead season.

Noting the increased positive visibility that media coverage of the Sherman Heights Day of the Dead exhibit (promoted in the *San Diego Reader*, the *Union*

Tribune, La Prensa San Diego, and *Fahrenheit Magazine*) brought to this predominantly Latino neighborhood, resident Louise Torio explains, "People from all over the place come to this inner city neighborhood—people who don't know about the neighborhood, or from what they've heard, they think of it is a bad neighborhood. Or they haven't been here for thirty years. So with this event, the impression of the neighborhood changes."[27]

Terry Alderete, chief coordinator of the annual Fruitvale Day of the Dead festival in Oakland California, similarly notes that media coverage of the event (in the *Oakland Tribune,* the *San Francisco Chronicle,* the *Bay Guardian,* television networks, Telemundo and Univision, AAA's travel magazine, Southwest Airline's in-flight magazine, English-language jazz station KBLX, Spanish radio stations, online news sources, and small local papers) has improved the public's perception of Oakland. Initiated in 1996, Fruitvale's Day of the Dead Festival is the "star" in a lineup of annual cultural events sponsored by the Mainstreets economic development initiative, and now attracts about a hundred thousand visitors annually from throughout the San Francisco Bay Area.[28] It is the largest one-day Día de los Muertos festival in the United States and has not only put Fruitvale on the map of the Bay Area arts scene, but has brought the neighborhood national acclaim, with a listing in the U.S. Library of Congress as a "Local Legacy" for the state of California.[29] Alderete explains. "In the late 1980s, Fruitvale was all boarded up, urban blight, crime. People wouldn't drive here for fear they might get shot at. From the 1970s and into the 1980s, it was like a war zone … [Now] we're getting a lot of publicity and this brings a lot of pride. Our Day of the Dead festival is even listed on the Smithsonian Institution's Web site."[30]

Ritual communication occurs not only when people attend Day of the Dead events in person, but also when they routinely see this tradition positively represented in the major media, strengthening the sense of imagined community felt by Mexican–Americans and other Latinos, and giving the general public an opportunity to learn more about Latinos. In so doing, the media have helped turn the ritual into an annual autumn activity for Americans of diverse racial and ethnic backgrounds.

Notes and References

1. Personal interview, La Jolla, California, April 29, 2003.

2. Some recent front-page coverage includes the El Paso Times (November 2, 2003), Chicago Weekly (October 26, 2004), the San Bernardino Sun (November 2, 2004), the Daily News of Los Angeles (November 1, 2004), the Weekend Calender supplement of the Los Angeles Times (October 27, 2005), and the Calendar Magazine supplement of the Boston Globe (November 1, 2006).

3. Many Web sites are created by teachers who freely share their Day of the Dead curricula with the public, offering instructions on how to make ofrendas, papel picado, or traditional foods. Other sites are created by artists, galleries, community centers, or university faculty (often from Spanish language or Latino Studies departments) to display photos of their Day of the Dead exhibits. Commercial sites sell Day of the Dead merchandise and tours.

4. Although Latinos are the largest minority group in the United States, representing 13.9 percent of the national population, they receive the least media coverage of any racial group (Alvear 1998, 49; Gerbner 1993; Hoffman and Noriega 2004, 6; Portales 2000, 56). A UCLA study of prime-time news, reality programming, dramas, situation comedies, sports, variety show, cartoons, and other television genres concludes that Latinos are "the most dramatically under-represented racial/ethnic group on prime-time." The report notes that 85 percent of all prime-time shows do not include Latinos as regular characters (Hoffman and Noriega 2004). A 1993 study by the Nieman Center for Journalism at Harvard University found that only 1 percent of national TV news focused on Latinos (Alvear 1998, 49), and research done at the Annenberg School of Communication reveals that on network news, "Latinos make up 1.5 percent of all newsmakers, only 0.3 percent of all news deliverers, and were not cited at all as sources, spokespersons or authorities—by far the lowest proportion of any other group" (Gerbner 1993, quoted in C. Rodriguez 1997).

5. The other spooky holiday, San Francisco Chronicle, October 26, 2003, Sunday Date-book, 17; Devorah Knaff, A lively attitude on death: Mexican Day of the Dead celebrations go beyond the ghoulish activities of Halloween, Press-Enterprise, Riverside, California, October 16, 1994, A16: Rich Barlow, Spiritual life, Boston Globe. November 16, 2002, Metro/Region, B2: Dirk Surro. Music to go with Raza's Day of the Dead, Los Angeles Times, November 1, 1991, Calender, 1: G. Pabst, Accepting death while celebrating life. Milwaukee Journal Sentinel, November 4, 2001, News, 2A.

6. People who are not employees, local residents, or constituents of an arts organization or community center are most likely to rely on media coverage to learn about activities.

7. Personal interview with Mary Ann Thiem. Oceanside, California, July 8, 2003.

8. Personal interview with Estela Rubalcava Klink, San Diego, California, June 12, 2003.

9. Personal interview with Rocky Behr, Pasadena, California, June 4, 2004.

10. Personal interview with René Yañez, San Francisco, California, June 3, 2003. A lack of publicity in the early days is corroborated in the research of Suzanne Morrison, who states that while working in the Mission District from 1974 to 1978, she heard nothing about Day of the Dead at La Galería de la Raza (Morrison 1992, 343). Paying particular attention to the Calender, Art Walk, and Family Guide to the Weekend sections in the Times, and the Events, Art, and Datebook sections in the Chronicle, I found that none of the autumn cultural happenings announced in any of these sections took place in the Latino neighborhoods of Los Angeles or San Francisco. Associated with crime, poverty, and violence, these neighborhoods were apparently not yet considered (by mainstream media) as suitable locations for family and arts activities.

11. Personal interview with Yolanda Garfias Woo. San Francisco, California, June 6, 2003.

12. Lon Daniels, The Day of the Dead: Mission district celebrates ancient Aztec festival, San Francisco Examiner, November 3, 1990, A1.

13. I surveyed nineteen journalists who have reported on Day of the Dead regarding their views on the rise of Day of the Dead in the news. Journalists were located by their bylines in articles retrieved from Lexis-Nexis. An initial sample of fifty-four journalists was contacted by e-mail. More than half of these no longer worked at the paper in question and could not be reached. Responses were received from nineteen reporters (64 percent of whom were Latinos) with journalistic experience ranging from a few years to more than thirty years in the news business.

14. Personal e-mail communication with reporter at the Los Angeles Times, June 10, 2005; personal e-mail communication with reporter at the El Paso Times, June 8, 2005: personal e-mail communication with reporter at the Boston Globe, June 11, 2005.

15. Personal e-mail communication with reporter at the San Antonio Express News, June 12, 2005; personal e-mail communication with reporter at the San Diego Union Tribune, June 22, 2005; personal e-mail communication with reporter at the Los Angeles Times, June 10, 2005; personal e-mail communication with reporter at the El Paso Times, June 8, 2005.

16. Personal e-mail communication with reporter at the San Diego Union Tribune, June 13, 2005.

17. Personal e-mail communication with reporter at the Houston Chronicle, June 13, 2005.

18. Personal e-mail communication with reporter at the San Diego Union Tribune, June 24, 2005; personal e-mail communication with reporter at the San Antonio Express News, June 27, 2005; personal e-mail communication with reporter at the Kansas City Star, June 27, 2005; personal e-mail communication with reporter at the San Francisco Chronicle, June 20, 2005.

19. Personal interviews with Tere Romo, San Francisco, California, June 2, 2003; and Carmen Lomas Garza. San Francisco, California, May 25, 2006.

20. Personal interview with René Yañez, San Francisco, California, June 3, 2002.

21. Personal interview with Yolanda Garfias Woo, San Francisco, California, June 6, 2003.

22. Personal interview with Patricia Rodriguez, San Francisco, California, June 2, 2003.

23. Angelica Martinez, Day of the Dead: A happy day, San Bernardino Sun, November 2, 2001. Local 1; Sandra Guerra-Cline, Altared states: Annual festival for the dead is whimsical, bittersweet. Fort Worth Star Telegram, October 13, 2001. Home, 1; Rico Mendez, A Grave Celebration. San Francisco Chronicle, October 30, 1997, Daily Datebook, E1; Marita Hernandez, Day of the Dead: Time to Celebrate, Los Angeles Times. November 3, 1985, Metro, 1.

24. Day of the Dead news coverage has helped educate the general public about Indigenous spiritual practices that assume a more fluid connection between the living and the dead than do traditional Western religions. Considered "sacrilegious" by mainstream society prior to the 1970s, Latin American Indigenous beliefs and practices now enjoy wider circulation among both Latinos and non-Latinos, in part because of media depictions of Day of the Dead as being spiritually profound. The growth of Day of the Dead in the United States also coincided with a rise in New Age spirituality, in which many baby boomers, disenchanted with traditional Western religions, sought alternative spiritual models from other cultures.

25. Information based on my conversations with René Yañez, Tere Romo, Carmen Lomas Garza, Yolanda Garfias Woo, David Avalos, Amalia Mesa Bains, and other Chicano/a artists.

26. Personal interview with Louise Torio, San Diego, California, November 15, 2003.

27. Mainstreets is an economic development project that provides funding to economically distressed communities throughout the United States to upgrade commercial infrastructure and public image, reduce crime, build community, and improve business.

28. Library of Congress, California Local Legacies, *http://lcweb2,10c.gov/diglib/legacies/CA/200002737.html* (accessed October 11, 2008).

29. Personal interview with Terry Alderete, Oakland, California, November 4, 2003.

Questions

1. What are some of the reasons for increased media coverage of the Day of the Dead in the US? How is this an example of cultural convergence?
2. What role have the media played in popularizing the Day of the Dead? What effect has that had on the ritual performance itself? How has the content adapted to new producers, performers, and audiences—or has it?
3. What other examples can you give of a ritual or performance that began in one culture but spread to numerous other cultures? What ritual performances do you participate in that could be defined as outside your own culture?

View

Web

"Dia de los Muertos" (AZ) http://www.azcentral.com/ent/dead/

"Day of the Dead in Mexico" http://www.dayofthedead.com/

"Dia de los Muertos" (LA) http://www.ladayofthedead.com/

"All Souls Procession" (AZ) http://www.allsoulsprocession.org/

Read

Awanohara, Yuri. "Mexico's Día de Muertos Celebration: Is it Dying?" *Mexconnect* 1 November 2008. Web. 4 October 2010.

Brandes, Stanley H. *Skulls to the Living, Bread to the Dead*. Malden: Blackwell Publishing, 2006. Print.

Carmichael, Elizabeth and Chloë Sayer. *The Skeleton at the Feast: the Day of the Dead in Mexico*. Austin: University of Texas Press, 1992. Print.

Performing Identity

In contrast to Marchi's examination of a culture writ large, Gunnels' "'A Jedi Like My Father Before Me': Social Identity and the New York Comic Con," examines how Schechner's delineation between "make-believe" and "make-belief" get blurred when individuals engage in cosplay at the New York Comic Con. Gunnels offers examples of how individuals both define and reorder their identities depending on how they are framing or contextualizing their identity performance, often using the character they are embodying as an idealization of values and beliefs they want to reinforce in their everyday lives.

Ideas

Comic-Con
Cosplay
Fan Studies
Identity Performance

"A Jedi Like My Father Before Me"

Social Identity and the New York Comic Con

By Jen Gunnels

Keywords: Comic Cons; Community; Cosplay; Fan studies; Generation X; Identity; Performance studies; Sociology; Star Wars.

---

1. Introduction

Obi-Wan looked amazing! [His costume was meticulously detailed, right down to a film-quality light saber. He walked a fine line between staying in character, which was delightful because he was *really* good, and discussing the well-organized Star Wars cosplay (costume role-play) fan base (figure 1). I became even giddier at finding no fewer than five slave Leias. And when asked by a storm trooper if I wanted to try on the helmet, I said, "Hell, yes" (figure 2). Examining identity and how people choose to perform it places me in unusual circumstances. In this case, the experience was both enjoyable and enlightening.

I was at the 2009 New York Comic Con to ask Obi-Wan and his friends why they did this. Very few venues exist for adults to play dress-up, with Renaissance festivals, comic and other media conventions, and live-action role-playing games comprising the bulk of these venues. This sort of behavior is expected of people in their formative years—children and teenagers—where they try on and receive feedback about the "range of possible extensions of the self" (Elliot 1986, quoted in Kaiser 1996:162). What might be the reasoning behind the behavior of adults doing so, especially after primary socialization has occurred? Susan B. Kaiser, in her study of clothing, wonders whether role-play dress is important "in terms of providing some means for 'escaping' from mundane daily routines, as well as for

Jen Gunnels, "'A Jedi like my father before me': Social Identity and the New York Comic Con," *Transformative Works and Cultures*, no. 3, 1–12. Copyright © 2009 by Transformative Works and Cultures. Reprinted with permission. *http://dx.doi.org/10.3983/twc.2009.0161*. doi: 10.3983/twc.2009.0161.

Figure 1. Obi-Wan Kenobi andAnakin, respectively (Star Wars III: Revenge of the Sith, 2009).

expression of creativity," but she concludes that "little is known about fantasy dressing; this is an area with a great deal of potential for contributing to an understanding of creativity and self-expression" (1996:163). Very little has been written on the subject, beyond mentioning that this behavior happens.

As my ongoing research is showing, the behavior isn't necessarily mere escapism. Adults engage in costumed role-play to explore an identity that may not be practicable in everyday life. For comic and other media conventions, the behavior also has a social, communal nature. In the case of Star Wars, members of Generation X, who saw the original Star Wars trilogy, are reminded of its effect on their childhood. Star Wars helped socialize this generation and may be providing a

Figure 2. Fans dressed as Storm Troopers.

template for their own parenting, especially because current socioeconomic issues are not dissimilar to those of 1977. In this way, cosplay, as a performed identity, can provide a means of permitting individual agency and social commentary on current and past social stresses.

Ordering Identity

When examining performed identities, such as those seen in Star Wars cosplayers, two things should be kept in mind: How is the identity being ordered? And what is the framework surrounding its construction? These are important not only because identity is fluid, but also because it can be perceived or misperceived on the basis of the social framework into which it is being projected. To answer the first question, Henry Tajfel (1982) posits that identity is self-determined, and that a person can have multiple identities in place. The individual determines the dominant identity through hierarchically organizing potential identities—for instance, I am a woman, an academic, a mother, and a friend, among other identities. However, the ordering of identity is largely based on the notion of framing, which determines not only how we decide to order our identity in that moment, but also how others will either read or misread what is presented (Goffman 1959). A frame is usually socially and historically determined: I wouldn't dress as slave Leia to go to work, and regardless of Leia's introduction to the cultural consciousness, no one would dress like that in the 1950s.

Cosplay and the New York Comic Con

Some identities can be performed and explored as cosplay. The study of cosplay and its practice specifically within the United States is sparse. Most studies of cosplay are framed within its expression within Japanese popular culture, particularly manga and anime, and its export to the United States and other points West (as can be seen at http://www.cosplay.com); other studies discuss cosplay in terms of gender. What has not been examined is its nature as performance and as identity play as found at sites such as conventions. The site of my fieldwork, the New York Comic Con, began in 2006. In 2 years, it has grown explosively from a total attendance of 33,000 to a total attendance of 67,000 in 2008. It is the second largest popular culture convention in the United States. The con is an amalgam of material, cultural, and visual consumption. In addition to vendors, areas are set up for gaming tournaments, demonstrations, film previews, and media podcasts; other activities include seminars and professional panels (with writers, artists, and other professionals), and artists autograph material and network for future work (like a job fair).

When I attended the Comic Con in 2009, very few of the audience chose to participate in costume—as an offhand guess, I'd estimate that perhaps less than 5 percent of the attending audience was in costume—although all of them were having a good deal of fun (figure 3).

The quality of the costumes varied but tended toward the virtuoso, with a great deal of detail, such as the costume worn by Obi-Wan, a cosplayer who became one of my interview subjects. In fact, I was surprised to find that many of the cosplayers drew from the Star Wars universe (figure 4). I took an informal tally that broke the character representations down as follows: one Obi-Wan Kenobi, one Anakin Skywalker (both from *Star Wars Episode III: Revenge of the Sith,* 2005), five slave Princess Leias (*Star Wars Episode VI: Return of the Jedi,* 1983), four Wookies, one Han Solo (*Star Wars Episode IV: A New Hope,* 1977), three Imperial officers (two men, one woman), and, at a conservative guess, a dozen Jedi and perhaps another 8 or 10 storm troopers from the 501st Legion, Vader's Fist, a national Star Wars costuming organization. All were networked with groups specifically created to assist people in cosplaying the characters from the Star Wars universe (note 1). Intrigued, I found myself examining the cosplayers' possible purposes for choosing these specific identities.

Fandom Through Performance and Fetish

When observing cosplayers, regardless of the universes they represent, some might wonder why they choose to connect with their fandom through performance, as opposed to other manifestations of fan engagement. Two reasons in particular come to the fore: the immediacy of the physical, and applying archetypes/fetishes to aspects of personal identity. Francesca Coppa (2006) notes that fanfic can be read as performative when viewed through the lens of Richard Schechner's well-known

Figure 3. Star Wars cosplayers. Photo by Nicole Fellows.

Figure 4. Leia, Wookie and company. Photo by Nicole Fellows.

ideas on performance. Fiction, however, lacks the level of real, constructed immediacy found in a true performance environment. Yes, you can imagine that you are Obi-Wan Kenobi as you read a fan text, but wouldn't you rather *be* him? Of course, this isn't possible, but cosplay serves as a middle ground.

Further, Schechner's concept of the subjunctive mood in performance (1985:37)—not me, not not me—allows people to incorporate aspects of the character into their own identity. This can, and sometimes does, lead to a fetishization of both costume and character. Donning the costume, or even simply carrying a small prop such as a light saber, allows cosplayers to tap into the character as archetype and the costume piece as fetish: "The fetish is empowering, transgressive of the realm of the everyday and mundane, and transforms the user, thus marking a return in a sense to the original meaning of the fetish" (Wetmore 2007:177). Essentially, both become a totem, or a meaningful emblem or symbol, and "people will act towards totems in such a way based on the meaning they have given the totem." Meaning will then manifest as social interaction (Garrard 2008:17).

In an interview I conducted on February 7, 2009, Obi-Wan shared with me his view of why he admires Obi-Wan—what meaning he has given his chosen totem: "The nobility, the warrior, the leadership, following the Jedi Code, all these things, I think, make him that great archetype that we've come to know and love." When I asked him more specifically if there were any aspects of Obi-Wan that carried over into his everyday life, he replied,

> [I'd like to think there's a lot, but I could certainly be more noble. I could certainly be a better leader in my own life. But when it comes right down to it … I could be a better person in my own life. Probably when I step into costume, into the role, I think I become a better person than I am in real life and could certainly aspire to be as good as Kenobi.

Becoming the character acts as transformative moment: he is not Kenobi, but not not Kenobi. As he remarks, aspects of the character are specifically tied to donning the costume. He may not believe that he carries specific aspects of character identity over into everyday life, yet they are available to his identity when in costume.

Another of my interview subjects, Steve Koets, a member of the 501st Legion, summed up being a storm trooper as a question of enjoying the sense of shared community. In an e-mail interview I conducted with him on January 22, 2009, he stated that he participates because he "never really let go of an aspect of childhood that lets you truly believe that you're a race car driver whilst peddling your big wheel down the sidewalk. Or Luke Skywalker flying down the Deathstar trench." An anecdote he shared further stresses the aspect of his childhood love of the Star Wars universe:

> A few years ago my wife threw a 40th birthday party for me. Knowing my closet love for Star Wars (from my childhood) … [she] surprised the dickens out me with a Star Wars theme party. Everyone came in a costume, Cantina Band DJ, full-size Jabba the Hut Statue, Millennium Falcon cake, my wife in a Princess Leia metal bikini … and my indoctrination into the 501st [Legion] … I absolutely was impressed by the squad of storm troopers, Darth Vader, Boba Fett and many more that marched into the room to present me with my present—an actual set of storm trooper armor. The costumes were very screen accurate and worth up to $3000 a piece after being "sworn to the empire" … what is cooler than being a storm trooper?

Indeed, what is cooler than being a storm trooper? Determined to find out why so many cosplayers were drawn to this role, I asked many storm troopers, all of whom were either already members of the 501st or were in the process of requesting membership, about the appeal of this role. Koets replied, "They are the 'misunderstood bad guys' ... the troopers began with the clone army—OWNED by the republic—they were the military force that protected the rights of Democratic government—that turned into one run by the emperor—but because they were owned—and had allegiance, they ended up with the bad rap" (e-mail interview, January 26, 2009). Another member of the 501st (figure 5), in an interview at the con (February 7, 2009), remembers being 7 years old: for him, the first guys who really stood out in the films were the storm troopers. Now that he's old enough, he "can afford to indulge in having wanted to be a storm trooper."

The most interesting similarity with nearly all of the Star Wars cosplayers was their ages. Most of them represented a spectrum of Generation X, which I'm defining following William Strauss and Neil Howe (1992) as members of the population born between 1961 and 1981. The release of the original trilogy films (1977, 1980, and 1983, respectively) meant that members of this generation were impressionable children. The content of the films becomes progressively more complex, thus presenting more complicated ideas concerning life to progressively older (and appropriately so for the messages) audiences. As an example, I fall into the middle range of Generation X. At the release of the films, I was 9, 12, and 15—very age appropriate for considering what the films had to say about navigating the path to adulthood and society.

Why Star Wars? Why now? Several cosplayers, particularly those who decided on characters from the original trilogy, pointed to a backward entry into cosplay: participation began with their children's interest in the franchise, even though they themselves had been fans since childhood. Koets, like many others I interviewed, found that he connected with his children through his own childhood love of Star Wars. Koets and one of the Wookies I interviewed were pulled into Star Wars cosplay through building an R2D2 robot with their children. Koets "hopp[ed] around the house for a good lightsaber battle [with his children]," and the Wookie cosplayer, after completing the R2D2 model, felt compelled to have a costume to go with it. When I met him at the 2009 Comic Con, he even carried his own childhood Chewbacca action figure.

The fact that they are parents is telling. Through their involvement, the adults reaccess their memories of seeing the original film and how this material helped them navigate the circumstances of their own childhood. They revisit these memories while immersed in similar social circumstances to their first viewings. Then, as now, a new generation of children are discovering Star Wars while the country is in dire socioeconomic circumstances. As children, members of Generation X found themselves thrust into a period of rapid value shifts, the breakdown of the nuclear family, and economic upheaval. In addition, the parenting style of the baby boomers, in opposition to their own strict upbringing, tended to leave their Generation X children to their own devices. This proved detrimental in bequeathing the cultural information—"the teaching of society's acceptable values, norms, beliefs, and actions" (Garrard 2008:9)—necessary for navigating a path to adulthood. Star Wars filled the gap.

Several scholars, such as Bruno Bettelheim (1991), explain how fairy tales and myths provide a vehicle for this teaching. Today's fairy tales and myths are expressions of popular culture—films, TV shows, video games. The Star Wars films are relevant here, as producer and film critic Dale Pollock acknowledges in his remarks about the mythic power behind the original Star Wars film: "Children get the message—they know eventually they'll have to leave home, take risks, submit to trials, learn to control their emotions, and act like adults. What they don't know is how to do these things. Star Wars shows them" (Garrard 2008:67). Children of Generation X understood, as most children eventually do, that they would need to learn to negotiate the world as adults. They knew the "what" but not the "how," and Star Wars bridged that gap: George Lucas used the structures of the mythic journey throughout the original trilogy, and Generation X in turn used it as a model for navigating their path to adulthood. All of this blossomed in 1977's sociohistorical context: economic downturn, rising housing prices, rising gas prices, rising inflation, and falling real wages (Garrard 2008:87). Sound familiar?

Conclusion

As with any area of study, particularly those (like this study) with scarce secondary literature to consult, my examination of Star Wars cosplay within the New York Comic Con raises more questions than it answers. Why do cosplayers choose the characters they do? How do cosplaying communities, like the 501st Legion, work on a larger scale? Are cosplayers at other comic cons portraying Star Wars characters for similar reasons? Why do people choose cosplay over other forms of fan participation—or do they participate in other fan areas as well? If so, to what extent?

The Star Wars cosplayers are clearly tapping into their childhoods: today's social context eerily mirrors the context that members of Generation X grew up in, and the children born to Generation X are growing up in parallel circumstances characterized by economic instability. For some cosplayers, dipping into the Star Wars universe may be a way to cope, as well as a way to share coping strategies with their own children—to pass on the same myth that enabled them to negotiate their own growth within our culture. Will we point them in the direction of Luke Skywalker and Obi-Wan Kenobi to learn how to best negotiate the times? In all honesty, I would like to think so. Perhaps they will forge a New Jedi Order to balance the mistakes of the Knights of the Old Republic.

Acknowledgments

A version of this paper was presented at the 2009 PCA/ACA Conference in New Orleans for the Faires and Festivals group. I thank Nicole Fellows for her assistance in gathering field material and shooting footage at the 2009 New York Comic Con.

Note

1. The cosplayer within the Star Wars universe can find enormous help and support online. My discussion with Obi-Wan Kenobi revealed two major sources for assisting the would-be Star Wars cosplayer: The Padawan's Guide (http://www.padawansguide.com) and Padme's Wardrobe and Closet (http://www.anakinsangel.net/PadmesPic.html). These provide sources and materials for organizations such as the 501st Legion (http://www.501stlegion.org/index.php), "the world's definitive Imperial costuming organization" and a national charity organization, the beginnings of which are outlined in the documentary film *Heart of an Empire* (2007).

Works Cited

Bettlelheim, Bruno. (1991). *The uses of enchantment: The meaning and importance of fairy tales*. New York: Penguin.

Coppa, Francesca. (2006). Writing bodies in space: Media fan fiction as theatrical performance. In *Fan fiction and fan communities in the age of the Internet,* ed. Karen Hellekson and Kristina Busse, 225–44. Jefferson, NC: McFarland.

Garrard, Todd Anthony. (2008). Remember, the Force will be with you … always: The electronic media and "Star Wars" and the socialization of Generation X. *Master's thesis, Univ. of Texas-San Antonio.*

Goffman, Erving. (1959). *The presentation of self in everyday life.* New York: Anchor Doubleday.

Kaiser, Susan B. (1996). *The social psychology of clothing: Symbolic appearances in context.* 2nd ed. New York: Fairchild Books and Visuals.

Schechner, Richard. (1985). *Between theater and anthropology.* Philadelphia: Univ. of Pennsylvania Press.

Strauss, William, and Neil Howe. (1992). *Generations.* New York: Harper Perennial.

Tajfel, Henri, ed. (1982). Introduction. In *Social identity and intergroup relations,* 1–11. Cambridge: Cambridge Univ. Press.

Wetmore Jr., Kevin J. (2007). Your father's lightsaber: The fetishization of objects between the trilogies. In *Culture, identities and technology in the "Star Wars" films: Essays on the two trilogies,* ed. Carl Silvio and Tony M. Vinci, 175–87. Jefferson, NC: McFarland.

Questions

2. What are some reasons given for adults to engage in costumed role-play (cosplay)? Why do fans choose to connect with their fandom through active performance?

3. How does this case study provide a generational perspective on popular entertainment? What examples does it provide?

4. If "today's fairy tales and myths are expressions of popular culture—films, TV shows, video games," what specific aspects or examples of popular entertainment have shaped *your* navigation of your childhood and adolescence? How has popular entertainment reinforced society's norms and beliefs in your life?

View

Web

Vader's Fist (www.501st.com)
Wookieepedia (starwars.wikia.com)
Comic Con (www.comic-con.org)
Dragon*Con (www.dragoncon.org)

Film/Video

Comic-Con: Episode IV – A Fan's Hope (2011)
Four Days at Dragon*Con (2010)

Read

Dorfman, Elena and Carlo McCormick. *Fandomania: Characters and Cosplay. New York: Aperture Foundation*, 2007. Print.

Goodale, Gloria. "How Comic-Con Went from Geek to Hollywood Megabucks." *Christian Science Monitor*. 21 July 2011. Web. 14 June 2012.

Gunnels, Jen and Carrie J. Cole. "Culturally Mapping Universes: Fan Production as Ethnographic Fragments." *Transformative Works and Culture* 7 (2011). Doi:10.3983/twc.2011.0241. Web. 14 June 2012.

Cultural Authenticity

Chen's "Authenticity at Burning Man" takes a historical perspective on a uniquely structured countercultural performance, bringing us back to issues of authenticity in cultural performance. Through interviews, Chen offers varied perspectives of cultural authenticity from the participants of the Burning Man Festival, who engage in this annual cultural performance as producers, performers, *and* audience simultaneously.

Ideas

Authenticity
Radical inclusion
Radical self-expression
Gift economy
Counter culture

Authenticity at Burning Man

By Katherine K. Chen

Burning Man, Black Rock City, Nevada

In the days leading up to Labor Day Weekend, more than 47,000 people travel to Nevada's Black Rock Desert. Each year, these people gather at this isolated site for Burning Man, an event named after its signature bonfire of a 40-foot tall wooden and neon sculpture. For a week, these adventurers form Black Rock City, a temporary desert metropolis with an expansive outdoor gallery of art.

The Black Rock City Limited Liability Company, more commonly known as the BOrg (the Burning Man Organization), or simply the Project, relies on a $10 million budget generated by ticket sales and an estimated 2,000 volunteers to produce this annual event.

During my years studying the organizing activities behind Burning Man, I've noticed that attendees, or Burners, struggle with a conundrum.

At one sunset during the 2008 event, while I strolled back to my camp along a temporary street pressed into the desert's dusty surface, a banner caught my attention. Large, hand-written letters proclaimed the camp's theme: "The Museum of It Was Better Last Year." It captured the simultaneous joy and angst evident in Burners' accounts of their event experiences.

When Burners long for the wonder and novelty of their first year participating in the festival, they may embark on a trip down memory lane. Their experiences every year after their first pose invidious and revealing comparisons about authenticity.

To validate worth or confer esteem, people seek out what sociologists call authenticity—that sense of meaning and dignity, or a connection with other people and experiences. People pursue authenticity in their workplaces and neighborhoods, or through consumption and relationships, and as their experiences change, so too do their perceptions of authenticity.

As Burning Man enters its third decade, several changes to the event have challenged hard-core Burners' conceptions of its authenticity. Some believe the event's longevity, exponential population growth, and increasingly complex rules and regulations have eroded its authenticity. In contrast, more supportive attendees uphold a dynamic conceptualization of authenticity: they view change as a creative process crucial to the event's rejuvenation.

Burning Man first debuted in 1986 as an evening bonfire at a San Francisco beach. Led by co-founders Larry Harvey and Jerry James, a small group of friends and family celebrated the summer solstice and mourned the end of Harvey's romantic relationship. In 1990, the eponymous bonfire relocated to the Nevada Black Rock Desert. The weekend desert camping trip of 90 people has since expanded in size and duration.

Artwork litters the desert.

Admirers gather around and climb inside large-scale, interactive artwork.

James described 1996 as a pivotal year for the event, an "exhilarating but very dangerous," "muted riot." Attendees could shoot guns, drive their vehicles at high speeds, and engage in other dangerous activities. After a death and a car accident that severely injured several bystanders, some organizers decided the event should end. These people quit while those that remained regrouped, and their decision to change the event and formalize their organizing efforts irrevocably altered its trajectory.

Over the years, organizers formed and disseminated guidelines for the event that emphasized creativity and community. "Participants," as attendees are called, are exhorted to take active roles in producing the event. The principle of radical self-expression encourages laypeople to produce art and other experiences alongside professionals. Participants undertake both small and large art projects that invite involvement and interaction with others.

For example, using electroluminescent wire, also known as EL wire or cool neon, Molly Ditmore and her boyfriend fashioned a jellyfish and a manta ray. Each night, they and their creations drifted across the desert. By chance, they joined a school of EL wire fish. The glowing sea creatures evoked the days when the desert, or playa, was a prehistoric lakebed bottom.

At the 2008 event, large-scale art projects included Jen Lewin's "Pool," an installation where the inquisitive could jump en masse upon concentric circles of discs, thereby illuminating patterns of colors. Art cars (modified and decorated vehicles) also promote audience engagement—a yellow rubber duck art car spews flames from its mohawk, rotates its green laser eyes, and plays techno music for the passengers dancing on its deck.

Flâneurs can also visit theme camps that line the city streets. While walking on stilts, Eric Waterman discovered a theme camp devoted to this activity. The camp "had made a stilt bar, a 10-foot-tall bar, with, like, the seats, and they had extra stilts for people to wear … All of the stilters are, like, walking around and drinking cocktails and stuff. It was just so fun," he exclaimed. Other camps offered body painting, disco roller-skating, games, or respite in a "chill space." A few camps specialized in satirizing bureaucratic banality through performance art. Back in 1998, by answering surveys or enduring absurd questioning, visitors could get information about their soulmates, a prized stamp in their passport, or mail postmarked and delivered.

> People pursue authenticity in their workplaces and neighborhoods, or through consumption, and as these experiences change, so too do their perceptions of authenticity.

Reminiscing about earlier events, a few fondly recall a brief period when participants could purchase burgers from "McSatan's" and beer, fireworks, and trinkets from small entrepreneurs. Today, though, Burning Man prohibits vending and corporate sponsorship, thus discouraging commerce and advertising (however, participants can purchase ice for their food and drinks, the sales of which benefit the near-by town's schools and other programs. At the Center Camp Cafe, which is run at cost, they can also purchase tea or coffee, the latter of which is considered a necessity for desert survival).

A gift economy encourages sharing hugs, conversations, art, and other experiences with participants without expecting reciprocity. Mary Ellen Burdwood, a.k.a. Dirtwitch, described to me a gift that serendipitously replaced a forgotten necessity. "The first day I was there, this man came over, and he was covered with this suit, and every inch of the suit was covered with toothbrushes in boxes, and he plucked one off from himself and gave it to me."

Some consider Burning Man's counter-cultural principles and activities a decommodified haven from conventional society. For a week, participants can live in a space that prohibits corporate sponsorship and advertising. Burners "want to be a part of what makes the event work because the event … inspires all of the dirty, rotten cool underground things that are not part of the corporate world that they have to live in every day," John Rinaldi, a.k.a. Chicken John, told me. "It's not about advertising or selling shoes; it gets them closer to [the] real … something that everybody has been looking for."

In sociological terms, then, people seek authenticity. However, the pursuit of the "real" or authentic can elevate expectations.

Some participants want to recreate the anarchy that characterized Burning Man during the mid-1990s. Joegh Bullock observed that attendees "want to see something go out of control because they want to feel like they're part of something dangerous." Flaming projectiles, conflagrations, and machinery cater to this desire. For example, one theme camp built a mini roller-coaster. Screaming passengers spun 360 degrees as their metal cage rattled up and down a U-shaped track through shooting flames.

Critics, though, deride contemporary Burning Man activities as meek substitutes for what happened at past events. For those invested in the countercultural history, the influx of newcomers and coverage by mainstream media outlets suggest Burning Man no longer rides the cutting edge of cool.

Self-reflective Burners poke fun at such yearnings for authenticity. In 2002, for example, email discussion lists forwarded a link to a news report that played on participants' fears about the event's future. Under the headline "MTV Gets Burning with the Man," the story announced the cable network had signed "an exclusive five-year broadcasting and merchandising deal" with the Burning Man organization. While stunned and outraged Burners railed that Burning Man had sold out, more astute readers noted the story's date—April 1, or April Fool's Day—and an unusual web address that redirected users to a personal web page (rather than the real CNN website), and they applauded the prank.

Unlike adherents to the past, volunteers I spoke to accept the event's continual changes. Jim Graham, who started attending in 1996, described how he made different realizations over successive years.

"The first year is this standard first year thing: 'Oh my god, why can't the rest of my life be like Burning Man?' And then the second year was, 'Oh my god, this isn't what it was like last year! It's gone completely corporate!' And then by year three, it was, 'Okay, this event changes every single year, and it's something different every year, but it can be equally good,'" he said. "It's not like a staid thing that's always going to be the same. It's always changing and they're experimenting with it to see if they can make it better."

Participant Susan Strahan looks forward to making discoveries at each event. "One of the exciting things about Burning Man is: what is going to happen next year?" she said.

Some consider Burning Man's countercultural principles and activities a decommodified haven from conventional society.

At first glance, a longing for the authentic seems harmless. However, some wield authenticity as a basis for making distinctions or scapegoating others. Some have blamed assorted problems, including littering and voyeurism, on an influx of Burning Man "virgins," "newbies," or "yahoos" unfamiliar with Burning Man norms. Critics have also accused various groups of promoting incompatible values, engaging in activities that could detract from the event, or being oblivious to the event's mission. On such grounds, critics have suggested excluding or harassing a variety of stereotyped bogeymen: the media, frat boys, hippies, rednecks, ravers, dot-commers, MTV viewers, and SUV drivers, among others. By denigrating such groups for lacking the desired authenticity, their provocations promote exclusion.

In contrast, others uphold the principle of "radical inclusion," which states that any interested individual can join Burning Man. When educated on the event's purpose and principles, newcomers often become active contributors. Enthusiastic newcomers have launched recycling efforts and a message service that are now part of the event's infrastructure. Organizer Michael Mikel thinks Burning Man's survival hinges on its inclusiveness and openness to such new ideas. In envisioning the event's future, Mikel admits, "my greatest fear is that it [Burning Man] would not continue to be organic and open and evolving. We need to continue to ... be open to more ideas. More input is very important."

The desire to preserve or expand authenticity isn't limited to Burning Man. Gentrifying neighborhoods reveal similar tensions about whether newcomers displace longtime residents and thus erode the area's authenticity. Church congregations divide over introducing new practices that may attract and retain new members at the cost of driving away existing members. Artists face constraints when creating innovative work—if their work doesn't adhere to cultural conventions, they may alienate clientele who prefer more familiar music, painting, or sculpture. These tensions tend to devolve into a zero-sum game of irreparable loss and corrosive disenchantment.

How people handle change at Burning Man shows one way of moving beyond a restrictive and divisive conception of authenticity. People can simultaneously acknowledge the importance of the past and redirect activities toward growth and flexibility. Instead of lamenting the loss of a past that may never have existed, the evolution of Burning Man suggests it's possible for us to both celebrate the present and look forward to future possibilities.

Katherine K. Chen is in the sociology department at The City College of New York and the Graduate Center, the City University of New York. She is the author of **Enabling Creative Chaos: The Organization Behind the Burning Man Event.**

Questions

1. How does this essay define authenticity?
2. How is this idea of authenticity problematic for the participants of Burning Man?
3. How does Burning Man define its authenticity by placing the festival geographically and philosophical beyond the influence of other cultures? Do you think this is a successful strategy?
4. Have you attended Burning Man or a similar festival? These could include music festivals like Coachella or Bonnaroo, Renaissance festivals, Mardi Gras or Carnival, or a pow-wow. Did you feel a sense of authenticity to your experience? Why or why not?

View

Web
Official Burning Man site (burningman.com)

Film/Video
Burning Man: Beyond Black Rock (2006)
Journey to the Flames: 11 Years of Burning Man (2011)

Read

Doherty, Brian. *This is Burning Man: The Rise of a New American Underground*. New York: Little, Brown and Company, 2004. Print.

Gilmore, Lee and Mark Van Proyen, eds. *Afterburn: Reflections on Burning Man*. University of New Mexico Press, 2005. Print.

Traub, Barbara. *Desert to Dream: A Dozen Years of Burning Man Photography*. Revised Edition. San Francisco: Immedium, Inc., 2011. Print.

Exercises

1. In "A Jedi Like My Father Before Me," Gunnels points out that identity is both self-determined and hierarchically ordered. List several potential identities you have in the hierarchal order you would identify yourself to your classmates. Now reorder them as you would identify yourself to a potential employer. Now your parents. Where are there similarities in how you frame your identity? Where is there the most divergence? What do you think that says about how you perform your identity in your culture?

2. In his essay, Schechner states "Tourism…allows the tourist to purchase the other, the past, the exotic, the sexy, the exciting…whatever is up for grabs. And if 'purchase' means to buy with money, it also means to get a hold on, to grasp firmly, to be in charge." Write a brief sketch of a recent time you were a tourist, focusing specifically on your memories of how culture was performed. Were you reconnecting with your own cultural past? Were you exploring a foreign culture? Were you experiencing an unfamiliar aspect of your own community? What did you "purchase" from this performance experience? Was it the same thing that was sold or packaged, or did you experience something at odds with the narrative of the performance?

3. Marchi's essay on the Day of the Dead shows how a culture can popularize an aspect of its ritual performance, while Chen's study of Burning Man contains examples of how participants in the culture want their experience to remain exclusive of outside influence. Choose one aspect of your own cultural identity that you would like to popularize through performance, and write a pitch to the audience about why they should attend.

Part 4

Performance of Sport and Competition

Part Four considers popular traditions that stage competition as performance. These competitions include both sporting events and of course, reality television programs. In these events, the spectacle is the spectacle of the real. It is real people performing for real people in events that serve to heighten, to extend, to transport the audience into other worlds and into the imagination.

Building on Part Three and the study of cultural entertainment, we begin with one of the oldest and most popular forms of sport—the Olympics. The Olympics provide the opportunity to bring together the study of competition and culture on the world stage in what Schechner calls "globalism's signature performance" (287). The games exemplify the globalization of the ancient ritual of the Athenian Games in which each host country has the opportunity to display their unique traditions and culture within. As a worldwide event and a mass-mediated event, the games are not without controversy and provide many countries an opportunity to carry political messages and statements to much larger audiences than they might normally have.

As in any spectator sport, one of the key attractions is the uncertainty of the outcome. While industry and media producers cannot control the outcome of the game itself, they can control the spectacle of the overall performance in order to maximize the entertainment value and continue to attract audiences. "The Big Business of College Game Day" draws our attention away from teams and nations and into the world of industry and sports as played out on college campuses.

The final essay in Part Four offers another perspective on competition. In recent decades, reality TV programming has developed competitions that feature contests of skills, talents, and/or intellect. Meizel's essay calls into question issues of authenticity as well as social prejudices and "the necessity of failure in the process of achievement" in the popular reality show *American Idol* (317). This essay interrogates how perceptions of race, gender, and class influence contestant's pursuit of and audience's reactions to fame and fortune in reality-based televised competitions. Returning to questions of authenticity and identity, Meizel places her essay within the context of the American Dream, illustrating the ways in which these types of mediated competitions have led to a reconceptualization of this ideal for the 21st century.

Team and Nation
Industry and Sports at the College Level
So you think you can ....? Reality Competition

Team and Nation

The ancient Olympiads were inspired by the funeral games described in Homer's *The Iliad*. In ancient Greece, spectators were treated to nine-mile chariots races with as many as forty contestants. Modern-day Olympics began in 1896 when Pierre de Coubertain had the idea to rekindle the spirit of the ancient Olympiads. The ideal, as in Grecian times, was that nations and people might put aside their differences and redirect their rivalries to the playing fields. While the ideal has not changed, the Olympics reflect the political, cultural, and social context of the era and the place where the individual games are held.

Today the Olympics are undoubtedly one of the greatest performances of spectacle in sports. Through television and the web, many of the performances are available to audiences across the globe. The Olympics carry the promise of competition at the highest level while at the same time foster a sense of community among athletes and people of all nations. Teams from individual nations compete against one another on a world stage but live together in the Olympic Village. The whole world can experience the same events within the same two-week period, and anticipates the arrival of the Games every two or four years. Spectacle, festival, ritual, and games are intertwined with the convergence of live and mediated performances.

Ideas

Olympic Ideal
Interconnected performance system: Spectacle, Festival, Ritual and Games
"Society's real unreality"
International Olympic Committee
Media convergence
Receptivity and interactivity between performance and audience.

The Olympics

Globalisim's Signature Performance

By Richard Schechner

The modern Olympic Games are the most popular performance event in history, a truly global phenomenon. More than 4 billion people watched some portion of the 2004 summer Olympics at Athens. Several million attended the Games in person. The 2004 Games featured 11,099 athletes from 202 nations competing in 300 events of 28 sports. By comparison, the United Nations in 2005 had 191 member nations. In addition to athletes, many thousands are involved as press, dignitaries, officials, technicians, snack and souvenir sellers, janitors, housekeepers, performers and other artists, scientists, and commercial exhibitors. Building arenas for the competitions and for housing athletes involves reconstructing large sections of cities, laying down roads and infrastructure, and uprooting neighborhoods. The new construction has reinvigorated urban areas. But the displacements and profiteering have also evoked strong protests. It all adds up to billions in investments and, during the Games, the spending of even more money by the media, sponsors, and those attending the Games.

The first modern Olympics took place in 1896 in Athens. The brainchild of Pierre de Coubertin, those first modern Games featured 245 white male amateur athletes from 14 European nations, the USA, Canada, and Australia. They competed in 45 events of nine sports ranging from racing and weight-lifting to swimming, tennis, and fencing (where a professional was allowed to compete). In the present-day Olympics, about 40 percent of the athletes are women, people from all over the world compete, and the distinction between professional and amateur has all but vanished because every athlete is either paid or sponsored. When the Games are over, many can look forward

> Pierre de Coubertin (1863–1937): founder of the modern Olympics movement and president of the International Olympic Committee from 1896 to 1925.

to lucrative careers built on their Olympic triumphs. This "impurity" is nothing new. Whatever the rhetoric of the founders, from the start, the modern Olympics combined

> **Homer** (eighth or ninth century BC): the legendary blind Greek poet, putative composer of the seminal epic poems, the *Odyssey* and the *Iliad*. Most scholars believe that Homeric tradition is oral. Only long after Homer's time were his poems set in writing.

sport, spectacle, ritual, festivity, performing arts, economics, and politics.

And although the International Olympic Committee (IOC) says it wants to keep the Games "above" politics, rifts in the global political landscape are played out at the Olympics. The Games were cancelled three times because of war: in 1916, in 1940, and in 1944. Ironically, the 1916 Games were scheduled for Berlin, the 1940 for Tokyo, and the 1944 for London. At Munich in 1972, terrorists murdered eleven Israelis. At the 1976 Montreal Games, 20 teams from Africa (plus Iraq and Guyana) withdrew to protest the New Zealand rugby team's tour of South Africa during the height of apartheid. Taiwan withdrew because it was not allowed to play under the banner of the "Republic of China." The USA and four other nations boycotted the Moscow Games of 1980 to protest the Soviet invasion of Afghanistan. The USSR retaliated by leading 14 nations in a boycott of the 1984 Los Angeles Games.

Despite all this, the Games keep growing in general popularity and national participation. The opportunity to use the Olympics as a showcase is too much to resist. The media event is too popular to forego. Although the original idea was for individuals not nations to compete, the flying of flags, the playing of anthems, the jockeying over where the Games are held, and the keeping of records proclaiming which nation has won the most medals—focus attention on national accomplishment.

The modern Olympics were meant to rekindle the spirit of the ancient Olympiads (776 BCE–369 CE), themselves a kind of recreation of the funeral games honoring the slain patrocolus described by Homer in book 23 of the *Iliad*. A key goal of the Olympics, modern and ancient, is to transcend the local and emphasize the "global" (however that is conceived). In ancient times, warfare was suspended for the games, in modern times, the games were suspended for war. The underlying Olympic ideal is for nations to put aside their differences and sublimate their rivalries on the fields of play. But "the world" of 2004 and beyond is not the world of 1896 no less that of the ancient Greco–Roman civilizations. At the end of the nineteenth century, the world was controlled by Europe and the European diaspora. But over time, with the end of colonialism and the emergence of multiple players on the world stage, more and more nations joined the Olympic movement.

In terms of the participating athletes and media spectators, the Olympics are a truly global event. However, at the organizational and structural levels the Eurocentricity of the Games remains intact. First, the IOC continues to be led by Europeans or North Americans. Second, although people everywhere run, jump, swim, play fight, and so on, the Olympic sports based on these activities are European. No effort is made to include non-European sports such as sumo wrestling, Trinidadian stick fighting, or the kind of mixed-terrain long-distance running enjoyed by the Tarahumaras of northwest Mexico. Third, venues remain overwhelmingly Western. Only Seoul in 1988 lay outside the West (if one considers Sydney culturally a Western city). Mexico City, host to the 1968 Games, is both Western and Third World; Moscow, site of the 1980 Games, is a European city even if, at that time, it was capital of the USSR. The 2004 Games returned to Athens and the 2008 Games will be in Beijing.

When in July 2001 the IOC selected Beijing, the decision was televised on large screens in China and more than 100,000 persons poured onto the streets of Beijing shouting, waving flags, and setting off fireworks. ... The joyous celebration was by far the largest free-flowing mass in the streets of the Chinese capital since the Pro-Democracy movement of May–June 1989. The Pro-Democracy demonstrators were shot, beaten, and crushed as the Chinese army used troops and tanks to clear Tiananmen Square. Clearly the crowds celebrating the Olympics had the blessing of the authorities. What were they and Chinese officials so happy about? As *The New York Times* put it: "Winning the Olympic bid is much more than a matter of civic or even national pride for people here. [...] As host to the Games, China believes it will stand as a respected member of the world community, a position it has long felt the West has denied it." Wanting to be a "respected member of the world community" is to enact a concept made real by globalization.

Aside from the sports competition, the Olympics have always featured sheer spectacle. The first modern Games commenced on Easter Sunday with Athens adorned in colorful bunting, streamers, and green wreaths inscribed with the letters "O. A." (the Greek initials for the games) and the dates "776 B.C." and "A.D. 1896" connecting the ancient to the modern. After the Greek King George I (1845–1913) opened the modern Olympic era, cannons were fired,

King George I of Greece (1845–1913): born William, Prince of Denmark, and proclaimed King of Greece in 1863. In 1896, George I inaugurated the first modern Olympics, hoping to restore some glory to Greece.

pigeons released, and the Olympic hymn sung. The present era features the arrival of the Olympic torch, elaborate opening-day ceremonies, raising the national flags of winning athletes, playing national anthems, and the constant media drumbeat.

The Olympics are a lot more than a sports competition. Surrounding the Games are all kinds of celebrations, artistic events, and commercial operations. The 1984 Los Angeles Olympics spawned the "Cultural Olympics," which in turn morphed into the Los Angeles Festivals of 1987 and 1990. The vast conglomeration of performances and exhibitions in 1990 included 550 events in 70 venues with more than 1,400 artists from 21 Pacific Rim countries. Although the 1990 LA Festival may have been the biggest, there have been many similar festivals around the world modeled on the Olympics and on similar gatherings: world's fairs and expositions. All of these super-conglomerations import, package, and stage events performed by persons from a variety of nations and cultures; they also display the latest scientific achievements and commercial products. The goal—sometimes stated, sometimes implicit—is to assemble, own, and display the largest quantity and widest diversity of peoples performing either culture-specific (the expositions and fairs) or "universal" activities (the Olympics).

What kind of performance are the Olympics? The Games can't be subsumed under a single category. According to anthropologist John J. MacAloon, the Olympics are a complex interplay of spectacle, festival, ritual, and play (see ... [the] MacAloon box). The largest, most inclusive category is spectacle (see Debord box). The global spectacle of the Olympics is crystallized in the opening-day show, which features thousands of performers, music, dance, and special effects. Spectacle both generates and is part of the overall festivity permeating the Games. Although this festivity is centered in the Olympic city, it extends to many parts of the world, where groups assemble to root for their national heroes. Then come the many rituals of the Olympics. On opening day there are the declaration that the Games are open, the arrival of the Olympic torch from Greece, and the parade of athletes. After each event, the winners are displayed before the crowds as the flags of their nations are raised and their anthems played. The Games close with more rituals and the promise of another Olympiad four years hence. At the center of all this are the games themselves. In appearance these maintain a relative purity determined by the rules. However, because of the intensity of the competition

John J. MacAloon (1947–): American anthropologist and foremost scholar of the Olympic Games. Author of *This Great Symbol* (1981) and *Brides of Victory: Nationalism and Gender in Olympic Ritual* (1997); editor of *Rite, Drama, Festival Spectacle* (1984).

John MacAloon
Genres of Performance in the Olympics

The genres [. …] spectacle, festival, ritual, game by no means exhaust the roster of performance types found in the Olympic Games. But they are semantically and functionally the most significant. The order in which they are discussed reflects a passage from the most diffuse and ideologically centrifugal genres to the most concentrated and ideologically centripetal. Spectacle and game appeared earliest, festival and ritual consolidated later, in Olympic history. […] These genres are distinctive forms of symbolic action, distinguished from one another by athletes, spectators, and officials alike. While certain features are shared between genres, others are in tension or in opposition, both categorically and in context. […] At the same time, the Olympic Games form a single performance system. The genres are intimately and complexly interconnected on all levels: historically, ideologically, structurally, and performatively. Thus we are forced to recognize that the Olympic Games represent a special kind of cultural performance, a ramified performance type, and we are forced to seek for new models and methods of analysis that will allow us to understand the relationships between the various forms of symbolic action without losing sight of their distinctive properties. […]

By the late 1920s and early 1930s, cultural history had, so to speak, caught up with the Olympic movement. Until that time, the semantic boundary "This is play," had remained more or less intact around the games of the Olympic Games. In turn, this protected the festival frame as well, and it afforded Olympic rituals a certain serenity within which to condense and elaborate. But largely due to the success of the Olympics themselves, a mass efflorescence of organized sport, first in Euro–American cultures, then worldwide, drew down upon the Games of the 20s and 30s ideological, political, and commercial interests of every sort. […]

The professionalization of sports and the transformation of athletes into celebrities, the growing number-fetishism and specialization in athletics, the increased role of technology and hyperextended training periods […], the growth of athletic bureaucracies, the recognition of sport's importance and the incorporation of sports success by the dominant world ideologies, the takeover of the selection, preparation, and financing of the teams by national governments and corporate interests, the counting of medals as propaganda and ersatz warfare, the attempts to co-opt the Games for chauvinistic purposes by host nations, and their use as a stage for "jock-strap diplomacy," saber rattling, regime building, and, finally, terrorism by insiders and outsiders alike: these developments represent in a general way the penetration of the "stuff of ordinary life" into the public liminality of the Games. And as ordinary life has changed, so have the Games been forced to change.

1984, *Olympic Games and the Theory of Spectacle in Modern Societies*, 242, 258–59, 262–63.

and the huge rewards awaiting both individuals and nations, performance-enhancing drugs and other manipulations are rampant. The ideal of free competition has been corrupted by the demand for victory at any cost. Additionally, all else aside, athletes

Guy Debord
Spectacle, Society's Real Unreality

The whole life of those societies in which modern conditions of production prevail presents itself as an immense accumulation of spectacles. All that was once directly lived has become mere representation. [...] The spectacle is not a collection of images; rather, it is a social relationship between people that is mediated by images. [...] Understood in its totality, the spectacle is both the outcome and the goal of the dominant mode of production. It is not something added to the real world—not a decorative element, so to speak. On the contrary, it is the very heart of society's real unreality. In all its specific manifestations—news or propaganda, advertising or the actual consumption of entertainment—the spectacle epitomizes the prevailing model of social life. [...]

The unreal unity the spectacle proclaims masks the class division on which the real unity of the capitalist mode of production is based. What obliges producers to participate in the construction of the world is also what separates them from it. What brings together men liberated from local and national limitations is also what keeps them apart. What pushes for greater rationality is also what nourishes the irrationality of hierarchical exploitation and repression. What creates society's abstract power also creates its concrete unfreedom.

1994 [1967], *The Society of the Spectacle*, 12–13, 46.

from poorer nations are at a disadvantage because they cannot afford the kind of training or facilities used by athletes from richer countries.

Questions

1. Which event in the Olympics do you think best illustrates Schechner's interconnected performance system of spectacle, festival, ritual, and game?
2. How is the performance of nationhood achieved through the various elements of a modern Olympic Games?
3. How has politics influenced the modern Olympic Games?
4. How has television changed audience receptivity to the games?
5. Consider the concept of society's real unreality and apply that idea to one particular Olympic Games. In what ways was this manifested in the many events of those games?

View

YouTube
"Jesse Owens and the 1936 Berlin Olympics" (2008)
"Black History: 1968 Olympics" (2008)
"1972 Munich Olympics Massacre of Israeli Athletes" (2010)

Web
Official Website of the Olympic Movement (www.olympic.org)

Film/Video
Tokyo Olympiad (1965)
Chariots of Fire (1981)
A State of Mind (2004)
Miracle (2004)
Sport at Heart (2005)
Munich (2005)

Read

Andrews, David L. "The Olympic Games and the Politicization of Everyday Life." *FlowTV*, 5 February 2010. Web. 14 June 2012.

Booth, D. "Olympic City Bidding: An Exegesis of Power." *International Review for the Sociology of Sport* 46.4 (2011): 367–386. Print.

International Olympic Committee. *The Olympic Charter*. Web. 2011. PDF file.

Klausen, Arne Martin. *Olympic Games as Performance and Public Event.* New York: Berghahn Books, 1999. Print.

Silk, M. "Towards a Sociological Analysis of London 2012." *Sociology* 45.5 (2011): 733–748. Print.

Industry and Sports at the College Level

Advances in media technology and the convergence of media platforms have provided producers the resources to control spectacle. Fans or enthusiasts loyal to a particular team anticipate positive outcomes while at the same time fear for the worst. And yet, if a team or individual is not performing well or if the score of the game is not particularly close, attention can wane. Producers use spectacle to heighten suspense and the entertainment value of the overall event.

Professional sports capture huge audiences through various media platforms. For many spectators, the attraction to professional sports begins in college. "The Big Business of College Game Day" focuses on the business of college sports and offers a critique of the attention paid to revenue at the detriment of education. In the early days, college sports in America were envisioned as a way to complement the ideals and values of the academy. Athletics was seen as a discipline or course of study and the focus was on the student. College athletics faces the challenge of negotiating how to respond to the industry and audience pressure that comes with the expectation for the level of spectacle and competition seen in professional sports.

Ideas

Industry
Technology
College athletics (intramural, recreational, intercollegiate)
Graduation rates
"One and done" rule
Campus life
Recruitment
NCAA

The Big Business of College Game Day

By Loftus C. Carson, II* and Michelle A. Rinehart**

I n July of 1859, two colleges came together on a field in Massachusetts to play a game of baseball that is now recognized as the first intercollegiate sporting event in the United States.[1] While the one-sided score of 73–32 may not have made for a hotly contested battle,[2] it did radically alter higher education and what we know as the collegiate experience.[3] For over two centuries prior to that game, American colleges and universities focused on educating young men (and women for a century prior) to be learned and engaged citizens.[4] The emphasis was on the development of their character and their minds.[5] Unfortunately, what is played out on the fields of college athletics 142 years later has nothing to do with the

---

1   Amherst College Athletics, *Amherst and Williams to Celebrate 150th Anniversary of First College Baseball Game*, (https://www.amherst.edu/athletics/teams/spring/baseball/articles/2009/0427_150th). Last visited Jan. 23, 2010.

2   Id.

3   Murray Sperber, (2000). *Beer and Circus: How Big-Time College Sports is Crippling Undergraduate Education* 45.

4   See generally John S. Brubacher & Willis Rudy, (2004). Higher Education in Transition: A History of American Colleges and Universities 3–100. (Providing an early history of American Higher Education.)

5   Id. at 23.

* B.S., Cornell University; M.Pub.Affs., Princeton University; J.D., Harvard University; M.B.A., University of Pennsylvania. Professor Carson holds the Ronald D. Krist Professorship in Law at the University of Texas School of Law.

** M.Arch., Tulane University; M.S. in Architecture, University of Michigan; Ed.D., University of Pennsylvania. Dr. Rinehart is Assistant Dean for Administration in the College of Architecture at The Catholic University of America.

The authors wish to thank Dr. Robert Zemsky of the University of Pennsylvania, for helpful comments on an earlier version, and Adam C. Harden, Esq. for research assistance.

character and minds of our students, but has everything to do with high-stakes entertainment. Gone are the days of the well-rounded student–athlete.[6] Instead, we have modern-day gladiatorial games that sacrifice the student–athletes for the sake of the audience's enjoyment.

The Disappearance of the Student–Athlete

In the early days of college athletics, the emphasis was on the student as an athlete.[7] The game of sport was a way to complement the ideals and values of the academy. The benefit to the students was clear: a sound body would lead to a sound mind.[8] Athletics also provided the opportunity to learn life's lessons. All students on campus were able to use athletics to learn the value of hard work, dedication, perseverance, sacrifice, and discipline.[9] Students also gained valuable collaborative and leadership skills.[10] All the while, the focus remained on the student.[11]

This changed, however, as colleges and universities began to embrace the many institutional benefits of athletics. Saturday game day was a time when the college community could put its hard work of the week behind it and focus on how best to beat the "other guy."[12] Students and faculty alike banded together in a sense of institutional camaraderie to prove that they were better than the college down the street.[13] It also became an opportunity to bind alumni to their college regardless of their geographic location.[14] With the advent of modern technologies (the radio, television, and now the internet), it was even easier to connect alumni to the

---

6   See, e.g., Paul C. Weiler & Gary R. Roberts. (2004). *Sports and the Law: Text, Cases and Problems*, 394. It was found at trial that, despite four years of playing football at the University of Arkansas, Gary Anderson had not learned to read; that was one reason he could not understand the various documents he had been signing as an NFL and USFL football player. But see Pete Thamel, *Myron Rolle Awarded Rhodes Scholarship*, The Quad: The NY Times C. Sports Blog (Nov. 22, 2008), (http://thequad.blogs.nytimes.com/2008/11/22/myron-rolle-wins-rhodes-scholarship).

7   See Brubacher & Rudy, supra note 4, at 131 (discussing the informal nature of early American college physical exercise).

8   Donald Siegel, Athletics and Education: The Union of Athletics with Educational Institutions, *Course Materials for Sport: In Search of the American Dream*, Smith College, http://www.science.smith.edu/exer_sci/ESS200/Ed/cd04/athletic.htm.

9   Id.

10   Id.

11   Id.

12   James J. Duderstadt, (2000). Intercollegiate Athletics and the American University 74.

13   Id.

14   Id.

campus. What was once a regional activity soon became a national phenomenon.[15] With its size and scale, it was only a matter of time before college athletics evolved into an entirely distinct financial enterprise, which has led college athletics to the pursuit of the almighty dollar (directly through ticket sales, the sale of broadcasting rights, merchandising, and conference tournament shares; indirectly through alumni giving).[16] College sports are now big business and are operated as such. The bigger, the better. In today's world of tighter state funding, this opportunity for increased revenue is simply too good to ignore, no matter what the cost to the institution.

The growing power of the media to influence college athletics has bound it to another big business—the entertainment industry.[17] Athletes and movie stars are the royalty of America.[18] Athletics as entertainment has permeated American society to such an extent that we have an overblown sports culture that goes from five-year-old pee-wee leagues to professional athletics.[19] All you have to do is watch the Olympics to see how we exalt athletes above all others as exemplars of a nation's might and power.

On college campuses, this mix of finances and entertainment has proved to be a toxic potion. Athletics on campus is no longer an extracurricular for all students, but rather is a commodity and its players are merely a labor force.[20] Just as in profes-

---

15   *TV by the Numbers, Florida Oklahoma Title Bout Concludes FOX's Most Watched BCS Game Ever.* (Jan. 9, 2009), (http://tvbythenumbers.zap2it.com/2009/01/09/florida-oklahoma-title-bout-deli vers-foxs-most-watched-bcs-game-ever/10553). The 2009 BCS National Championship game drew a record 26.8 million viewers.

16   Melissa McNamara. (Mar. 19, 2007). March Madness is Big Business, *CBS evening news*, (http://www.cbsnews.com/stories/2007/03/19/eveningnews/main2585960.shtml). The article states that CBS paid $6 billion to the NCAA for broadcasting to college basketball's "March Madness."

17   Id. McNamara's article also states that over 130 million viewers tuned in to watch the 2006 NCAA college basketball tournament.

18   See, e.g., Adam Jones (Mar. 9, 2009). Star Receiver Accepts Seat on UA Senate, *Tuscaloosa News*, (http://www.tuscaloosanews.com/article/20090309/NEWS/903081944). Alabama Crimson Tide freshman wide receiver Julio Jones was elected as a student body senator despite not running or campaigning for write-in votes. The previous year, Jones finished third in voting for Alabama's student body president despite not being enrolled at the University due to the fact Jones was still a senior in high school.

19   See, e.g., Youth Coach Charged with Attacking Player, *USA today*, (Sep. 6, 2006), (http://www. usatoday.com/sports/preps/2006-09-06-youth-coach-charges_x.htm).

20   See Mike Freeman, N.C.A.A. Tournament—East; For One, a Laugh and an Ax to Grind, *N.Y. Times*, (Mar. 26, 1993), (http://www.nytimes.com/1993/03/26/sports/college-basketball-ncaa-tournament-east-for-one-a-laugh-and-an-ax-to-grind.html). University of Cincinnati senior forward Terry Nelson stated, "College players are glorified slaves. The NCAA is nothing more than a system of institutionalized slavery … It's sick." Id.

sional sports, the allegiance is to the bottom line. The average College Joe isn't even able to walk on the football field, much less learn the life's lessons to be gained from participating in college athletics. Even the late Myles Brand, former head of the NCAA, recognized that this shift toward professionalism will lead to a diminished value to the institution.[21]

The commodification of student–athletes has fundamentally changed their role on campus. Where student–athletes once walked, we now see athletes parading as students.[22] College sports are no longer in the service of the academy.[23] Instead, they are ruled by the professional sports enterprise in the United States.[24] For football and basketball, the premier college sports, college teams have essentially turned into farm or feeder programs for professional athletics, all under the guise of the higher ideals of the academic institution.[25]

---

21   News Release, NCAA President Myles Brand, NCAA Response to the House Committee on Ways and Means concerning the NCAA's tax-exempt status 5, (Nov. 15, 2006), (on file with author) ("'Professional sports' sole purposes are to entertain the public and make a profit for team owners. The purpose of the collegiate model is to enhance the education development of student–athletes").

22   See Pete Thamel. (May. 28, 2009). *Coaches Don't Go by Book When It Comes to N.C.A.A.*, The Quad: the N.Y. Times C. Sports Blog, (http://www.nytimes.com/2009/05/29/sports/ncaabasketball/29memphis.html), (pointing out that fixed transcripts for athletes are as much a part of college basketball as exciting finishes); Chip Brown, (Feb. 19, 2008), *Still Deep in Texas: Young's Return to Classes Causes Quite the Stir on Campus*, Dall. Morning News, at 8C. Upon returning to class, Vince Young received a standing ovation from classmates for his on-field performance in the Rose Bowl game.

23   See Andy Katz. (May 13, 2008). *One-and-Dones Have Low Academic Requirements Too*, ESPN. com, (http://sports.espn.go.com/ncb/columns/story?columnist=katz_andy&id=3393470), (interviewing faculty members at various institutions who expressed their feelings about the negative academic implications of the NBA's age requirement).

24   See Tim Griffin, (Mar. 2, 2009). *NFL Snub Inspires Kindle in his Changing Role*, ESPN.com, (http://espn.go.com/blog/big12/post/_/id/1646/nfl-snub-inspires-kindle-in-his-changing-role). This is a prime example of a professional enterprise dictating what should happen to college athletes. As a junior and without loss of his amateur status, a college football player may ask the NFL for an evaluation from NFL scouts and a projected draft grade. If the NFL scouts wish for the player to leave college early, they will give him a glowing report and a high draft projection. If the NFL scouts, for whatever reason, do not want the player to become a professional, they will lowball his draft projection, which will almost always lead the player to return to college.

25   Major League Baseball and the National Hockey League have well-established, multi-tiered minor league systems and are therefore not as susceptible to this phenomenon.

The "One-and-Done" Phenomenon

In 2006, the National Basketball Association implemented new rules that prevent teams from drafting a player until a full year has passed after his high school graduation and he reaches 19 years of age.[26] The result is what has become known as "one-and-done"[27]—promising players attend university for one year, play for one season, and then drop out after entering the draft.[28] Because of these restrictions, high school phenom players have no choice but to play college basketball in order to be drafted into the professional ranks.[29] Freshman players are required to pass only six credit hours in the fall semester, and could, in theory, miss all classes during the spring and still be eligible to declare for the NBA draft at the conclusion of the season.[30] After the season-ending tournament, they drop out of their spring classes, leave campus, and bide their time until they can start in the NBA.[31] As a result, more often than not, colleges attract athletes who are less interested in education than they are in following the only true path to professional sports.[32] Colleges and universities are able to lure talented young athletes to their campuses with the promise of a lucrative career as a professional athlete combined (occasionally) with a good education,[33] when the reality is that most Division I-A athletes rarely achieve either.[34] There has been a cry from some in the athletics community

---

26   Eric Brady & Steve Wieberg. (May 15, 2008). *Merits of One-and-Done rule in NBA Face Fresh Scrutiny*, USA today, (http://www.usatoday.com/sports/college/mensbasketball/2008-05-14-nbadraft-freshmen_N.htm).

27   Id.

28   Marlen Garcia. (June 5, 2009). *One-and-Done Players Leave Behind a Mess; Scandals Shake Schools, Spur Call for NBA Age-Limit Repeal*, USA Today, (http://www.usatoday.com/sports/college/mensbasketball/2009-06-05-freshmen-cover_N.htm).

29   See id.

30   Dana O'Neil. (May 21, 2010). *College Basketball Doesn't Pass the Test*, ESPN.com, (http://sports.espn.go.com/ncb/columns/story?columnist=oneil_dana&id=5206806).

31   See id.

32   See Scott Bernarde, Brice Butler. (Feb. 6, 2008). 3 Years at USC, then NFL, Atlanta J. Const., (http://www.ajc.com/sports/content/shared-blogs/ajc/cfbrecruit/entries/2008/02/06/brice_butler_3.html). At the high school senior's signing day press conference, Brice Butler announced his intentions for his collegiate career: "Three good season [sic] and then to the NFL Draft." Id. Note that in order to be eligible for the NFL draft, an athlete must be three years removed from high school, so three seasons is the bare minimum. NFL Collective Bargaining Agreement art. XVI, § 2(b).

33   Id.

34   See Letter from Bill Thomas, House Ways and Means Committee Chairman, to Myles Brand, NCAA President. (Oct. 5, 2006). Available at http://www.usatoday.com/sports/college/2006-10-05-congress-ncaa-tax-letter_x.htm). Rep. Thomas noted that, at the Division I-A level, only 55% of football players and only 38% of basketball players graduate—compared to 64% of the general student

to change the NBA eligibility rule to a "two-and-done" system, in order to give student–athletes the extra time to develop physically and mentally before heading to the professional leagues.[35] Proponents argue that such a change would serve both the athletes, few of whom are emotionally or even physically ready to embark on a professional career at age 19,[36] and the professional teams, who would get an extra season to evaluate the potential of draft candidates.[37] While a two-and-done system might benefit teams because they would receive players with an additional year of training and preparation, and perhaps some extra height and muscle, the question remains whether an extra year of college would make a palpable difference in the emotional maturity of a student–athlete. This also fails to address the underlying problem of placing athletic involvement above the student's educational experience in the university.

Athletics and the Academy

This shift in focus from academics to athletics has not gone unnoticed by those in the academic community, but many are conflicted about the implications of the "one-and-done" system. While college athletics may offer a number of students the opportunity to attend a university that they otherwise would not have, some faculty have expressed concern about the quality of education that these student–athletes are getting.[38] Ostensibly, the NCAA monitors the academic performance of each

---

body. Rep. Thomas specifically noted that the then-defending nation champion in football only graduated 29% of its players as compared to 74% of the university's student body for the class of 1998.

35   Garcia, supra note 29; Jon Saraceno. (Jun. 12, 2009). *Debate is One for the Ages: 'One-and-Done' Rule has Plenty of Detractors*, USA Today, at 8C; Marc Stein. (Jun. 23, 2009). *NBA Should Impose 'Two-and-Done' Limit*, ESPN.com, (http://sports.espn.co.com/nba/columns/story?columnist=stein_marc&page=AgeLimit090622).

36   University of Memphis Coach John Calipari has commented on the physical and emotional preparedness of student–athletes in their late teenage years. See Dana O'Neil, One-and-Done not Expected to be as Prevalent in 2009, ESPN.com (May 23, 2008), (http://sports.espn.go.com/ncb/columns/story?columnist=oneil_dana&id=3405089).

37   Stein, supra note 36.

38   Ohio State University Faculty representative John Bruno, who holds positions in both the psychology and athletic departments, has voiced such concern to ESPN.com. See Katz, supra note 24 ("We understand the opportunity that athletics brought some of these kids with respect to the opportunity to go to college when they may never have gone to college before ... but on the other hand you sort of shudder. You're frustrated because you know that there is a real good chance that this person isn't going to take full advantage of this opportunity.").

team through the Academic Progress Rate (APR).[39] The APR is a two-point system, with one point awarded each term for each scholarship student–athlete who meets the NCAA's academic-eligibility standards, and an additional point for each student–athlete that remains in school.[40] The APR equals the team's total points at any given time, divided by the total points possible;[41] the cutoff score is 925, which represents a 60% graduation rate.[42] While the APR system rewards teams if their players stay at the university past their first year, it has clearly not deterred student–athletes from quitting without finishing their freshman year.[43]

The commodification of college sports has also led to the exploitation of our student–athletes. While it can be argued that student–athletes of every creed and color have been exploited by the "college sports as entertainment" complex, we contend that the exploitation of African–American athletes is by far the most troubling and signals how far we have fallen from the higher ideals of the academy. Today, African–American athletes dominate the college playing fields in the premier sports of football and basketball.[44] On average, nine out of ten of the first and second All-American basketball teams of the past two decades have been African–American. Given the extent of the domination of African–American athletes on college campuses, their exploitation is particularly egregious.[45]

The 1950s and 60s were a time of experimental integration on our campuses. Discovering the rich talent pool found in the African–American community, colleges and universities began recruiting black athletes.[46] At the time, it was seen as a win–win situation: the colleges showed their socially progressive attitudes by "integrating" their campuses and black athletes were given the rare opportunity to receive a quality and "equal" education. The broad acceptance of the African–American

---

39   *How is the Academic Progress Rate Calculated?*, NCAA, (http://www.ncaa.org/wps/wcm/connect/public/NCAA/Academics+OLD/Division+I/How+is+APR+calculated), (last visited June 15, 2010).

40   Id.

41   Id.

42   Id.

43   Garcia, supra note 29. Bruno admitted to advising one of his students, Ohio State University freshman B. J. Mullens, not to enroll for the third quarter once Mullens decided to enter the draft, saying that he did not want the school to "take another APR hit. ... 'The academic in me feels very conflicted,' Bruno says. But the advice, he adds, 'is totally defensible and sensible.'"

44   Richard Lapchick (Oct. 24, 2007). *The Buck Stops Here: Assessing Diversity Among Campus and Conference Leaders for Division I-A Schools in 2007–08*, DeVos Sport Business Management Program. The Institute for Diversity and Ethics in Sports (TIDES) reported that 50.4% of the football student–athletes who played Division I-A football during 2007 were African–Americans.

45   C. Richard King & Charles Freuhling Springwood. (2001). *Beyond the Cheers: Race as Spectacle in College Sport*, 10.

46   Charles K. Ross, (2004). *Race and Sport: The Struggle for Equality on and off the Field*, 127.

athlete in intercollegiate athletics followed a sustained effort that initially was a pitched battle for access.[47] It was thought that intercollegiate sports would present the same opportunities for individual African–Americans that whites, who were cheering for "our blacks," received in other sectors.[48] At the time, it was regarded as progress in race relations and was celebrated in *Ebony* magazine, the barometer of the prosperous and elite African–American community.[49] But what may have had the most honest of intentions at its inception has now become a caricature of its former self. Desperate for success on the playing field, colleges and universities have tossed aside their values and their moral compasses to recruit talented African–American athletes irrespective of the cost.[50]

Preferential treatment in the admissions process,[51] especially for African–American athletes, has virtually eliminated any requirements for academic rigor on the part of a talented athlete.[52] In today's hot recruitment market, it seems that little in an athlete's background disqualifies him from admission as a student–athlete,[53] especially if his vertical leap is over thirty-eight inches or his forty-yard time is 4.6 seconds or under. Admittedly, the University of Miami football program has reputedly stopped recruiting any players with a "rap sheet" longer than two pages, though it is also interesting to note that the practice has coincided with a decline

---

47   Id. at 199.

48   See Duderstadt, supra note 12, at 213.

49   Richard E. Lapchick (1986). *Fractured Focus: Sport as a reflection of Society*, 82–83.

50   Id. at 1. Dr. Lapchick writes that Walter Byers, former president of the NCAA, stated that "many good college players are making up to $20,000 a year" and that "the nation's best 'big men' were said to receive $100,000 when they signed with certain universities." Lapchick also notes instances at Tulane and Texas Christian Universities where players were paid substantial amounts to attend those institutions.

51   Duderstadt, supra note 12, at 193.

52   Lapchick, supra note 50, at 2. North Carolina State University admitted Chris Washburn, a star basketball player, with a combined 475 College Board score when the average student there has achieved a 950. Tulane University experienced a similar situation when "Hot Rod" Williams was admitted with close to the minimum score.

53   See, e.g., Ray Brewer. (Mar. 27, 2009). *Gorman Athlete's Ex-Girlfriend was Granted Restraining Order*, Las Vegas Sun, (http://www.lasvegassun.com/news/2009/mar/27/gorman-seniors-ex-girl-friend-was-granted-restraini). This article details a recent incident involving Justin Chaisson, one of the nation's top defensive ends, from national powerhouse Las Vegas Bishop Gorman. Chaisson had committed to play football for the University of Oklahoma before allegedly kidnapping his girlfriend, driving her to the desert, and holding a screwdriver to her throat while threatening to kill her. This incident happened one day after his girlfriend had a restraining order placed against him. Chaisson was arrested and charged with multiple felonies, but, after pleading down to misdemeanor charges, Chaisson's scholarship was honored by Oklahoma football coach Bob Stoops. Chaisson is currently enrolled in summer classes and listed on the 2009 Oklahoma Sooner depth chart.

in the team's success on the playing field.[54] Once enrolled, the low hurdle in the admissions process is replaced by even lower hurdles for the student–athlete, such as phantom courses, ghost writers, and inflated grades.[55] Too many of our black athletes are enrolled in a menu of courses designed to keep them eligible to play but provide little in terms of a broad knowledge base or application to a profession.[56] They select majors that do not challenge them or provide the skills necessary to earn a living once their athletic careers are over.[57] This is, of course, provided that they graduate at all.[58] Granted, a few do have lucrative professional careers, but those opportunities are few and far between.[59]

Schools exploit African–American athletes in many ways. Perhaps the most obvious, and therefore most troubling, is that black athletes are heavily recruited as a way to create instant diversity on campus.[60] Unfortunately, the nature of high-stakes

54   Football Archives, University of Miami Athletics (Oct. 30, 2010, 1:15 pm). (http://hurricanes-sports.cstv.com/sports/m-footbl/archive/mifl-m-footbl-archive.html.)

55   See, e.g., Bill Kaczor. (Sep. 26, 2007). *Nearly 2 Dozen Florida State Athletes Accused of Cheating*, USA Today, (http://www.usatoday.com/sports/college/2007-09-26-floridast-cheating_N.htm). An investigation revealed that a tutor had typed papers for five FSU athletes and provided answers for an online exam to 23 FSU athletes.

56   Walter Byers with Charles Hammer. (1992). *Unsportsmanlike Conduct: Exploiting College Athletes* 315. Mr. Byers, the former president of the NCAA, states, "[b]elieve me, there is a course, a grade, and a degree out there for everybody," in reference to the case of the curriculum for some NCAA student–athletes.

57   Jill Lieber-Steeg, Jodi Upton, Patrick Bohn & Steve Berkowitz. (Nov. 19, 2008). *College Athletes Studies Guided Toward 'Major in Eligibility'*, USA today, at 1A. Former Boise State safety Marty Tadman admitted to taking the easiest classes when he was in school. "You're going to school so you can stay in sports," Tadman said in this article. "You're not going for a degree … It's a joke."

58   Lapchick, supra note 45, at 1. Dr. Lapchick cites that the nationwide graduation rate for the 1985 NCAA basketball season was 27%. Dr. Lapchick also notes that the graduation rate for Final Four participant Memphis State University was a shocking 6%.

59   King & Springwood, supra note 46, at 10; Wilford S. Bailey & Taylor D. Littleton. (1991). *Athletics and Academe: An Anatomy of Abuses and a Prescription for Reform*, 84. It is estimated that only 64 out of the roughly 150,000, or one out of every 2,344, senior participants in high school basketball will make professional teams.

60   Pete Thamel. (Nov. 22, 2008). *Myron Rolle Awarded Rhodes Scholarship*, The Quad: The N.Y. Times College Sports Blog, (http://thequad.blogs.nytimes.com/2008/11/22/myron-rolle-wins-rhodes-scholarship). Thayer Evans. (Feb. 7, 2008). *Twist in the Scott Recruiting Story*, The Quad: The N.Y. Times College Sports Blog, (http://thequad.blogs.nytimes.com/2008/02/07/twist-in-the-scott-recruiting-story). This article states that the mother of Darrell Scott, the top running back recruit in the nation for the class of 2008, was alleged to have received a job at a bank in Colorado in exchange for her son signing with the University of Colorado. See also Thayer Evans. (Dec. 25, 2008). *Ending a Recruiting Battle*, N.Y. Times, (http://www.nytimes.com/2008/12/26/sports/ncaafootball/26recruit.html). This article states that the mother of Jamarkus McFarland, one of the nation's top defensive tackles, claims to have been offered interest free loans if her son would sign with a particular

athletics never allows these black athletes, especially those in the premier sports, to become integrated into everyday college life.[61] While they are segregated from the general student population by living in jock dorms, eating with jocks, and taking fluff courses,[62] their images are plastered across university viewbooks and admissions materials, giving prospective students, parents, and society-at-large the impression that the college is more diverse than it actually is.[63] But once this dirty little secret is exposed, the hypocrisy of the academy is in full view and its professed commitment to fair-play and non-discrimination is undermined.

While African–American student–athletes make up approximately 50% of college football's foremost division, known as the Football Bowl Subdivision (FBS), formerly known as Division I-A, African–American coaches and front office administrators are virtually nonexistent, especially at the upper echelon of the group.[64] According to a 2007 study conducted by the University of Oregon, there were only 15 African–American athletic directors among the 119 NCAA member schools in Division I-A—or 12.6%—and only twelve of those schools compete in Division I-A football.[65] Conversely, 102 of the 119 schools, or 86%, employed white persons as their Athletic Directors[66] during the 2007–08 academic school year. The study also found that, out of the 119 head coaching positions available in the FBS, only five—or 4.2%—were occupied by African–American head coaches.[67] The marked incongruity between the amount of African–American football players (50%) and the amount of African–American head coaches (4.2%) serves to showcase the disparate treatment that African–Americans have seen in the realm of collegiate sports.

---

university. Additionally, Jamarkus claims to have attended recruiting parties on college campuses where recruiting hostesses were "sitting on the laps of all the players, … drugs were prevalent with no price attached," girls were "taking off their tops and pulling down their pants," and other girls "were also romancing each other." See also King & Springwood, supra note 46, at 10.

61   Robert Samuels. (Mar. 4, 2004). *The Black Line: Black Athletes Struggle to Juggle Sports, Social Demands*, the Daily Northwestern, (http://www.dailynorthwestern.com/2.13921/the-black-line-1.1982647).

62   Id.

63   See King & Springwood, supra note 46, at 10.

64   Richard Lapchick. (Nov. 6, 2008). *The Buck Stops Here: Assessing Diversity Among Campus and Conference Leaders for Division I-A Schools in 2008–09*, DeVos Sport Business Management Program.

65   Lapchick, supra note 45, at 1.

66   id.

67   Id. However, with the termination of Washington's Tyrone Willingham and the resignation of Kansas State's Ron Prince, that number has since decreased to three.

A Call for Change

College sports, as we know them, no longer provide the promise of opportunity to exploited black athletes.[68] In fact, they are equally harmful to individual African–Americans and to the African–American community in general by helping to perpetuate the idea of the African–American as "other," that is, substantially different in biology from whites.[69] This concept of "otherness" is echoed on college campuses, where African–American athletes are exploited, treated like second-class citizens, and segregated from the rest of the academic community.[70] These behaviors are easily replicated off-campus. The academy should not take comfort in the example that it has set and that others have quickly followed.

Here we find a double-edged sword: we uphold the system of college athletics because of the revenue and media exposure that we receive,[71] while at the same time bemoaning our drift from the core values of the academy. We are perfectly willing to turn a blind eye and let our athletics programs exist as entities unto themselves, pretending all the while that they are acting in the best interest of the academy. This is far easier than acknowledging the hypocritical situation in which we are mired.

The purpose of the academy is not to entertain the American public with athletic prowess, nor is it to line the pockets of over-paid coaches and merchandising executives.[72] The priorities of the academy should serve a greater good to society—educating future citizens and addressing the larger problems of society such as health care, war and peace, and the environment.[73] It would be difficult, at best, to claim that our college sports programs serve any greater good. Colleges

---

68 King & Springwood, supra note 46, at 31,

69 John Hoberman. (1997). *Darwin's Athletes: How Sport Has Damaged Black America and Preserved the Myth of Race*, 4. Hoberman argues that the outcome of the illusion in African–American communities that social acceptance and monetary success will come through athletic achievement has created an unrealistic perception of reality and cultivates a focus on athleticism that directs young people away from advancement in education and academic achievement and has helped propagate stereotypes about racial differences in physical and mental ability.

70 Samuels, supra note 62; Duderstadt, supra note 12, at 205.

71 See Richard Sandomir. (Nov. 19, 1999). *CBS Will Pay $6 Billion for Men's N.C.A.A. Tournament*, N.Y. Times, (http://www.nytimes.com/1999/11/19/sports/college-basketball-cbs-will-pay-6-billion-for-men-s-ncaa-tournament.html). The NCAA signed an 11-year, $6-billion contract with CBS in which CBS gets broadcast rights to the NCAA college basketball tournament.

72 Steve Wieberg & Jodi Upton. (Dec. 5, 2007). *College Football Coaches Calling Lucrative Plays*, USA Today.

73 See Duderstadt, supra note 12, at 107 (discussing how collegiate athletics, as currently run, are based on values that are antithetical to the academy and its academic mission).

and universities should advance programs (academic, athletic, and otherwise) that support the ideals and values of the academy.

Colleges and universities are expected to convey knowledge to students through teaching, to develop knowledge, and to serve society by applying the fruits of their efforts. American higher education needs to get out of the sports entertainment business, whether that product is currently showcased on a large stage (Division I-A) or on a smaller one (Division III). Our institutions of higher education should focus on harnessing our intellectual capital, a task to which they are uniquely suited. As a society we cannot continue to allow the substantial diversion of colleges and universities away from their mission and professed ideals.

Is it possible to de-commercialize and de-commodify college sports now that the horse is out of the gate? The only way to accomplish this is to dismantle the "college sports as entertainment" complex. Athletics must be realigned with the ideals of the academy. We need to see a return of the student–athlete, where a student's achievement is lauded over athletic prowess. One potential solution is to eliminate freshman eligibility so that our student–athletes are able to enjoy a year to integrate into the life of the college as well as develop their intellectual abilities.[74] Additionally, colleges must focus on the welfare of the student–athlete by reducing the time commitment required to participate in athletics and by eliminating the performance anxiety that can result when scholarships are based on the ability to perform on the field. Admissions preferences for athletes must be eliminated to place emphasis, first and foremost, on an applicant's academic ability and not his or her skills on the field.

Colleges must also distance their sports programs from professional athletics.[75] The college farm system that now acts as a gateway to the professional ranks for the premier sports must be eliminated. Compensation for coaching should be restructured to be on par with salaries in the academy rather than that of their professional counterparts. Media contracts and other financial incentives for college sports similar to what is seen in professional athletics must be rejected. This entails eliminating the major "college sports as entertainment" events, such as the Bowl Championship Series (BCS) and the Final Four Tournament.

---

74   Id. at 201. Duderstadt argues, "there is no better example of the conflict between educational and competitive values than the issue of whether first-year students should be eligible to compete at the varsity level." For the majority of the 1900s, freshmen were not allowed to compete on the varsity level. However, this rule was lifted in the 1970s, when football coaches needed the additional athletes to keep up with the contemporary movement to not have players start on both offense and defense.

75   Id. at 302.

None of these recommendations will be easy to implement. The ultimate question is who can fix it? Certainly not the NCAA or others working within the college athletics system.[76] They are too financially and professionally invested in the system.[77] Maintaining the status quo continues their livelihood—why bite the hand that feeds you?[78] Professional athletics will not address the problem. Its members are far too reliant on colleges and universities to provide them with what are, in effect, professional athletes straight out of college who need no additional training or investment from their new team and who can be moneymakers from their very first game.[79] Society at large will not call for change. It prefers the latest fantasy football league or winning the office's Final Four pool to recognizing the higher purpose of the academy.

Looking inside the academy, it is clear that faculty are not likely candidates to change the "college sports as entertainment" complex. Despite expressing their outrage at how athletics undermine the values of the institution, they are simply too interested in their own research or the politics of their own department to effect any change.[80] They complain that athletes are given preferential treatment in admissions and then have lax course requirements.[81] They also claim that the sports machine on campus distracts the student body as a whole, which helps to lower overall academic performance.[82] Ultimately, however, they do nothing but turn a blind eye to the situation in what may be a "Devil's Bargain" with the administration—you let us do our own thing and we will let you keep your sports programs and their revenues. This represents a much deeper, and far more problematic, shift in faculty priorities from the education of students to the advancement of their own research and careers.

While we assert that higher education itself must take an active role in any athletics reform movement, we also recognize that change cannot come purely from

---

76   See id. at 202. Duderstadt states, "[i]n 1999 the NCAA commission concerned with reforming college basketball floated a trial balloon of freshman ineligibility, only to find that 74% of university presidents, coaches, and athletic directors opposed the change."

77   Byers, supra note 57, at 369. Byers, a former NCAA president, wrote, "[t]he rewards of success have become so huge that the beneficiaries—the colleges and their staffs—simply will not deny themselves even part of current or future spoils."

78   Id.

79   Kevin Durant's Statistics, NBA.COM (Oct. 30, 2010, 04:30 PM), (http://www.nba.com/player/file/kevin_durant/career_stats.html).

80   See generally Duderstadt, supra note 12, at 305–18 (detailing the current state of discontent among faculty towards celebrity coaches, the potential power they wield, and their limited action).

81   Id.

82   Id.

within the academy. This issue has been debated for far too long at the highest levels of American colleges and universities, and reform still has not come. In 2003, there was a movement to address the relationship between athletics and the academy. Led by Scott Cowen of Tulane University and James Duderstadt, President Emeritus of the University of Michigan,[83] it culminated in the National Symposium on Athletics Reform.[84] This was a step in the right direction, but it was simply not enough.

Tackling the Giant in Court

One avenue that shows promise is to change the legal framework surrounding college sports. Existing statutes and regulations, as well as the common law, can be interpreted in a manner that supports the dismantling of the "college sports as entertainment" complex. The NCAA, along with joint athletic activities of colleges and universities, could be more harshly subjected to the existing antitrust laws for anticompetitive collusion. Several key cases support this legal approach. In *Bob Jones University* v. *United States,*[85] the Supreme Court determined that the IRS could revoke a university's tax-exempt status if its actions are contrary to broader public policy.[86] Courts have also held that an institution may be held accountable by student–athletes who were promised an education and were subject to misguided education advice constituting education malpractice.[87]

While the Court has not always held the NCAA to be anticompetitive, it has done so on occasion. In the second set of cases we find *United States* v. *Brown University,*[88] in which the federal government alleged that MIT and eight Ivy League institutions violated the Sherman Antitrust Act in their financial aid policies.[89] The Supreme Court has also held the NCAA to be under §1 of the Sherman Antitrust Act in the landmark case *NCAA v. Board of Regents of the University of Oklahoma.*[90]

---

83   Id.

84   National Symposium on Athletics Reform, Symposium Transcript and Photos (last visited Oct. 30, 2010, 4:15 PM), (http://symposium.tulane.edu).

85   Bob Jones Univ. v. U.S., 461 U.S. 574 (1983).

86   Id. at 605.

87   See, e.g., Ross v. Creighton Univ., 957 F.2d 410 (7th Cir. 1992), in which plaintiff Ross, a Creighton basketball player from 1978–1982, left the University with the overall language skills of a fourth grader and the reading skills of a seventh grader.

88   U.S. v. Brown Univ. in Providence in St. of R.I., 5 F.3d 658 (3d Cir. 1993).

89   Id. at 661.

90   NCAA v. Bd. of Regents of Univ. of Okla., 468 U.S. 85 (1984).

In this case, the Court held that a television agreement between the NCAA and two broadcasting networks had "significant potential for anticompetitive effects" because the NCAA was effectively creating a pricing regime that was unresponsive to consumer demands and unrelated to any price that a competitive market would support.[91] Thus, the agreement violated the Act by imposing an unreasonable restraint on trade. It is important to note, however, that the Court in dicta acknowledged that the nature of collegiate sports under the purview of the NCAA is such that "horizontal restraints on competition are essential if the product is to be available at all."[92] Further, the Court stated that the NCAA "plays a vital role in enabling college football to preserve its character, and as a result a product to be marketed which might otherwise be unavailable ... and hence be seen as precompetitive."[93] The Court goes on to note that "most of the regulatory controls of the NCAA are justifiable means of fostering competition among amateur athletic teams and therefore precompetitive because they enhance public interest in intercollegiate athletics." [94] Thus, although the Court found the NCAA's behavior to be in violation of current antitrust law in this instance, the overarching judicial attitude nevertheless remains one in which the NCAA is given immense latitude in its self-regulation and organization in spite of what seem to be anticompetitive practices. This extended leeway is highlighted in *Gaines* v. *NCAA*,[95] in which the petitioner Gaines alleged that the "no-draft" rule allowed the NCAA to engage in an unlawful exercise of monopoly power in violation of §2 of the Sherman Antitrust Act. The *Gaines* court was unconvinced that the NCAA's "no-draft" rule was unreasonably anticompetitive and reasoned that the NCAA eligibility rules have "primarily precompetitive effects in that they promote the integrity and quality of college football and preserve the distinct 'product' of major college football as an amateur sport."[96] The court went on to state that the NCAA rules, as a whole, "benefit both players and the public by regulating college football so as to preserve its amateur appeal ... [and] in fact makes a better 'product' available by maintaining the educational underpinnings of college football and preserving the stability and integrity of college football programs."[97]

---

91 Id at 105–06.
92 Id. at 101.
93 Id. at 102.
94 Id. at 117.
95 Gaines v. NCAA, 746 F. Supp. 738 (M.D. Tenn. 1990).
96 Id. at 746.
97 Id. at 745.

While there is precedent to hold the NCAA under the Sherman Antitrust Act umbrella, the Courts have failed to do so on several recent occasions.[98] The Courts' citing of the student–athlete paradigm is both naive and farcical as evidenced by the "one-and-done" phenomenon[99] and the multiple incidents the Courts have seen where student–athletes have been made to or allowed to sacrifice education in favor of athletics.[100] Moreover, it is our contention that the Courts should not be so solicitous to the NCAA and its member institutions in light of the reality that big-time college sports are indeed a business. Ultimately, these cases provide sufficient precedent for examining intercollegiate athletics through a legal lens and holding the NCAA accountable in the legal forum. Doing so, or, perhaps, even having the requisite ability to do so, might well provide greater leverage to college and university presidents for athletics reform.

Conclusion

What is needed here is a strong, concerted movement by university and college presidents to reaffirm the values and ideals of the academy in tandem with a reexamination of the legal issues surrounding college sports. However, it will take an especially aggressive stance by a sitting president of a high-profile, big-time sports university for any reform to take root. He or she must stand up and say "enough is enough." Until a major Division I-A institution steps up to the plate and re-affirms its commitment to the academy as a whole, and the student–athlete in particular, we will continue with sports being "business as usual."

---

98   See e.g., Banks v. Nat'l Collegiate Athletic Ass'n, 977 F.2d 1081 (7th Cir. 1992).
99   NCAA v. Bd. of Regents of Univ. of Okla., 468 U.S. 85, 120 (1984).
100   Freeman supra, note 20;, Lieber-Steeg, Upton, Bohn & Berkowitz, supra note 58.

Questions

1. Think back to a recent sporting event you attended or watched. What are some examples of how technology enhanced spectacle throughout the game? In what ways did those instances of spectacle influence your enjoyment of the game?
2. Have you thought about college sports as part of the big business of sports in general?
3. Do you think colleges are trying to control athletics and achieve more balance between academics and sports?
4. Do you think intercollegiate athletes should be paid for their participation? If so, for all sports or just some? Which ones?

View

Web

ESPN: The Worldwide Leader in Sports (espn.go.com)
The Official Website of NCAA Championships (ncaa.com)
National Collegiate Athletic Association (ncaa.org)

Film/Video

ESPN College GameDay (1986-)
Hoosiers (1986)
Rudy (1993)
Hoop Dreams (1994)
Coach Carter (2005)
Glory Road (2006)

Read

Cummins, R.G, B.H Nutting, and J.R Keene. "The Impact of Subjective Camera in Sports on Arousal and Enjoyment." *Mass Communication and Society* 15.1 (2012): 74–97. Print.

Jones, G. "In Praise of an 'Invisible Genre'?: *An Ambivalent Look at the Fictional Sports Feature Film*." Sport in Society 11 (2008): 117–129. Print.

Mehus, I. "The Diffused Audience of Football." *Continuum: Journal of Media & Cultural Studies* 24.6 (2010): 897–903. Print.

Smith, Anthony F. and Keith Hollihan. *ESPN: The Company: The Story and Lessons Behind the Most Fanatical Brand in Sports*. Hoboken, N.J: John Wiley & Sons, 2009. Print.

Stauff, Markus. "The Faces of Athletes: Visibility and Knowledge Production in Film/ Television Sport." *FlowTV*. 16 October 2009. Web. 14 June 2012.

So you think you can ...? Reality Competition

Unlike spectator sports, competition-based reality programming does not rely on participants who have practiced or trained to perform at the highest level possible. In reality programming, the emphasis is on "everyday" people competing to win but also competing for audience attention. For the everyday folks watching, the attraction is in the suspense of not knowing the outcome and in the inherent and intimate drama of choosing who to root for and who to root against in each episode. Reality programming examines the illusion of authenticity through the combination of what Schechner refers to in Part One as "make-believe" with "make-belief" (77). Producers create the illusion of contestants playing themselves (make-belief) while at the same time demand a certain amount of pretending or role playing (make-believe) from them in order to heighten the stakes for the fans. Further, the relationship between audience and performer is intentionally blurred. Those who are diehard fans are most often those who regularly audition or interview to be contestants.

As Meizel illuminates in her essay, winning may not always be the ultimate goal. *American Idol* is arguably one of the most successful reality shows on television today. Using the game show format first made popular in the 1950s coupled with the talent search shows from the 1980s, *American Idol* heightens the competition by creating intense interactions between the contestants and judges and eliminating contestants one by one until the end. Audiences are invested from the beginning as they can vote for who continues in the competition. As is seen in Meizel's example, audiences can also determine the future success of a contestant, whether or not he is a winner on the show.

One of the dangers of reality programming is an over-reliance on stereotypes. Given the paucity of minorities on mainstream television, there is a tendency for an individual to end up being a representative for an entire group. Social prejudices centered on race, gender, and ethnicity are brought to light through the interactions between audience and performer/contestant and can influence a contestant's ultimate success. Meizel locates her discussion of social prejudices and identity within the context of the "puzzling intersection of success and failure in the show's negotiation of the American Dream" (318). Foundational to the American Dream is opportunity and possibility. Any individual has an opportunity for success "each according to his ability or achievement" (319). This is key to Meizel's argument and to the commercial success of both *American Idol* and the individual contestant.

Ideas

Reality programming
Game shows
Make-believe/Make-belief
Authenticity
Identity
Stereotype
Social Prejudice
Race, gender, ethnicity
American Dream
Ability
Achievement

Making the Dream a Reality (Show)

The Celebration of Failure in American Idol

By Katherine Meizel

In *American Idol,* fame is as readily won through harsh rejection as it is through approbation. As millions tune in each season to watch the dismissal of a tragic–comic parade of anti-stars, it becomes clear that something beyond mere reality-show ridicule is at work here. In failing, those rejected from *American Idol* succeed in authenticating certain understandings of the American Dream—obligatory ambition, individuality, and the necessity of failure in the process of achievement. This paper examines the negotiation of failure in *American Idol,* and addresses the question of why, in the end, losers sell just as well as winners.

On a rainy afternoon in May 2006, I stood among a crowd of several hundred spectators at the Artichoke Festival in Castroville, California, waiting for a pop idol to take the outdoor stage. When he arrived, those around me rushed forward from their makeshift hay-bale seats, cheering, brandishing cameras and cell phones. One woman held up a sign asking, "Will You Marry Me?" The singer, crowned Artichoke King the previous day, shared the royal title with no less than Marilyn Monroe, Castroville's first Artichoke Queen in 1947. But the object of adoration on this day was not a star in the conventional sense associated with Monroe, though he was a celebrity nevertheless. William Hung's rise to fame is as much a story of failure as of success, his remarkable career launched with a nationally televised rejection from Fox's talent competition *American Idol.*

Each year, the preliminary episodes of *American Idol* detail the third round of auditions, in which singers perform for the show's three judges—Simon Cowell, Randy Jackson, and Paula Abdul—who will also preside in the later episodes. Two sets of auditions, not broadcast, precede those that make it to the air. The producers accept many talented contestants, but turn away others to make room onscreen for would-be idols to be presented as entertaining laughing-stocks. The popularity of the rejection segments has generated several "specials" reviewing the most cringe-inducing moments of one or more seasons, as well as a cumulative DVD devoted to the "Worst Auditions" and a 2005 program that expanded the concept to global proportions, *American Idol Presents: The World's Worst Auditions* (aired on Fox, 19 May 2005). At first glance, it may seem that these episodes merely reflect a sadistic streak in televisual culture—in *Idol* creator and judge Simon Cowell's words, "the modern day version of the lions and the Christians" (*Best & Worst of American Idol Seasons 1–4*)—or that they just bolster the viewer's ego ("I can sing better than that guy"). However, upon deeper inquiry, it becomes clear that rampant *Schadenfreude* is not the whole story and that more than the measure of talent is at stake.

An online advertisement for the 2005 season of *American Idol* featured photographs of aspiring contestants, overlaid with the successive captions, "American Idol. American Music. American Dream" (idolonfox.com, accessed 3 December 2004). Every broadcast season of *American Idol* chronicles the dual construction of this "dream," in its realization for a happy few and in the corresponding failure of thousands of hopeful singers. The American Dream is a fluid concept whose definition is often presupposed as a standardized and teleological success narrative. However, as Scott A. Sandage points out in *Born Losers*, success is not the sole defining characteristic of the Dream. Rather, it is defined by motivation, not action, by ambition, not its fruition, and "success" is only one possible result. Sandage writes: "Ours is an ideology of achieved identity; obligatory striving is its method, and failure and success are its outcomes" (265). But the *chiaroscuro* of the *American Idol* experience supports the idea that these two outcomes (success and failure) may better represent points on a continuum[1] than a fixed binary. Furthermore, the polarity of these points is in question, as what Matthew Stahl has called *American Idol's* "narratives of failure" (224) are interwoven with narratives of success. This essay, part of a larger study of identity politics in *American Idol* investigates the puzzling intersection of success and failure in the show's negotiation of the American Dream.

Setting the Stage for the Rise of the Anti-Idol

Though rooted in earlier American religious–political doctrines, the mores of Manifest Destiny and the "spirit of capitalism" (Weber),[2] the phrase "American Dream" entered popular discourse from the "melting-pot" crucible of the Great Depression—as Sandage observes, the nation's archetypal expression of success, emerging from the tremendous national failure of the 1929 stock market crash. In his 1931 book *The Epic of America*, James Truslow Adams described an "*American dream*, that dream of a land in which life should be better and richer and fuller for every man, with opportunity for each according to his ability or achievement" (415). Ability *or* achievement. This subtle distinction has proven to be key, not only in *American Idol*, but over the long history of American music. It has been significant in the discursive genres of camp and of outsider music, in which artists who deviate severely from expected aesthetic and/or social parameters may nevertheless be received as embodiments of a certain kind of individualistic authenticity.

William Hung is certainly not the first such artist. It happened during the Depression, concurrent with the birth of "American Dream" discourse, when a soprano named Florence Foster Jenkins was at the height of her impressively long career. Jenkins was a socialite with a passion for opera and the funds to support it. Though she was extremely popular and performed in numerous recitals—culminating in a 1944 Carnegie Hall appearance at the age of 76—her audience attended for reasons other than deep respect for her artistic merit. But there *was* a curious sort of respect, all the same. She has been described as "sincere" (Peters 22, quoting Alix B. Williamson), "genuine" ("*genuina*") (Helguera 102), and "happy in her work" (Helguera 102, quoting Roger Bager in *New York World Telegram*). Her longtime companion, St. Clair Bayfield, said after her death, "There was something about her personality that made everyone look at her. … People may have laughed at her singing, but the applause was real" (Peters 23). *Personality*, as in this situation, is considered to be a fundamental element in stardom and in its opposite, and crucial to twenty-first-century ideas about success and failure. Success and stardom are often attributed to possession of an "it factor," an intangible quality inherent to an individual's nature. And, as Sandage proposes, failure is no longer only a question of deficient finances or bad luck, but of an entire *identity* centered on personality—being a "loser" is not about what you cannot do, but about who you are. If failure is taken as equivalent to your identity—and consequently to your personality—then does not a spectacular failure indicate a spectacular personality worthy of stardom?

Singers following in Mrs Jenkins's footsteps have included Elva "Mrs" Miller in the 1960s, who was reviewed as "off-pitch for profit" (Bonafante), and more recently the Hong-Kong born Wing Han Tsang ("Wing"). But the 2004 season of *American Idol* launched the unparalleled international cross-media career of a new anti-star, William Hung. Hung was at that time a student in civil engineering at the University of California, Berkeley, and an avid karaoke performer. A victory in his dorm talent competition inspired him, and he auditioned for *American Idol* in San Francisco. His audition, in which he sang Ricky Martin's 2000 hit "She Bangs," was aired early in the broadcast season. His performance for judges Simon Cowell, Paula Abdul, and Randy Jackson was received with laughter and dismissal by the two men, while Abdul seemed pleasantly amused. Hung was interviewed briefly before entering the audition room, and the televised episode included his assertion that he would like to make a living in music. After the disappointing reaction from the judges, Hung seemed unfazed, telling them, "I already gave my best, and I have no regrets at all" (*American Idol*, 27 January 2004). Cowell, Jackson, and Abdul heartily approved of this attitude, but still sent Hung on his way. And that was that.

Only it wasn't: somehow, Hung caught viewers' attention and, soon after the 27 January broadcast, a fan website was established, attracting four million hits in its first week. An online petition, encouraging *American Idols* producers to bring him to the show in Hollywood, accumulated nearly 117,000 signatures. He was indeed asked to appear again, on an episode titled "Uncut, Uncensored, and Untalented" that aired on 1 March 2004. For this performance, he was surrounded by back-up dancers, whose choreography was built on Hung's own distinctive movements. From there he rose to an ambiguous position that could be described either as international fame or as international infamy. He has recorded four albums for Koch Records (a label unaffiliated with *American Idol*), made a music video and DVD, appeared on the Fox Television series *Arrested Development*, and played a sizable role in a Hong Kong film. Last spring, he returned to the realm of *American Idol*, appearing in a set of television commercials for one of the show's major sponsors, Cingular Wireless. The first album was reportedly recorded in a single weekend, under the supervision of Giuseppe D (who had worked with the Backstreet Boys and Celine Dion, among others) (Chi 2). Incidentally, the process of Florence Foster Jenkins's recordings has been described as similarly effortless: "Simply, she sang and the album was recorded" (Helguera 100, my translation). Regardless of this haste, Hung's album debuted in the *Billboard* top 40 and attained a #3 ranking on Amazon.com. His voice has also been featured in widely circulated mash-ups. In this genre, anyone with the necessary—and easily available—technology may create a new musical product from diverse pre-existing tracks. Here, the elevation of Hung's own ordinariness facilitates the participation of other ordinary individuals in creative musical processes.

While everyone on *American Idol* starts out as ordinary, hoping to be recognized as extraordinary, for a lucky few it proves to be only the kind of illusory ordinariness found in comic-book superheroes. Gifted singers only *appear* to be mild-mannered waiters and farm girls, but, when thrust into the spotlight, reveal hidden qualities of superstardom. Others typically remain bespectacled and unrespected Clark Kents. But it was William Hung's very ordinariness, if perhaps exceptional, that earned him recognition on a similar scale. The tension between this image of averageness, to which a sense of personal authenticity is attached, and the unashamed artifice of the Idol enterprise can make even the pinnacle of success on the show seem a somewhat dubious accomplishment. It was in acknowledgment of this kind of tension that Bob Dylan crafted his own image in the 1960s. Dylan is named by Sandage for his early advancement of a cultivated "loser chic," and for his philosophy positing "failure as the only remaining moral identity, the only true success" (270).

Sense, Sensibility, and Sincerity

The mechanisms of Hung's unexpected career are less than clear, but it plainly appears to validate the prevailing ideological components of the American Dream: the obligatory ambition, the projection and perception of an "authentic" personality as factors in success, and the requirement of failure as a stepping-stone to achievement. His ambition is clear in the broadcast of his audition; he would like to make a living as a singer, though he admits that he has, at that time, never had a lesson. In terms of personality, there seems to be something of the Florence Foster Jenkins phenomenon at work in the media portrayal of both his apparent cluelessness and his determined confidence during the notorious audition. His resolute optimism about his singing makes him innocent, *naïf*. For this quality, his cult following may be located within what Susan Sontag called the "sensibility" of "camp." Sontag identified the main component of "naïve" camp (or "pure" camp) as *seriousness*, specifically "a seriousness that *fails*" (Sontag 295, emphasis added). "What it [camp] does," she wrote, "is to find the success in certain passionate failures" (302). On the DVD by Koch Entertainment, Hung is heard to say, "I might not be the best singer in the world, but I sing from my heart, and I sing with passion" (*Hangin' with Hung*

2004). These qualities seem to imbue Hung with a musical authenticity based not in technical proficiency, but in sincerity.

For Sontag's contemporary John J. Enck (174), camp comes from an amateur who does not recognize the limits of his skills. But, while Hung's sanguinity may strike his audience as an inaccurate gauging of his ability, it becomes part of his appeal and his public identity. His "honesty" and his "genuine" character are referred to frequently in the media, and his unperturbed reply to the *American Idol* judges ("I have no regrets") establishes him as what Glenn Dixon calls the "Nathan Hale of the karaoke nation." Hung himself acknowledges that the positive outlook he presented on *American Idol* has been a crucial factor in his success; when I asked him for his thoughts about why he had attracted so much interest, he replied, "Probably because of my attitude, or inspiration. … Never give up, and you can succeed in life." He also repeated this last advice later in our conversation, when asked how he would counsel aspiring singers. Hung believes that his experience might encourage others to audition for *American Idol,* or other competitions, since he has demonstrated that "there's nothing wrong with losing." His statements reinforce the idea of failure as only a temporary obstacle, a fundamental and necessary experience on the road to success. He has expressed similar sentiments during public appearances. When he returned to *American Idol* about a month after his audition aired, host Ryan Seacrest asked him about his studies in civil engineering. He admitted that he was struggling a bit in school, and then continued, "I'm struggling with pretty much most of the things I do in my life." At the audience's laughter, he responded, "No, what you need to understand … is that everybody goes through struggles to succeed" (*American Idol,* 1 March 2004). This statement was greeted with cheers and applause. Like that of Florence Foster Jenkins's fans, this applause is real, or at least *about* real-ness, as befits a reality television audience.

Alterities and Amateurism

An examination of Hung's audition is illuminating. While his musicianship is continuously under fire, I would argue that his competence in fact exceeds that assigned to him by his critics. His rendition of "She Bangs," and Ricky Martin's own track from the 2000 album *Sound Loaded,* are both precisely in F# minor. When I asked Hung if he had received his starting pitch before he began singing, he seemed confused by the question, and told me that he already knew how to perform the song from his many hours of listening and practice. Since he had not been listening to it just prior to his audition, we may infer that he sang in Martin's key from memory. In addition, the range of the song exceeds the pitch (around E_3, by the system of the Acoustical Society of America) at which untrained young male voices tend to encounter problems. Hung's greatest musical difficulty lies in the distancing of the solo vocal line from its originally accompanied context. This is a furthering of certain processes inherent in karaoke, particularly, an intensification of absence—*kara* means "empty," in reference to the omission of the vocal melody from the soundtrack (Hesselink 56). In the *American Idol* auditions, the *oke* (from "orchestra") is absent as well. For many singers, a loss of the instrumental accompaniment to which they are aurally and psychologically accustomed creates problems with timing. With the less than simple patterns of syncopation required in "She Bangs," for Hung this leads to a shortening of the pauses between phrases, and a subsequent loss of fixed meter. However, the rhythmic relationships *within* phrases are correct, matching Ricky Martin's singing almost exactly.

So, if he isn't such a bad singer, what is it about the performance that provokes the judges' reactions? His movement is the most visible target—if Florence Foster Jenkins has been retroactively called an "anti-Callas," then Hung's dancing presents him as a kind of "anti-Martin." Language expectations may also factor in the judges' response, though, in spite of his accented English, Hung's diction is entirely intelligible. However, *American Idol* has a history of ridiculing those with discernible accents. And in the fourth season, the audition episodes featured a segment entitled "The Incomprehensibles," in which the performances of a South Asian man and a Japanese woman were presented with phonetically transcribed subtitles that amounted to nonsense. Of course, it may be said that the aforementioned are by no means the *only* criteria for derision on *American Idol*. Alterities of race and ethnicity, gender and sexuality, psychology, and musical genre are all equally fair game.

To some, Hung's success, or successful failure, is representative of deeply embedded social prejudices regarding Asian–Americans. This is less than surprising, as the adoration is certainly not devoid of sinister qualities; Hung's innocence is fascinating, but innocence is not enough. With the captivation of his audience, he is also held captive to a combination of racializing and commercial motives. As Deborah Wong reminds us, "race, as a cultural construct, is neither natural, innocent, nor apolitical and is intimately linked to processes of commodification and control" (4). In season six of *American Idol*, eventual semi-finalist Paul Kim was featured in a segment ostensibly meant to provide guidelines for *Idol* hopefuls.

His performance accompanied the recommendation "Seek Inspiration." After a brief flashback to Hung's infamous audition, the Korean American Kim was shown telling the cameras, "It kind of bothers me [that] when people think about 'Asian singer,' they think William Hung … and I'm not hatin' on William Hung, but I mean, come on—there are many talented Asian people out there, you just don't see them. I mean, they don't get an opportunity in the entertainment industry at all" (*American Idol*, 7 February 2007). This is a telling statement, especially considering Hung's relative success in terms of opportunity and visibility. For Kim, that success doesn't count. It is an inspiration in the negative, a set of failures (Hung's, the entertainment industry's, America's) that he is motivated to transcend in his own *Idol* expression of the American Dream.

More than one writer has seen in Hung's televised appearance an uncomfortable reference to historically essentialized performances of Asianness. Journalist Emil Guillermo believes that Koch Records and the music channel Fuse (which aired Hung's video) have made of him an updated version of Mickey Rooney's "Mr. Yunioshi" in the 1961 film *Breakfast at Tiffany's*. Sharon Mizota compares this kind of representation to blackface minstrelsy, and describes the commodification of William Hung as a new form of "yellowface." She points to his performance on *The Today Show* in the spring of 2004, during which members of the audience enacted this analogy almost literally, holding up masks with photos of Hung's face. Additionally, both she and David Ng find Hung's popularity an example of the discursive de-sexualization of Asian–American men. Asian men, Ng writes, "rank somewhere below white women" when it comes to "virility." Mizota sees the Asian–American man as a "heterosexual 'subaltern,'" in the mainstream perception dating from early immigration policy. Hung is constructed not only as an ethnic/immigrant "subaltern," but also as an archetypal "nerd"—a socially awkward, academically inclined engineering major—and has spoken in public about his desire to remain a virgin until marriage. Mizota calls him a "righteous nerd." His "nerdiness," intellectual trade, and approach to sexuality diminish the masculinity of his image to a level acceptable in Asian–Americans within the conventions of US popular culture.

This way, Hung remains a paragon of the "model minority," an assimilation success myth about Asian–Americans that Frank H. Wu identifies as being actually aimed at African–Americans. It implies the accusation: "They made it; why can't you?" (Wu 49). In the process, it places Asian–Americans, in "making it," closer to (though separate from) whiteness. There is a paradox here for Hung, though, because in popular culture that very whiteness, or at least a lack of blackness, can be fatal. "Do you know what a nerd is?" musician and theorist Brian Eno famously asked in a *Wired* interview, and then answered his own question: "A nerd is a human being without enough Africa in him or her" (Kelly 149). In the case of William Hung, his choice of "She Bangs" presents a related problem. An extension of the late-'90s explosion of "Latin" music in mainstream radio, Ricky Martin's song is tied to hyper-sexualized images of Latino performers, and by association to the discursive hyper-sexualization of Afrodiasporic cultural influences. Hung's physical performance isn't "Latin" enough, isn't "African" enough—his body and his embodied voice are not appropriate—to satisfy these expectations. But his failure at pop culture is, once again, ambiguous, since as an Asian–American he symbolizes a key success story all the same.

In light of these contradictory problems of representation, it is somewhat surprising that Hung has found enthusiastic audiences in his native Hong Kong, and in other Asian communities with large ethnically Chinese populations. However, Sheng-Mei Ma suggests a kind of strategic essentialism in the re-appropriation of body and language stereotypes within Chinese–American literature. In the context of increasingly globalized popular culture, the worldwide adoration of Hung could exemplify such a re-appropriation. It is also possible that, for some fans, Hung is simply a different kind of karaoke hero than the type offered in actually elected American Idols. According to Deborah Wong and Mai Elliot, karaoke in Asian contexts generally emphasizes the participatory rather than exceptional skill; the authors point out that "while good singing is admired, bad singing isn't maligned" (Wong and Elliot 158). In the karaoke-like atmosphere of *American Idol*, the categorical collapse of success and failure parallels the simultaneous collapse of amateurism and professionalism effected through the show.

On William Hung's debut CD, *Inspiration*, the instrumentation is overwhelmingly synthesized, and at the Castroville Artichoke Festival his performance also followed this model, as he sang Barry Manilow's "It's a Miracle," Billy Ray Cyrus's "Achy Breaky Heart," and, of course, the much-anticipated "She Bangs." The absence of a live band in his performances restricts Hung to karaoke practice, and symbolically confines him to the status of a kind of professional amateur. The juxtaposition in his career of professional structure (he is hired and paid to sing) and amateur content (karaoke settings) raises the question of whether celebrity has anything to do at all with either professionalism or amateurism, or whether it might be a discrete category of its own, grounded less in the economic processes of American capitalism than in its myths. In this context, the seemingly incongruous coincidence of William Hung and Marilyn Monroe as Artichoke monarchs is not so unimaginable, and serves as a reminder of Hollywood's fundamental place in American Dream ideology. The judges' expression of approval, "You're going to Hollywood," means explicit permission to live that Dream, win or lose. William Hung may have arrived there through a side door, but nevertheless, there he is.

A Closer Look at the American Idol Dream

According to Simon Cowell, he and creative partner Simon Fuller took the idea for the *Idols* format unsuccessfully to the United States before they produced it in the UK. They "tried to sell it initially as the great American dream, which is somebody who could be a cocktail waitress one minute, within 16 weeks could become the most famous person in America" (King). The idea was turned down at first—a failure—so Cowell and Fuller took it home and turned it into the sensation *Pop Idol.* It is somewhat ironic that an explicit expression of the American Dream sold in the United States only after it became a hit in the UK, but we have a history of such appropriative cycles in our popular music, and the *Idols* version of the Dream has, in the end, been tremendously successful here.

American understandings of fame intertwine perceptions of ordinariness and extraordinariness. This dichotomy is typically imploded in American Dream discourses of possibility, of the potential mutability of identity and status, but is simultaneously reinforced in the social distance implicit between the star and the fan. During the course of an *American Idol* season, that distance is ostensibly narrowed as the boundaries that separate producer, consumer, and product/star are blurred. Anyone (within a certain age group) may audition, anyone may make the transition from the living room couch to the living rooms of millions; audience voting, available to every viewer with a telephone, seems to recast the viewer/consumer as producer. In this apparent democratic redistribution of cultural power, the ordinary and the extraordinary, failure and success, can be assigned comparable value.

The various modes of democratic authenticity associated with the American Dream are played out explicitly in *American Idol.* In her study of the UK's *Pop Idol,* Su Holmes observes the significance ascribed to class-related definitions of ordinariness, and the same is true for the American version. Here are Cowell's cocktail waitresses, accompanied by other young people struggling to escape all manner of troubles. First-season winner Kelly Clarkson worked as a (cocktail) waitress prior to her audition, and, as she explained during one broadcast, lost an apartment and all of her possessions in a fire immediately before the audition. Third-season winner Fantasia Barrino was a single teenage mother. Such backgrounds and hardships are displayed often throughout each season. During a broadcast that focused on interviews with the final five contestants, Barrino told host Ryan Seacrest, "I want to see Zion [her daughter] have the best, things that I didn't have, I want to see her have it" (*American Idol*, 3 May 2004). Here is the generational, temporal articulation of the Dream—the potential to improve the class status of one's children, to acknowledge and surmount past social "failures," and to ensure a future in which the Dream is no longer even necessary.

The American Dream and the significance, of authenticity in relation to stardom are directly tied to hallmarks of capitalism: an emphasis on individualism (Holmes 157) and the "benefit of the few at the expense of many" (158). The "mediated identity" of a star involves the negotiation of individualism in the extraordinary context of reality television, where tension between the on-stage (-screen) self and the off-stage self must be worked out in a way that satisfactorily serves to "close the gap" between the two (Holmes 160). In this process, the importance of a particular kind of personal authenticity is also implied. Simon Cowell says of Barrino, "What you see on-camera is exactly the same as you see off-camera" (The TV Guide Channel, 30 May 2004). As if to confirm this assessment, Barrino told the TV Guide Channel, "I came into this competition being me, and I'm going to always be me" (The TV Guide Channel, 30 May 2004). The second quality of capitalism mentioned above is apparent both in the audition elimination process, as Holmes notes, and in the contracts 19 Entertainment has made with *Idols* finalists. An Associated Press article early in 2004 reported that Simon Fuller collects as much as 25 to 50% of all earnings in some of his *Idols* relationships (MSNBC.com 2004). The contestant who sells his or her voice to 19 Entertainment for the chance at a "break," instead of perhaps more financially satisfying remuneration, must believe in the value of fame itself as a commodity. It is fame as a reified concept, and not the labor that leads to it, whose value appears to have been naturalized by the hopeful singers.

Television viewers are as eager to see Americans self-destruct as they are to applaud the classic self-made man. Humiliation is a hallmark of reality television, and, as William Hung observes, rejection from *American Idol* is "the norm, not the exception," but this clear and present danger fails to deter the thousands who attend the *American Idol* cattle calls. A "personal release" form supplied at the show's website spells out the risks involved in auditioning, requiring the potential contestant to acknowledge that information "of a personal, private, embarrassing or unfavorable nature" may be made public, "which information may be factual and/or fictional" and which might result in "public ridicule, humiliation, or condemnation" (Idolonfox.com 2005). The hazards inherent in the decision to audition for *American Idol* raise questions about why, nevertheless, so many make that choice, and about why viewers tune in to the mocking rejection of the "worst auditions."

The answer to the first question appears to involve that patented American ambition, the requirement that one seize opportunity when it appears. I spoke with several singers who told me that they auditioned "just to say I did it." I heard that phrase from a young man, Matthew Maimoni, who had auditioned four times, and would try yet again. He told me that he never expected to "make it," but that a persistent "little bit of hope that you're going to make it through" can be enough to keep a singer coming back for more. He, along with others, also considered the attraction of a seemingly easy path to fame and fortune, for those who "just kind of want to go from their nothing lives to something big," and, though he recognizes that much work is done behind the scenes of the show, he has a sense that "this is an easy way to go for it". Another singer, Branden, explained it this way:

> I look at it as this. … It is sort of like winning the lottery. A mass, fun, mainstream get-rich-quick scheme. It allows you the opportunity to put yourself in a fantasy—in the process; and to dream big while [you are] actually seeing a road ahead that TV has created from other seasons. There is hope in that fantasy and the possible outcome makes you feel good about yourself. That is the scary part about the power of this show, *American Idol.* Nonetheless, it was an experience, just like venturing to New Jersey and waiting in a line [for] 3 hours for a $100 million jackpot lottery ticket is. (I did that once.) The odds are against you, and the notion is somewhat insane, but the allure is a great force. It was a life experience. There was no enrichment as an artist or even a useful way to practice an audition. Merely an experience. An "I did that when" sort of thing.

Matthew Maimoni and Branden both have an understanding of the *Idol* opportunity as chiefly a televisual, manufactured, and somewhat suspect one, but the promise of an "experience" and even the very slim odds of success made gamblers out of both singers. After all, as Matthew put it, "who wouldn't want to be the American Idol?".

And at least one audition judge also sees the power in taking that chance. Associate Music Director Michael Orland, who evaluated singers during the season five audition tour, reported that in each site he had attended, he would encounter someone who froze when his turn came, and refused to audition. He described his reaction:

> Uh-uh, no way, you're going to do it. You just waited in line that whole time, you're going to—I don't care if you sing one line to me and do it badly, you're not going to leave here and say you didn't do it … so I made these kids, *just to say they did it.* (10 September 2005, emphasis added)

Taking the *Idol* opportunity is a merit badge of sorts, then, a story one can tell to prove one's sense of ambition, one's dedication to the American Dream. And the Dream pursued at the *Idol* auditions mirrors quite precisely Adams's *Epic* Dream, the same one represented concurrently in the Golden Age of cinema and in *Idol* predecessors like the *Major Bowes Amateur Hour* (originally for radio)—those who are "discovered" are literally invited to Hollywood, to the place where the Dream lives.

As for the viewers who watch the dozens of frequently cruel *Idol* rejections in the early broadcast season, there is certainly more than one possible attraction. William Hung proposes that the rejection segments are, beyond their "entertainment value," in fact educational for potential contestants. Viewers may learn from them what to do and what not to do when it is their turn, "what the *American Idol* judges are actually looking for." *Idol* vocal coach Debra Byrd suggests a kind of morbid curiosity. In response to my question regarding why audiences might be drawn to these segments, she asked, "You ever been on the freeway, when there's an accident on the other side?" But she also cites another element, which, she points out, "makes fantastic television." This is the quality of "bravado" in the hopeful singers, a sense of confidence or pride that does not match the evaluation of the judges, or possibly of the audience; as Byrd describes it, these singers engage viewers' interest when they display "more guts than talent." Though the unfortunate are turned away for such hubris, Byrd's assessment is still consistent with the American admiration of ambition, of the attempt to fulfill the Dream.

How do people deal with public *Idol* rejection? Of course, there are the rants and the curses encouraged and recorded at the auditions ("If we say you suck … get to a camera" urged producer Nigel Lythgoe at the season four auditions in San Francisco—field notes, 5 October 2004). But some, like William Hung, take the experience gracefully in stride, "grateful for the opportunity." "Regardless of how they portrayed me," he maintains, "showing me on TV is like opening doors."

In May 2004, in the wake of William Hung's early success, the WB Network aired a short series in which unwitting contestants mistakenly believed that they were participating in a search for the best singer in the country. In fact, *Superstar USA* was aired as a search for the "worst" singer in America. Its format was an overt parody of *American Idol*, but immediately eliminated any singers who might have been competitive in the real *Idol* context. The show came under a bit of ethical fire in the press,[3] but primarily because one of the producers had told the paid studio audience that the singers were part of a charity program for seriously ill youths. (An apology was eventually issued; see Shain.) When the finalists and winner were at last informed that they had won thousands of dollars for their incompetence instead of in recognition of their talent, none of them showed the expected outrage. They had, after all, been paid handsomely, with victor Jamie Foss receiving a $100,000 prize and contract. A soundtrack recording of the contestants was produced on Koch Records, the same company responsible for William Hung's albums. After the show aired, Foss told *TVGuideOnline* about her response to the revelation of *Superstar USA's* hoax:

> My reaction was definitely fine. I was a little shocked, and there was a kind of frustration. But then I thought about it, and, like, a minute later, I was like, "This has been the time of my life. I would have done it even if I had known it was a joke!" I mean, I got to work with choreographers, I got a makeover, I was in Hollywood for three weeks. … It was awesome! (Katner)

It seems, then, that even when living the Dream is just that, a brief and illusory dream, the "allure" can be irresistible, and the simulacrum can be fulfilling enough.

In Conclusion

The celebration of William Hung's rejection from *American Idol* is the result of more than just public sadism or a delight in the humiliation that characterizes reality television programming. Hung's voice has been styled as that of a *bona fide* everyman, of the humble but determined, of blind ambition and blind faith in the

American Dream. His kind of celebrity begins to answer the question of why, in the face of almost certain rejection and the strong possibility of very public ridicule, up to 100,000 people attend auditions each season, and millions tune in to every brutal dismissal. It is about selling the Dream, regardless of whether it results in success or failure—and about the enactment of an ideology that hovers at the edges of any discourse about American morality. It is the potential of great ambition, rather than of great talent, that drives these hopefuls and inspires their fans. William Hung's devotion to his new vocation evokes the famous words of Florence Foster Jenkins: "Some may say that I couldn't sing," she allowed, "but no one can say that I *didn't* sing" (Peters 23).

Notes

1. Sandage himself recognizes this, to a degree, in an interview published in *Cabinet* (no. 7, 2002), (http://www.cabinetmagazine.0rg/issues/7/inventi0n0ffailure.php).
2. This essay's author further investigates the relationships among the American Dream, Weber's "Protestant ethic," and the "spirit of capitalism" in her 2007 PhD dissertation, "America Singing: The Mediation of Identity Politics in *American Idol*" and in "A Singing Citizenry: Popular Music and Civil Religion in America," *Journal for the Scientific Study of Religion* 45.4 (2006): 497–503.
3. A 10 May item in the *Los Angeles Times* (Collins) inspired apologies from the WB Network, as well as some further media commentary about the public's appetite for (public) humiliation (e.g., Shain; de Moraes; Oldenburg).

Works Cited

Adams, J. T. (1933). *The Epic of America.* 1931. Boston, MA: Little, Brown.

The Best & Worst of American Idol Seasons 1–4. (2005). Capital Entertainment and Fremantle Media, CEE0013.

Bonafante, J. (22 Sept. 1967). "Mrs. Miller Is Off-Pitch for Profit: A Most Unlikely Lark." *LIFE Magazine*; reprinted at *Mrs. Miller's World.com.* (20 Feb. 2006). (http://www.mrsmillersworld.com/story_bin/STunlikelylark.html).

Byrd, D. (31 Jan. 2006). Telephone interview.

Chi, M. (8 May 2005). "William Hung: Biography." (http://music.yahoo.com/ar-308192 bioWilliam-Hung).

Collins, Scott. (10 May 2004). "In Reality, It's a Super-Duping; The Coming Series 'Superstar USA' Trips Up the Audience in a Bid to Turn 'Idol' Upside-Down." *Los Angeles Times*: E1.

De Moraes, L. (2004). "Fox Puts Foot In Its Mouth, Kicks Self." *The Washington Post*, 14 May 2004. 20 Dec. 2007. (http://www.washingtonpost.com/wp-dyn/articles/A25870-2004May13.html).

Dixon, G. (7 May 2004). "What It Means to Be Hung." *Washington City Paper*. Copy provided by Glenn Dixon, pers. comm, 18 Apr. 2006.

Enck, John J. (1966)."*Campop*." Wisconsin Studies in Contemporary Literature 7.2: *168–82*.

Guillermo, E. (7 May 2005). "William Hung: Racism, Or Magic?" *SFGate.com*. 6 Apr. 2004. (http://www.sfgate.com/cgibin/article.cgi?file=gate/archive/2004/04/06/eguillermo. DTL8rtype=printable).

Hangin' with Hung. (2004). Koch Entertainment, LLC, KOC-DV-9607.

Helguera, Pablo P. (2000). "Florence Foster Jenkins: La Diva del Cuarto Tono." *Pauta* 75–76: 96–102.

Hesselink, N. (1994). "Kouta and Karaoke in Modern Japan: A Blurring of the Distinction between Umgangsmusik and Darbietungsmusik." *British Journal of Ethnomusicology* 3: 49–61.

Holmes, S. (2004). 'Reality Goes Pop!' Reality TV, Popular Music, and Narratives of Stardom in *Pop Idol Television & News Media* 5.2: 147–72.

Hung, W. Telephone interview.

James, B. (Oct. 2004). "Re: Idol Thoughts." Email to Katherine Meizel.

Katner, B. (12 July 2006). "Superstar Jamie Squeals!" *TVGuideOnline,* 15 June 2004. (http://144.198.225.50/News/Insider/default.htm?cmsRedir=true&rmDate=0615004& cmsGuid=%7B4FEF0722-A7F7-4C4C-ABD9-DF1FB5E6F8DA%7D).

Kelly, K. (May 1995). "Eno: Gossip Is Philosophy." *Wired*: 145–58.

King, L. (27 Mar. 2006). Interview with Simon Cowell. *CNN Larry King Live,* 17 Mar. 2006. (http://transcripts.cnn.com/TRANSCRIPTS/0603/17/lkl.01.html).

Ma, Sheng-Mei. (1993). "Orientalism in the Chinese American Discourse: Body and Pidgin." *Modern Language Studies 23.4*: 104–17.

Maimoni, M. (22 Oct. 2004). Interview, University of California, Santa Barbara.

Mizota, S. (7 May 2005). "Can the Subaltern Sing? Or Who's Ashamed of William Hung?" PopMatters, 4 May 2004. (http://www.popmatters.com/tv/features/040504-william-hung-mizota.shtml).

MSNBC.com. (2004). "Simon Fuller: 'American Idol' Svengali—Music Mogul's Earnings at Issue." 20 Jan. 2004. 19 Jan. 2004. (http://www.msnbc.msn.com/id/3943498/).

Ng, D. (7 May 2005). "Hung Out to Dry: What We Laugh about when We Laugh about *American Idol*'s Most Famous Reject." *The Village Voice*, 6 Apr. 2004. (http://www.villagevoice.com/news/0414,ng,52441,1.html).

Oldenburg, A. (20 Dec. 2007). "Can't Sing or Dance? Give 'Superstar' a Shot." *USA Today*, 17 May 2004. (http://www.usatoday.com/life/television/news/2004-05-16-wb-superstar_x.htm).

Orland, M. (24 Sept. 2004). Telephone interview.

———. Telephone interview. 10 Sept. 2005.

Peters, B. (2001). "Florence Nightingale." *Opera News* 65. 12: 20–3.

Sandage, S. A. (2005). *Born Losers: A History of Failure in America.* Cambridge, MA, and London: Harvard UP.

Shain, M. (11 May 2004). "'Superstar' Producers Lied to Studio Audience." FoxNews.com, 13 July 2006. (http://www.foxnews.com/story/0,2933,119593,00.html).

Sontag, S. (2000). "Notes on Camp." *Partisan Review* 1964. *The Best American Essays of the Century.* Ed. Joyce Carol Oates and Robert Atwan. (pp. 288–302). Boston, MA: Houghton Mifflin.

Stahl, M. (2004). "A Moment Like This: *American Idol* and Narratives of Meritocracy." *Bad Music.* (Ed.) Christopher Washburne and Maiken Derno. (pp. 212–32). New York: Routledge.

Weber, M. (1904–1905). The Protestant Ethic and the Spirit of Capitalism. Trans. Talcott Parsons. (1930). London and New York: Routledge. (2004).

(www.williamhung.net). (Est. 2004). by Don Chin.

Wong, D. A. (2004). *Speak It Louder: Asian Americans Making Music.* New York and London: Routledge.

Wong, D., and Elliot, M. (1994). "'I Want the Microphone': Mass Mediation and Agency in Asian–American Popular Music." *TDR (1988-)* vol. 38: 3: 152–67.

Wu, F. H. (2002). *Yellow: Race in America beyond Black and White.* New York: Basic Books.

Questions

1. Select a reality program that stages competition. As you view the program consider the following:
   - What is the primary theme/concept at play?
   - What are the competencies and/or skills that the participants display?
   - Is there a thirst for knowledge, power, and/or authority?
   - Is there a narrative of hero and underdog?
   - Are gender, race, and ethnicity associated with body images?
   - Is national identity a factor in the event?
   - What is at stake in "winning" or "losing"?
2. Do you think audiences are believe that reality TV is real? What calls into question authenticity in reality programming?
3. How do you see the American Dream displayed in other reality competition programs?

View

Film/Video

The Real World (1992-)
Big Brother (2000-)
Survivor (2000-)
Pop Idol (2001, 2003-2004)
American Idol (2002-)
The Bachelor (2002-)
America's Next Top Model (2003-)
The Reality of Reality (2003)
Project Runway (2004-)
Ultimate Fighter (2005-)

Read

"Competition and Game Show Reality Television." *RealityShows.com* 7 June 2012. Web. 14 June 2012.

Gardels, Nathan and Mike Medavoy. *American Idol after Iraq: Competing for Hearts and Minds in the Global Media Age*. Malden, MA: Wiley-Blackwell, 2009. Print.

Holmes, Su and Deborah Jermyn. *Understanding Reality Television*. London and New York: Routledge, 2004. Print.

Hoerschelmann, Olaf. *Rules of the Game: Quiz Shows and American Culture*. Albany: State University of New York Press, 2006. Print.

Huff, Richard M. *Reality Television*. Westport, Conn: Praeger Publishers, 2006. Print.

Kivka, Misha. *Reality TV*. Edinburgh: Edinburgh University Press, 2012. Print.

Miller, T. "The New World Makeover." *Continuum: Journal of Media & Cultural Studies*. 22.4 (2008): 585–590. Print.

Slocum Charles B. "The Real History of Reality TV Or, How Alan Funt Won the Cold War." *Writers Guild of America*, (2012). Web. 14 June 2012.

Smith, Matthew J. and Andrew F. Wood. "Survivor Lessons: Essays on Communication and Reality Television." Jefferson, N.C.: McFarland & Company, Inc., 2003. Print.

Wang, G. "A Shot at Half-Exposure: Asian Americans in Reality TV Shows." Television and New Media 11.5 (2010): 404–427. Print.

1. Select a country and design an Olympic opening ceremony that will highlight what is unique about that country.

2. Watch a college sporting event on television and note the variety of technology that is used to increase audience investment and interest in the event.

3. Investigate the organization of athletics on your campus. What is the budget for intercollegiate sports? How much are coaches compensated in relation to other faculty? What are the graduation rates for athletes in the various sports?

4. Create your own "so you think you can..." competitive reality performance. Consider the following:
   - The skill or ability the competitors must display
   - The venue—both the venue for the competition and for the audience and how the audience will participate
   - The structure and rules of the performance
   - The stakes for the competitors (individual and/or team), the audience, and the judges.